london

D1114759

![NATIONAL GEOGRAPHIC TRAVELER]

london

by Louise Nicholson
photography by Alison Wright

National Geographic
Washington, D.C.

CONTENTS

Pages 2–3: Changing of the Guard at Buckingham Palace
Opposite: Henry VII's Lady Chapel at Westminster Abbey

TRAVELING WITH EYES OPEN

Alert travelers go with a purpose and leave with a benefit. If you travel responsibly, you can help support wildlife conservation, historic preservation, and cultural enrichment in the places you visit. You can enrich your own travel experience as well.

To be a geo-savvy traveler:

- Recognize that your presence has an impact on the places you visit.

- Spend your time and money in ways that sustain local character. (Besides, it's more interesting that way.)

- Value the destination's natural and cultural heritage.

- Respect the local customs and traditions.

- Express appreciation to local people about things you find interesting and unique to the place: its nature and scenery, music and food, historic villages and buildings.

- Vote with your wallet: Support the people who support the place, patronizing businesses that make an effort to celebrate and protect what's special there. Seek out shops, local restaurants, inns, and tour operators who love their home—who love taking care of it and showing it off. Avoid businesses that detract from the character of the place.

- Enrich yourself, taking home memories and stories to tell, knowing that you have contributed to the preservation and enhancement of the destination.

That is the type of travel now called geotourism, defined as "tourism that sustains or enhances the geographical character of a place—its environment, culture, aesthetics, heritage, and the well-being of its residents." To learn more, visit National Geographic's Center for Sustainable Destinations at *www .nationalgeographic.com/travel/sustainable.*

london

ABOUT THE AUTHORS & THE PHOTOGRAPHER

Louise Nicholson, a London resident for 25 years, considers it the world's most exciting city. She is an art historian, conservationist, and journalist, and her 26 books mostly concern London and India. She won the London Tourist Board's "best book of the decade" award and was a finalist for the Thomas Cook Travel award. She is also author of *National Geographic Traveler: India.* In 2001 she moved to New York, gaining valuable new perspectives on the expectations of visitors to London. She received the 2010 Woman of the Year award from the National Association of Professional Women of America. Her website is *www.louisesindia.com.*

Alison Wright, a New York–based documentary photographer, has spent a career capturing the human spirit through her photographs, traveling to all corners of the globe photographing endangered cultures and people. Her photography is represented by the National Geographic Image collection and is published in a number of National Geographic books and publications. Wright is a recipient of the Dorothea Lange Award in Documentary Photography and a two-time winner of the Lowell Thomas Travel Journalism Award. Her memoir, *Learning to Breathe: One Woman's Journey of Spirit and Survival,* was published in 2008.

Larry Porges updated and wrote new features and sidebars for the 2011 edition. He lived in London for five years and is currently a travel book editor at the National Geographic Society in Washington, D.C. He misses London, especially the *London Evening Standard,* Little Venice, and being surrounded by people who know the lyrics to "Blue is the Colour."

British-born **Tim Jepson,** who updated the Travelwise section for the 2011 edition, is widely traveled and has written several titles for National Geographic, but home is Notting Hill, in west London.

Charting Your Trip

This sprawling city of 7.5 million souls, spread over 610 square miles (1,580 sq km), is not something you're going to conquer in a few days. The city bursts at the seams with relics and reminders of its 2,000 years of rich history, including some of the world's most celebrated architecture and repositories of art and culture. London is a destination to tackle with a sense of humility.

Getting Around

The London public transportation system is excellent. The subway system (the Tube) and London's famous red buses can take you to every corner of the city, while the Docklands Light Railroad (DLR) to the east and the overground suburban train service fill in gaps and connect stops. Even Thames riverboat commuting is possible; services are frequent and varied (see sidebar p. 53). The Tube, however, is in the process of a major (and needed) upgrade, and delays and temporary closures, especially on weekends, are common. The Transport for London website (*tfl.gov.uk*) is an excellent resource for maps and route information for all these services, Travelcards, as well as temporary closures.

Black taxis are plentiful and convenient, but pricey—they can be hailed anytime on the street. (The signal that the cab is free is if the rooftop light is lit.) Radio cabs are also available, but need to be called in advance. See p. 237 for a list of companies.

Don't even consider renting a car to tour central London. Traffic congestion is a major issue, plus construction for Crossrail—a new rail line being built through north central London—will mean temporary street closures and detours around some of London's busiest districts until the project is completed in 2018.

If You Have Only a Week

Begin your week where London began: the original City, the Square Mile that the Romans first called home. First stop on **Day 1** can be Sir Christopher Wren's 17th-century masterpiece, St. Paul's Cathedral, located on Ludgate Hill. From here, it's a short walk north to the fascinating exhibits of the Museum of London. Backtrack south across the Thames on the pedestrian-only Millennium Bridge to Tate Modern, one of the world's leading modern art exhibition spaces. From the Tate, walk east along the riverbank to the re-creation of Shakespeare's famous Globe Theatre in atmospheric Southwark. Then cross London

The imperial state crown in the Tower of London

Bridge back to the north side of the Thames. One Tube stop east brings you to the Tower of London, where Beefeaters, Crown Jewels, and tales of beheadings will fill the rest of your day. A Thames boat ride from the Tower or St. Katharine's Wharf is a relaxing way to head home.

Day 2 takes you to Westminster, the royal and political center of the capital. Begin at Westminster Abbey, home to Poets' Corner, beautiful cloisters, and tombs of English monarchs. It's a short walk across the street to the neo-Gothic Houses of Parliament. A loop north and west takes in Downing Street, the expanse of the Horse Guards Parade, lovely St. James's Park, and the queen's London house at Buckingham Palace. Head back to Westminster Bridge and walk south over the Thames—the views back to Parliament are the stuff of picture postcards. Across on the lively South Bank you'll find the towering London Eye observation wheel, the Sea Life London Aquarium, and the Southbank collection of art, film, and concert venues. The excellent Imperial War Museum lies a ten-minute walk farther south.

The lively West End, London's main entertainment district, can be the focus of **Day 3.** Start with a stroll around Trafalgar Square, the epicenter of the action—the treasures of the National Gallery and the National Portrait Gallery are only steps away. Wander north into Leicester Square, where a booth provides reasonably priced theater tickets to

NOT TO BE MISSED:

Discovering the opulent majesty of St. Paul's Cathedral   60–63

A visit to Gothic Westminster Abbey   74–77

Taking a stroll in royal park, such as St. James's   81, 87

Buckingham Palace for the Changing of the Guard   89

Exploring the National Gallery and National Portrait Gallery   110–117

Seeing a play in one of London's many theaters   118–120

Visitor Information

Both the excellent **Visit London** website *(www.visitlondon.com)* and *LondonTown.com* provide a wealth of online information on hotels, restaurants, shopping, and anything else you need to know about visiting London. See p. 239 for a list of other useful websites.

The **Britain & London Travel Centre** *(1 Regent St., W1, tel 08701 566366)* provides brochures and maps and sells theater tickets, discount passes, and tours.

Be sure to check out *Time Out,* a weekly magazine with the latest information on movies, theater, museum exhibits, events, restaurants, and clubs around the city.

West End shows. Piccadilly Circus, Soho, and Chinatown round out your roamings father north, while electric Covent Garden to the east beckons with shops, restaurants, and street entertainers.

Visit Bloomsbury and the British Museum's massive collection to start **Day 4.** Just south, at the north end of Lincoln's Inn Fields, is the Sir John Soane's Museum, crammed full of fine art and quirky artifacts. From there, an eclectic range of sites are all within walking distance: the Charles Dickens Museum to the northeast, the quiet lanes and courtyards of the Inns of Court to the south, and the renowned Courtauld Institute art collection south along the Thames at Somerset House.

Start **Day 5** at royal Kensington Palace—its refurbished exhibits, gardens, and grounds open again in May 2012.

Climate

In general, London enjoys defined seasons. Winter (Nov.–March) is cold with frosts and sometimes snow. Spring (April–May) warms up. Summer (June–Aug.) can be warm enough to eat dinner outside and may even become humid and sticky. And fall's (Sept.–Oct.) chilly mornings can become warm sunny days. See p. 236 for more information.

One note: London's famous fogs of the last centuries were not functions of climate but were actually blankets of heavy industrial pollution. They were eliminated by the Clean Air Act of 1956.

A short walk southeast through Kensington Gardens takes you to the ornate Albert Memorial, while the impressive Victoria & Albert, Natural History, and Science museums are all nearby, a short walk south on Cromwell Road. From here, the siren call of Harrods and Harvey Nichols department stores lures shoppers a half-mile (1 km) east up Brompton Road.

Devote **Day 6** to touring East London, one of the city's fastest growing areas. A weekend visit is best to take in the markets at Spitalfields and Petticoat Lane, but any day is good to explore South Asian culture and food around nearby Brick Lane. Be sure to leave time to take the DLR to Canary Wharf and the excellent Museum of London Docklands, as well as a few hours to explore lovely Greenwich a couple miles beyond, south across the Thames.

Day 7 can be your chance to buy all those last-minute gifts for yourself and others, with some refined culture mixed in. Start on Oxford Street, one of the world's busiest retail strips. Head west from Oxford Circus to stately Selfridges department store and dozens of other retailers. A detour north a quarter mile (0.4 km) or so brings you to the art and armor of the Wallace Collection. Before Marble Arch, turn south to walk through Mayfair backstreets to indulge in a traditional afternoon tea at one of the great hotels—perhaps Claridges or the Dorchester.

If You Have More Time

There's so much to see and do in London, a week really won't cut it. A venture to northern London takes in **Regent's Park** and its beautiful rose garden, **Madame Tussauds's** kitschy but fun wax museum directly to its south, **Camden Town's** huge and lively weekend markets off the park's northeast corner, and the lovely canals of **Little Venice** and St. John's Wood with **Abbey Road** (of Beatles fame) to the west. A longer excursion 15 miles (24 km) west brings you to Henry

Discount Passes

London is a very expensive city—there's no shame in taking advantage of as many discounts as possible. For public transport, the convenient Oyster card and a variety of Travelcards allow you reduced fares on the Tube, buses, overground rail, Docklands Light Railway, trams, and many mainline railway services. Check *www.tfl.gov.uk/tickets* for complete information.

The London Pass (*www.londonpass.com*) provides entry to more than 55

major attractions for one price and offers the option to add on a London Transport Travelcard. The card also allows you to skip the line at some locations.

Combination tickets are available for many of the city's popular (and high-priced) attractions, such as the London Eye and Madame Tussauds. These can offer big savings in the long run. The London Eye website (*www.londoneye.com*) lists all their options.

London's friendly pubs—such as the Sherlock Holmes in Westminster—offer respite for visitors.

VIII's stunning **Hampton Court Palace,** best reached by cruising up the Thames.

London is also full of intriguing small museums and houses that often fly under the mainstream radar. Very much worth a visit are the **V&A Museum of Childhood** and the **Geffrye Museum** of the history of the domestic home, both in east London; the 19th-century **Old Operating Theatre** in Southwark; and elaborately decorated **Leighton House** near Holland Park in west London.

Sports fans may want to take in a **football (soccer) match**—the Barclays Premier League is often touted as the finest league in the world. Chelsea (*www.chelseafc.com*), Arsenal (*www.arsenal.com*), and Tottenham (*www.tottenhamhotspur.com*) are the top London clubs. If you cannot get a ticket, join Londoners watching the games in the pubs, or book a stadium tour. If cricket is more your style, Middlesex (*www.middlesexccc.com*) plays its home matches at Lord's, near Regent's Park, and Surrey's home ground is at the Kia Oval (*www.kiaoval.com*), south of the Thames.

If you need a break from the bustle of the capital city, London is an excellent base for excursions. **Windsor Castle,** Shakespeare's **Stratford-upon-Avon,** the seaside reort of **Brighton,** idyllic **Cambridge,** the Georgian spa town of **Bath, Stonehenge's** ancient stone circles, and the other destinations listed on pp. 219–234 are all within relatively easy reach on Britain's excellent National Rail (*www.nationalrail.co.uk*) lines or by rental car. All major U.S. car rental companies operate in the U.K., or try Europcar (*www.europcar.co.uk*).

Tipping

In restaurants, check if the service charge has already been added; if not, the usual tip is ten percent. In pubs and bars there is no tipping except for table service. Taxi drivers expect a ten percent tip, more if they help with luggage or have to wait. There is no tipping in theaters, cinemas, or concert halls.

History & Culture

Above: Detail of the Buckingham
Palace gate
Opposite: A Yeoman stands tall at
Hampton Court Palace.

London Today

London is a living and constantly changing city. Some cities depend on impressive historic buildings for their greatness, others on being the center of government or culture or finance; still others are exciting because they are new. What makes London unique is that it is all of these in one. It is simply the most culturally rich, stimulating, and dynamic city in the world.

There is, delightfully, too much to do, to see, to visit, and to explore. First-time visitors almost always return to revisit favorite haunts or to explore a little bit more. In fact, about 25 million people visit each year.

London's 7.75 million residents find this great city just as exciting. More than 30

Abbey Road's zebra crossing has become a London landmark.

percent were born elsewhere. Of the remainder, many are second- or third-generation immigrants. Some have fulfilled a childhood dream of moving from another part of Britain to the capital. Some have come from much farther afield, choosing to leave homelands such as India, Pakistan, and the Caribbean when the British Empire ended after World War II. Others have arrived fleeing political unrest in China, Cyprus, Italy, Kenya, Uganda, and elsewhere. London is truly cosmopolitan. Almost 200 languages are spoken. English may be predominant, but you might hear Chinese dialects, Gujarati, Urdu, Punjabi, Bengali, Turkish, Arabic, Italian, and Spanish on any street corner.

The core of London is spread along the north bank of the twisting Thames River, the capital's backbone.

Entering this pulsating mass for the first time takes one's breath away. Nowhere else offers such quality in such quantity. For instance, most people know that they want to visit the British Museum or the Victoria & Albert Museum, but few are aware that there are some 300 other museums

to choose from—plus myriad commercial art galleries that make London the world center of the art trade. London's theater is legendary, and visitors naturally want to sample it. But they are often surprised that they have to choose among more than 100 theaters staging plays or musicals at any one time; some of the best shows may be in theaters well away from the main theater district, the West End.

The museums and theaters are often superb buildings themselves, each telling a tiny part of London's history. Indeed, the quality of London's historic buildings may not surprise the visitor, but the quantity—almost 17,000 protected buildings tucked into every corner of this sprawling city—most certainly does. For instance, Buckingham Palace is not the only royal palace; you can visit six others including the palaces of Westminster, Hampton Court, and Kensington. These palaces are spread out across the expanse of London, so that Hampton Court Palace in the west is about 18 miles (29 km) from Greenwich Palace in the east.

Grasping the general layout of this vast city is the first challenge for any visitor. The core of London is spread along the north bank of the twisting Thames River, the capital's backbone. The oldest part, confusingly known as the City, is the tightly packed financial hub. The City's sleek buildings, soaring around the dome of St. Paul's Cathedral and 100 other City churches, are the destination for many of the million or so sharp-suited commuters who, from Monday to Friday, flood into London by train or car. Other City workers cross the capital on the Tube (as the Underground train system is now officially called) or squeeze into red buses.

Outside the City's east wall stand the riverside Tower of London and Tower Bridge. Behind stretches the East End, where the story of London's immigrants and dockworkers unfolds in

The London Eye provides views up and down the Thames both day and night.

the streets of Whitechapel and Spitalfields—French Huguenot silk-weavers' fine houses, Jewish synagogues, the Cockney traders of Petticoat Lane market, and the spice-scented streets where many Bengalis now live. Here, too, lives Europe's greatest concentration of artists, designers, and musicians, many using old warehouses as studios. East of the Tower, 11 miles (18 km) of docks left silent when the port moved to Tilbury have been revived. Known as the Docklands, the area has its own elevated Docklands Light Railway, some daring new buildings, and, farther north, extensive sports facilities—it is here that the 2012 Olympic Games will be held. Opposite the Docklands, on the South Bank lie ancient Greenwich Palace and Greenwich Peninsula with its landmark O_2 Arena (formerly called the Millennium Dome).

Hard by the City's north wall, Clerkenwell with its monastic remains leads north to Islington with its elegant houses, thriving fringe theaters, and a plethora of restaurants.

West of the City lies Westminster, London's political and royal center. Here, north of Westminster Bridge, stand the Houses of Parliament, Westminster Abbey, and the government's sprawling Whitehall offices. Buckingham Palace and St. James's Palace are nearby, surrounded by St. James's and Green Parks. This is where smart residential London first grew up, and the area has retained its status—St. James's and Mayfair contain some of London's most stylish shops, art galleries, and restaurants, as well as gentlemen's clubs, both Christie's and Sotheby's auction houses, and deluxe hotels such as the Ritz. London continues westward into the elegant residential and shopping districts of Belgravia, Knightsbridge, and Chelsea. Still farther west lie Kensington, Holland Park, and South Kensington, home to the Science, Natural History, and Victoria & Albert Museums. In these areas look for building facades that often have decorated doorways, terra-cotta friezes, or blue plaques noting that a person of historical importance lived at that address. Farther west are former aristocrats' country mansions, now swallowed up by the suburbs: Osterley, Syon House, Kew Palace and Gardens, and finally Hampton Court Palace.

London between the City and Westminster has a distinct character. On the north bank of the Thames, the old lanes and squares of Holborn, Bloomsbury, Covent Garden, and Soho contain the West End theaters and a rich concentration of museums and restaurants. Meanwhile, along the south bank of the Thames, a strip of entertainment centers running from Tower to Westminster Bridges includes the National Theatre, Shakespeare's Globe theater, and the Tate Modern museum.

London's legal Inns of Court extend through Holborn from Gray's Inn to the riverside Inner and Middle Temples. Leafy Bloomsbury squares are the setting for the British Museum, much of the University of London, and a string of specialist museums stretching down to Covent Garden, a center for theaters, restaurants, shops, and street entertainment. To the west of Covent Garden is Trafalgar Square, where the National Gallery looks down over the fountains to Whitehall and St. James's. A few minutes' walk north from Trafalgar Square, Leicester Square—a focal point of the night scene—marks the start of Soho. Its southern part is London's Chinatown;

> ## EXPERIENCE:
> # London Walking Tours
>
> With 2,000 years of history hidden in every nook and cranny, London is a perfect city for guided walking tours.
>
> The best-known and best-organized tours are led by **London Walks** *(tel 020 7624 3978, www.londonwalks.com)*, which offers daily walks covering topics such as the Blitz, the Beatles Magical Mystery Tour, and the Hidden Pubs of Old London Town.
>
> **Citisights** *(tel 020 8806 4325, www.chr .org.uk)* prides itself on high academic standards, while **Blue Badge** tour guides *(www .blue-badge-guides.com)* offer higher priced (and high-quality) personalized half- and full-day tours. Additionally, **Londontown .com** lists a variety of free do-it-yourself walks at *www.londontown.com/London/ Walking_in_London.*

its northern part is a mixture of bars, restaurants, and food shops. Theater-lined Shaftesbury Avenue slashes through Soho to Piccadilly Circus. Regent Street, lined with upmarket shops, sweeps elegantly north from here, along Mayfair's eastern edge and up toward Regent's Park. Beyond lie the residential areas of St. John's Wood, hilltop Hampstead, and Highgate.

Despite this variety, Londoners and visitors need to find peace. While the financial markets buzz, there are many ways to relax. In 2005 *Gourmet* magazine named London the world's best place to eat. It has more than 6,000 restaurants to choose from; 5,000 or so pubs and bars, many in old buildings or in pretty locations along the river, also serve food; some have music and even theaters.

If relaxation means shopping, try Oxford Street, the longest retail street in Europe. London's two greatest department stores are Selfridges, on Oxford Street, and Harrods in Knightsbridge. Some 350 street markets include Portobello Road's antiques shops and stalls. If relaxation means a walk in a park, make the most of London's parkland. If it means music, you can enjoy the sweet notes of more than 1,000 concerts a week taking place in concert halls, music colleges, churches, and museums.

Despite this banquet of choice, visitors to London can sometimes find themselves choked by crowds of other visitors, unable to taste the essence of the city they have come to visit. If this happens, it is best to leave the lines at Madame Tussaud's or the Tower of London behind and hop on a bus or take the Underground to one of London's more colorful areas. Try Soho or Islington, or take a walk along the south bank of the Thames from Westminster to Tower Bridge.

The Making of London

The twisting, slow-flowing Thames, Britain's longest river, was for centuries London's nerve center. Roman London stood on its north bank, alongside its vital port. A thousand years after the Romans arrived, Edward the Confessor established his new riverside palace and monastery upstream to the west, on the marshes of

Hyde Park is one of many London parks offering a refuge within the city.

Westminster, and so London's second city was born. William the Conqueror consolidated Westminster's position as the royal, political, and religious capital of his new land, while later sovereigns enjoyed a string of palaces built on the banks of the Thames from Hampton Court to Greenwich.

London grew fast. By 1700 its population was 575,000, making it the largest and fastest-growing city in Western Europe. Soon London was 20 times the size of the next biggest English city and contained one-tenth of the country's population. The city expanded westward, northward, and, in the 19th century, southward over new river bridges, as well as eastward around the docks. By the 1930s, its population peaked at 10 million.

The river is still a key factor in London's development. Docklands has been the largest urban renewal site in Europe, and historic riverside buildings such as the Tower of London and the Houses of Parliament are joined by new ones, including Embankment Place, and the world's largest dome at Greenwich Peninsula.

Parks

Londoners seeking escape on weekends do not need to leave their city. Parks of all kinds enrich the capital, about 1,700 in all. They range from the walled Chelsea Physic Garden and handkerchief-size City churchyards to the great expanses of Richmond Park and the formal Royal Botanic Gardens. Indeed, nearly 11 percent of Greater London is parkland, a total of 70 square miles.

It was the monarchs who first protected large open spaces for their hunting. Today, these hunting grounds survive as the magnificent royal parks. Hyde Park, formerly considered the fashionable center of London, has fine landscaping and plenty of activity available. The childlike serenity of neighboring Kensington Park, with its palace backdrop, is quite different. Regent's Park retains the grandeur of its original aristocratic country estate plan. St. James's Park, close to Buckingham Palace, is the one for pageantry, and nearby Green Park offers tranquility and shady trees. In the far west of London, Richmond, the largest royal park, has wonderful views from its hills, while Bushy Park, with its grand chestnut avenue and deer, shares its history with Hampton Court Palace. In the east, Greenwich Park sweeps up from gleaming Queen's House to provide the finest panoramic viewpoint of London.

London Plane Trees

London is lucky to have met the plane tree. This hearty, quick-growing shade tree has claimed the city as its own, standing sentry along its busy streets, filling the peaceful parks, and providing a green canopy for its famous squares.

The London plane can grow to heights of about 165 feet (50 m) and is especially adept at urban living. Air pollution gets absorbed in the tree's thick outer bark, which is then shed as needed, revealing a healthy layer. The plane can be easily transplanted and does well in the typical hard-packed London soil. Plus, its strong limbs can survive wind and ice storms better than most, helping it stand tall when other trees might cry uncle. The plane's ability to thrive, even during London's most darkly polluted days, is a fine example of evolution in action.

London's other green spaces have evolved in different ways. Hampstead Heath was once common grazing ground. Victoria Park and Battersea Park, opened in 1846 and 1858 respectively, were created to improve local conditions. Peace and quiet can be found in cemeteries and churchyards—St. Dunstan-in-the-East, a secret garden within a ruined church, is especially magical.

Wildlife & Nature

London not only supports a population of around 7.75 million people, it is a nature sanctuary whose diversity and importance are unrivaled by those of any other capital. London bees produce a good honey, and Richmond Park's 200 species of beetle have helped make it a Site of Special Scientific Interest.

Great, thick forests once encircled London, before they were pushed back for agriculture. Vestiges include the spinneys of Highgate Woods and Holland Park and some of the ancient oaks of Richmond Park. The 18th-century Enlightenment and Picturesque movements awakened Londoners to nature's beauties, both tamed and untamed. It was at this time that Kew's Royal Botanic Gardens were planted.

In the 19th century, the Victorians replaced many traditional limes, elms, and chestnuts with plane trees (see sidebar above). They also controlled their parkland vistas by introducing evergreen oaks, copper beeches, false acacias, arbutus, and trees of heaven.

Other parts of London are truly wild, notably the neglected cemeteries where hedgehogs, weasels, frogs, and foxes have resettled. And birds—redstarts, kestrels, and herons—are returning to London, to join the pigeons, sparrows, and seagulls. ∎

History of London

It is people who have, over the centuries, shaped the London we know today. Some have left a tangible legacy: The Romans left their Temple of Mithras, Samuel Pepys his vivid diary, and William Hogarth his caricatures of 18th-century life. London today is the city created by all those who have taken part in its 2,000-year history.

Roman London

London might have been born in 54 B.C. when Julius Caesar and his Roman army attacked the Catuvellauni forces who held two hills beside the Thames, at the point where it stopped being tidal and could easily be forded. But Caesar instead returned to Gaul (France). It was under Emperor Claudius, in A.D. 43, that the Romans came back and founded Londinium port on the same spot. They built the first London Bridge, linking their ports on the southeast coast (now Kent) to Camulodunum (Colchester), capital of their British province.

After a revolt of the British tribes, led by Queen Boudicca of the Iceni, who burned the city down in A.D. 61, the Romans made Londinium their capital. A tall, thick wall protected its 30,000 to 60,000 inhabitants. Public buildings included baths, temples, gardens, a basilica, and a forum. But in 410, mirroring Rome's decline, Roman troops left London.

> The young Viking Dane Cnut (R.1016–1035) chose London, not Winchester, as his capital—a position it would never again lose.

Saxons & Vikings

After the Romans left, London dwindled. However, its location ensured that trade continued—and its wealth attracted invaders. Over the next three centuries, Angles and Saxons from northwest Germany gradually established small kingdoms in England—Kent, Mercia, Wessex, and others. Saxon London, called Lundenwic, was sited along the Strand. Through the sixth and seventh centuries it prospered with international trade.

But there were other eyes on London. Viking longships left Norway, Sweden, and Denmark to raid England. In 842 and 851, Danish Vikings stormed London, and in 872 they made it their headquarters. It was Alfred (R.871–899), the Christian king of an enlarged Wessex, who recaptured the city in 886 and made peace with the Danes. Although Winchester was the royal capital, Alfred made Lundenwic the power base. He moved the earlier Saxon settlement from the Strand, where enemy longships could easily beach, back inside the walls and renamed it Lundenburh. He repaired the defenses and invigorated international trade, devising a countrywide code of law and a system of taxation and instituting military service. When the Danes returned in 980, the state was strong enough to hold firm, even if hefty "Danegeld" tribute was needed to buy off war.

But these payoffs didn't protect England from the eventual arrival of the Danes as rulers of England. The young Viking Dane Cnut (R.1016–1035) chose London, not Winchester, as his capital—a position it would never again lose. Cnut brought prosperity to the country and patronized the Church.

Medieval London

In the years 1042 to 1485, Westminster was established as the seat of the monarchy, while the City's merchants exercised more and more control over their city and their kings.

When Edward the Confessor (*R.1042–1066*) dared not make his pilgrimage to Rome (he feared a coup if he left the country), Pope Leo permitted him to restore the modest Westminster Abbey instead. Thus began one of London's greatest

The Battle of Hastings in 1066 brought Normans into England and into London.

Street Names That Tell a Story

Doesn't Pudding Lane sound like a charming cobblestoned alley, evoking images of good-natured vendors selling sweets to happy children? Think again. "Pudding" was actually the medieval term for animal guts, and Pudding Lane was a street by the riverside that housed many a butcher shop. Animal innards were tossed out the overhanging windows, and gravity, time, and the occasional broom would funnel the pudding down the sharply pitched street into the flowing waste removal system known as the Thames.

London is full of evocative street names. Many derive their names from the ancient businesses plied there: It's pretty clear what was sold on Wood Street, Poultry, Milk Street, Honey Lane, and Bread Street, all located near or on the old market at Cheapside. Less obvious is the origin of Friday Street's name, until we learn it led directly to Cheapside's fishmongers.

Other street names tell different stories: Houndsditch, at the east end of the City, was a ditch just outside city walls where, in the Middle Ages, the bodies of dead dogs were unceremoniously tossed; Cockpit Steps, in Westminster, was the site of royal cockfights; Old Jewry, a street near the present-day Guildhall, was a Jewish settlement in Anglo-Saxon times; and Clink Street in Southwark marks the location of the old Clink prison (long since gone), which endowed the language with a short and sweet English nickname for a jail.

building projects: the monastery, abbey church, and royal palace of Westminster. But it was Edward's cousin, William (R. 1066–1087), Duke of Normandy, who established Westminster as the seat of royal and state power. Invading England in 1066, he crushed Edward's successor, Harold, at the Battle of Hastings. Norman rule, with imported administrators and soldiers, replaced Anglo-Saxon; and, to keep watch over the City merchants, William built the Tower of London.

William's great tax survey of England, the Domesday Book, reveals an ordered society that would thrive under Norman and Plantagenet rule. This was a period of Crusades abroad and monastic building at home. Between 1077 and 1136, 13 monasteries and 126 churches were built in and around London's wall, including St. Bartholomew's Church and Hospital. At Westminster, Henry III (R.1216–1272) began the Gothic rebuilding of the Abbey in 1245.

In the City, the merchants won the right to be self-governing in 1191. In 1215 King John (R.1199–1216) put his seal to the Magna Carta, which curbed his powers. By 1295, the Model Parliament of Edward I (R.1272–1307), government was by consent, not rule.

The next century witnessed the Black Death (1348–1350) epidemic, when half of London's population died; the Peasants' Revolt of 1381, which Richard II (R.1377–1399) quelled at Smithfield; and the Wars of the Roses (1455–1485) inheritance dispute. On a happier note, in 1477 William Caxton produced the first book printed in England on his Westminster press.

Tudor London

When Henry VII (R.1485–1509) came to the throne, ushering in Tudor rule (1485–1603), London's prosperity and status surged forward, out of the medieval world into the Renaissance and onto the international stage.

War-torn England recovered under strong rulers, and the benefit was felt most in London. Commerce expanded. Wharves lined the riverfront. In 1566, Thomas Gresham built the Royal Exchange to enable London financiers and merchants to compete with Antwerp. London's population leaped from 75,000 to 200,000, making it the fastest-growing European city, and equal in size to Paris and Milan.

Trade boomed as merchant-adventurers opened up new trading routes, to Asia for silks and spices and to America for tobacco and sugar. At Deptford and Woolwich, a navy was built up that would quash Philip II's Spanish Armada in 1588 and enable Francis Drake, Walter Raleigh, John Hawkins, and others to explore new trade routes, laying the foundation for the British Empire.

The Church, however, was turbulent. Henry VIII (R.1509–1547), lacking a male heir, instructed his lord chancellor, Cardinal Wolsey, to win permission from the Pope to divorce Catherine of Aragon. When he failed, the king dismissed him, took over his palatial homes at Hampton Court and Whitehall, and from 1532 to 1534 broke with Rome to become Supreme Head of the English Church. The Reformation began. It promoted Protestant ideas, English-language Bibles and, most radical of all, the Dissolution of the Monasteries (1536–1540). About 800 religious houses were closed, 20 of them in and around London. The capital's atmosphere and character were profoundly altered as secular power replaced the religious influence.

Henry was succeeded by his son, the boy-king Edward VI (R.1547–1553), his daughter Mary I (R.1553–1558), and then his younger daughter, Elizabeth I (R.1558–1603).

The Palace of Westminster was the principal London royal residence until Henry VIII.

With her heady mix of intelligence, charm, and arrogance, she gave her name to an age: the Elizabethan Renaissance. This was the age of the first custom-built theaters (where Shakespeare's plays were performed), of art patrons, and of pageantry.

Stuarts & Revolution

Londoners greeted King James VI of Scotland as their James I of England (R.1603–1625) with eight triumphal arches. But Stuart rule (1603–1714, except for 1649–1660, the period of the Republic) failed to unite Catholics and Protestants.

Parliament turned against the extravagant, well-meaning monarchs. Protestants left for the New World—the Pilgrim Fathers sailed on the *Mayflower* from Rotherhithe in 1620. Papists threatened the king's life—Catholic conspirators tried to blow up the royal family and Parliament in 1605. Finally, after Charles I (R.1625–1649) was executed for treason (see sidebar this page), Oliver Cromwell and his Puritan followers formed the Commonwealth (1649–1653), and then the Protectorate (1653–1659).

Their Puritan London did not last. Soon after Cromwell's death, the monarchy was restored and Charles II (R.1660–1685) took the throne. This marked the start of the Restoration, where dramatist John Dryden, composer Henry Purcell, scientist Isaac Newton, painter William Hogarth, and architect Christopher Wren were key figures in a creative outburst. But Parliament's attempts to restrict royal power soon broke down.

When Charles's Catholic successor James II (R.1685–1688) fled to France, the bloodless Glorious Revolution witnessed Parliament inviting the Dutch Prince William of Orange (R.1689–1702) and his wife, Mary (R.1689–1694), both Protestants, to take the throne. They signed the Bill of Rights (1689), defining and limiting the monarch's power and excluding Catholics from the throne. In Parliament, modern elements of government evolved, such as political parties, cabinet government, and the limited parliamentary term. Later, under Queen Anne (R.1702–1714), Scotland and England signed the Act of Union (1707).

Meanwhile, Londoners had suffered the Great Plague, which killed some 110,000 in

The Execution of Charles I

In 1648, with the English Civil War finally over, a tribunal assembled by Oliver Cromwell and his Parliamentarians sentenced defeated king Charles I to death, citing his "wicked design to erect and uphold in himself an unlimited and tyrannical power to rule according to his will, and to overthrow the rights and liberties of the people of England."

The sentence of beheading was carried out on January 30, 1649. Charles was led through Banqueting House, then part of Whitehall Palace, to the makeshift scaffolding erected outside. He wore extra-heavy clothing, as the day was very cold and he was concerned that visible shivering would be construed as cowardice by the thousands of spectators in the crowd.

The king acted with poise and dignity on the scaffold. Charles asked the executioner that the fatal blow not be struck until he had stretched his hands out wide by his side, signaling his readiness. After adjusting the executioner's block, the king lay in position, spoke softly to himself, and gave the agreed-upon signal. Charles was beheaded in one stroke. By all accounts, the act was greeted with a woeful combination of groans, cries, and stunned silence.

SILVER JUBILEE OF HER MAJESTY QUEEN ELIZABETH II.

GEORGE II.
1727 – 1760

GEORGE III.
1760 – 1820

GEORGE IV.
1820 – 1830

45c

St.Vincent

1977

A 1977 St. Vincent stamp shows English kings George II, George III, and George IV.

1665, then the Great Fire of London, which raged for four days in 1666 and destroyed four-fifths of the wood-built City. Afterward, the wealthy moved westward and Wren's St. Paul's Cathedral and churches gave new character to the City. A financial explosion stimulated by William Paterson's new Bank of England (1694) generated ideas that would produce the Stock Exchange, the Baltic Exchange, and Lloyd's.

Georgian London

When Queen Anne died without a direct heir, the crown went to the great-grandson of James I, the German-speaking Elector of Hanover named George. Thus began the Hanoverian line that continues today, called Windsor since 1917.

Under the Georges—George I (R.1714– 1727), George II (R.1727–1760), George III (R.1760–1820), and George IV (Prince Regent 1811–1820, king 1820–1830)—London prospered as never before. Trade and the arts flourished, and the population doubled to one million. London became Europe's largest city.

This huge metropolis needed houses. The wealthy moved westward again, first toward the Court at St. James's and then over the Bloomsbury fields, and northward up to Islington, Hampstead, and Highgate. Inspired by Inigo Jones's Covent Garden Piazza of 1631 and Henry Jermyn's lucrative development of St. James's Square in the 1660s, developers coated aristocrats' London estates with terraces and squares to create Mayfair, Marylebone, and later Belgravia. London also expanded southward: Westminster Bridge opened in 1750, and others followed. Northward, the flamboyant Prince Regent and his architect, John Nash, laid out Regent Street and Regent's Park and Canal in 1811–1828.

Grand private mansions were also built, such as Apsley House, Kenwood, Syon, and Osterley, where the Scottish architect Robert Adam introduced his delicate neoclassicism. Indeed, classicism and intellectual inquiry were fundamental to the 18th-century

Enlightenment movement. In London it found expression in David Garrick's classical theater, Lord Burlington's Palladian villa at Chiswick, and in the establishment of learned and artistic societies such as the Royal Society of Arts (1754) and the Royal Academy (1768).

London's wealth rested on trade. The industrial revolution and the expansion of the empire made London the world's largest port in 1800—up to 8,000 ships might be on the Thames at any given time. To thwart pilferers and speed up the unloading of cargo, the merchants built walled, enclosed docks, an 11-mile-long system completed in 1921.

Victorian London

In 1837 the young Victoria ascended the throne to reign for 63 years. She gave her name to an age of change, invention, growth, and contrast, particularly in her capital—now the center of an empire that stretched across the world. Colonialism became Imperialism; in 1877, Victoria became queen-empress of India.

During the 19th century, London's population exploded from one million to more than six million people. Despite London's wealth, the problems of transport, water supply, sewerage, and slums posed huge challenges. Nevertheless, entrepreneurs, philanthropists, and entertainers prevented the city from grinding to a standstill.

London was now too big to walk across, too widespread to be served by the Thames ferries. In 1829, London's first regular public bus service started. Electric trams followed in 1901, motor buses in 1905.

> **Despite London's wealth [in the 19th century], . . . transport, water supply, sewerage, and slums posed huge challenges.**

London's first railway opened in 1836. Two years later, Euston terminus was built; there were a dozen more by 1899, making the capital easy to visit. From 1851, the North London Link brought workers from outlying London villages to the docks. The railway companies' need to issue precise timetables resulted in the establishment of British Standard Time in 1884, and it was soon adopted around the world. The world's first underground railway had opened in 1863; the first deep-dug lines for electric trains followed in 1890, soon known as the Tube.

People migrated from the countryside in droves. There were also waves of immigrants. Following the Irish potato famine of 1845–1848, 100,000 Irish arrived, cramming into speculators' tenement housing, which, lacking drainage and running water, quickly became slums. Later, in the 1880s, more than 100,000 Jews arrived, fleeing anti-Semitic pogroms in Russia and Eastern Europe. Many settled in Whitechapel in the East End.

London had been seriously overpopulated since the 1830s, and its hygiene infrastructure collapsed. More than 400 sewers emptied into the Thames. Typhus, smallpox, and

Firemen hose down wreckage after a Saturday-night bombing during World War II.

cholera were rampant. After the 1848–1849 cholera epidemic and the Great Stink of 1858 (when the stench of a hot summer and the overflow of human waste finally jolted the city into action), engineer Joseph Bazalgette designed London's first sewage system. He then created the Embankments, built between 1864 and 1874, reclaiming land from the Thames to house a trunk sewer, an underground railway, gas mains, and a water conduit, with a road and public gardens above.

Prince Albert, Queen Victoria's Consort, realized his grand plan for promoting learning and trade. On May 1, 1851, his Great Exhibition opened, displaying "the Works of Industry of all Nations" in a great glass hall in Hyde Park, designed by a gardener, Joseph Paxton. Six million people visited it, a third of the British population. Afterward, Albert was the vision behind a permanent showcase of science and the arts in South Kensington. Beginning with the Victoria & Albert Museum in 1855, museums, colleges, and institutions soon covered an area fondly known as Albertopolis.

Londoners needed lighter entertainment, too. By the 1890s, London had 38 West End theaters and was the theater capital of the world. In the East End, Marie Lloyd was one of the stars who sang in more than 30 music halls, each seating up to 1,400. Meanwhile, countless heroes of empire, science, and the arts were honored with public

St. Pancras International

While London may best be known as a city of ancient tradition, St. Pancras train station is a symbol of its future. The station was dramatically refurbished recently and in 2007 became the London terminus of the Eurostar trains to Europe.

A shiny new train terminal, built below the original 250-foot (75 m) arching roof of the Gothic Victorian structure, greets visitors stepping off from Belgium and France with a range of shops, restaurants, cafés, pubs, and wine bars, including an impressive 315-foot-long (96 m) champagne bar.

But all is not metal and glass. Keep an eye out for statues of wyverns—mythical winged reptiles with the heads of dragons—that were the emblem of the Midland Railway Company who built this fine terminus for their railway in the 1860s.

statues, most notably Admiral Lord Nelson in Trafalgar Square, named for the battle in which he died defeating the French.

Twentieth-century London

Under Edward VII (R.1901–1910), Victorian grandeur acquired a certain extravagance and decadence that was halted by World War I. George V (R.1910–1936) saw his capital suffer unemployment, overcrowding, and an influx of refugees. George VI (R.1936–1952) witnessed the World War II bombs of the Blitz, the arrival of Polish refugees, the dissolution of the Empire, and, in 1948, the creation of the Commonwealth. Since 1952, his daughter Elizabeth II has reigned over a truly multicultural London, whose cosmopolitan outlook continues to enable waves of cultural innovation to influence the rest of the world.

The 20th century saw great physical change in London. It began when Aston Webb laid out a royal processional route from Buckingham Palace, along The Mall to Admiralty Arch. After World War II, bomb sites such as the Barbican were rebuilt as high-rise housing, while developers took advantage of the property slump—most of Mayfair's mansions were destroyed at this time. This gave energy to the burgeoning conservation movement, whose advocates fought to save Covent Garden, Islington, and other areas.

After London Port was moved to Tilbury, the docklands slowly closed down. Then, in 1981, the world's largest urban renewal program began, heavily backed by the government. The profitable deregulations of the financial markets in 1986—"the Big Bang"—led the City to rebuild half of its office space; the following year saw Rupert Murdoch's revolution in newspaper production silence London's home of printing, Fleet Street.

London's people changed, too. When the population of Greater London peaked at ten million in the 1930s, housing was short, the smog was unhygienic, and one million worked on the docks. Political refugees were also arriving by the thousands: Jews went to the East End, then to northern areas such as Golders Green, Edgware, and Stamford Hill; Turkish Cypriots settled in Haringey and Stoke Newington, and Italians in Clerkenwell. After World War II, more than one million Londoners left for the verdant suburbs. Their houses were often divided up for the thousands of immigrants coming from the Commonwealth—Jamaicans went to Brixton and Stockwell, Trinidadians and Barbadians to Notting Hill, Asians to Southall, Greek Cypriots to Camden, and Hong Kong Chinese to Soho.

Amid these crises and upheavals, London witnessed many landmark events—the first radio broadcast in 1922, all women over 21 winning the vote in 1928, the first television broadcast in 1936, and in 1951, the Festival of Britain. Held on the south bank of the Thames to raise Londoners' morale after postwar austerity, the festival marked a release of new creative energy. The south bank now has one of Europe's largest arts complexes.

The Swinging Sixties followed, and then an outpouring of innovative music, art, architecture, and fashion. Terence Conran, Andrew Lloyd Webber, Norman Foster, Vivienne Westwood, and many more lifted London's status. The city was once again a fashionable and exciting place in which to live and work.

The Twenty-first Century

The eve of the millennium witnessed Eurostar trains running from London to Paris via the Channel Tunnel and a revitalization of the London riverscape for public buildings, such as Tate Modern at Bankside, and residential warehouse conversions.

The city and nation suffered a painful blow on July 7, 2005, when 52 people were killed in four coordinated terrorist bombings on the London public transportation system. A memorial to the victims stands quietly at the eastern edge of Hyde Park.

More recently, the Westminster Abbey wedding of William, Prince of Wales (second in line to the throne) to Kate Middleton on April 29, 2011, was much celebrated and watched by billions around the globe.

Looking to the future, all eyes will be on the 2012 Olympics, which will continue the revitalization of the East End. Meanwhile, an important new rail line, Crossrail, is being built through north central London (and out to the eastern and western suburbs). The project, slated for completion in 2018, will connect dozens of existing rail and Tube stations in a new configuration and should help ease some of the city's travel congestion. ∎

The new Duke and Duchess of Cambridge ride off after their wedding in April 2011.

The Arts

London is remarkable not for its cultural cohesion but for its cultural diversity. Almost everything you might ever want is here—it is merely a question of finding it: a thousand years of architecture, painting stretching back to early Gothic delights, statues from the Romans onward, and music and theater of every description. London's museums, galleries, churches, and open houses can be overpoweringly rich, but if the Victoria & Albert Museum is too exhausting to contemplate, you can always visit smaller galleries.

Art is unavoidable. Commercial galleries and auction houses show art on the move. Sculptures spangle London's streets and parks. Both private houses and impressive public buildings may be decorated with fine ironwork or terra-cotta friezes—you have only to lift your eyes above street level to see them.

Architecture

London has superb examples of virtually every British architectural style. Westminster's story leads through grand public buildings, such as Westminster Abbey, the royal palaces and parks, and the aristocrats' mansions and amusements. In the City the remains are a rich mix of livery halls, offices, dealing rooms, and markets that culminate in Broadgate and the Dockland's Canary Wharf developments.

> Westminster's story leads through grand public buildings, such as Westminster Abbey, [and] the royal palaces and parks.

Pre-Norman Remains: Evidence of occupation in the London area goes back to about 500,000 B.C., but the most substantial pre-Norman remains are Roman. Archaeologists have located the forum, basilica, amphitheater, governor's palace, and public bath sites. The Museum of London possesses some fine mosaic floors and a wall painting from Southwark. In the City, there are thick chunks of Roman wall at Trinity Square and on Tower Hill and a section of amphitheater beneath Guildhall Art Gallery.

Norman Castles & Churches: The houses of London's Saxon, Norman, and medieval merchants and craftsmen were built of wood and plaster, so they did not last. Just before the Norman Conquest, the Saxon King Edward the Confessor built Westminster Abbey (consecrated 1065), inspired by buildings at Jumièges and Caen in France. The Romanesque style he adopted, with its chunky piers, rounded arches, galleries, and open timber roof, was so widely used by the Normans that in Britain it is known as Norman style.

William I built a ring of castles, including Windsor, around his capital, and his White

(continued on p. 34)

St. Paul's, built in the 17th century, is England's only domed cathedral.

Traditional English Food

Like airplane food, English cuisine suffers from a serious lack of respect. Never mind that London is one of the hottest cities on the planet for fine dining—it's the traditional fare that usually takes the brunt of the jokes. But what's not to love?

Fish and chips shops are a traditional, but increasingly rare, London sight.

The English custom of boiling vegetables beyond recognition is largely a thing of the past, but if it's comfort food you're looking for, London delivers.

The Traditional English Breakfast

Start your day with a traditional English breakfast, which is usually made up of eggs (most often fried, though sometimes scrambled or poached), back bacon, grilled tomatoes, baked beans, fried mushrooms, black pudding, English sausages, and toast. Sometimes kippers (smoked salt herring—with "salt" being the operative word) is on the menu as well. Nearly all hotels and cafés offer some variation of the English breakfast, though many pubs also offer the meal throughout the day. Stand-out breakfasts can be had at **Simpson's-in-the-Strand** (100

Strand, WC2, tel 020 7836 9112, www.simpsonsin thestrand.co.uk), the **Wolseley** restaurant (160 Piccadilly, WI, tel 020 7499 6996, www.thewolseley .com), or at any of the four **Richoux** (www .richoux.co.uk) restaurants around the city.

Pub Grub

If, by chance, you find yourself in a pub during lunch, there will most likely be several reliable dishes on the menus, all falling under the rubric of "pub grub." Try the Ploughman's Lunch, a very serviceable and hearty meal that usually consists of a thick slab of farmhouse cheddar cheese, tangy relish (called "pickle" in England), salad greens, pickled onions, and fresh, crusty bread. Other tasty fare to try includes meat- and/or vegetable-filled savory pastries (called pasties) and pies (steak & kidney being the most famous, but many others are available); English sausages with mashed potato, gravy, and peas (aka bangers and mash); shepherd's pie; and a traditional Sunday roast of beef, pork, or lamb.

Meanwhile, gastropubs are taking pub food firmly into the 21st century. What began as an isolated effort to upgrade the offerings of pub kitchens with fresh, refined, and creative menus has blossomed into a major foodie movement. Gastropubs are sweeping across London and can be found in nearly every neighborhood; check with your hotel concierge or local friends for recommendations. Some of the tried and true include the **Eagle** *(159 Farringdon Rd., EC1, tel 020 7837 1353)* in Clerkenwell, the **Charles Lamb** *(16 Elia St., N1, tel 020 7837 5040, www. thecharleslambpub.com)* in Islington, and the **Gun** *(27 Coldharbour, E14, tel 020 7515 5222, www. thegundocklands.com)* in Docklands.

Dinner Fare

In addition to the traditional dinnertime roasts, several restaurants specialize in British meats and game. Established in 1798, **Rules** *(35 Maiden Lane, WC2, tel 020 7836 5314, www.rules. co.uk)* in Covent Garden is the oldest restaurant in London and the place to go for seasonal game, including grouse, pheasant, and deer.

St. John *(26 St. John Street, EC1, tel 020 3301 8069, www.stjohnrestaurant.com),* appropriately located near the Smithfield meat market, is a highly celebrated restaurant that specializes in "nose-to-tail" dishes that waste no part of the animal—but its menu is extensive enough to also please those less enamored with offal.

Pie & Mash

An East End staple for centuries, the traditional pie and mash shop is sadly on the endangered species list. The bill of fare consists of a hearty minced-meat pie accompanied by a spoonful of mashed potatoes, all buried in a ladleful of green "liquor"—a seasoned parsley-based broth that has nothing to do with alcohol. Jellied or stewed eels are usually the only other offerings, but you won't be run out of town if you decide against them.

A few authentic pie and mash shops remain around London. Two old-timers: **F. Cooke** *(150 Hoxton St., N1, tel 020 7729 7718, www.realhoxton .co.uk/f-cooke.htm)* in East London's up-and-coming Hoxton neighborhood; and **M. Manze's** *(87 Tower Bridge Rd., SE1, tel 020 7407 2985, www .manze.co.uk)* south of the Thames (and at two other locations).

EXPERIENCE: Sampling Fish & Chips

Another dying tradition to bemoan: the decline of corner fish and chips shops, which used to be found in every neighborhood but now are few and far between. Even so, the renowned hot battered-and-fried fish (usually cod, plaice, or haddock) and the thick wedge potato fries (served with salt and vinegar) are worth seeking out. A high-end option is the **Sea Shell of Lisson Grove** (49–51 Lisson Grove, NW1, tel 020 7224 9000, www.seashellrestaurant.co.uk), near the Marylebone Tube station, which has been serving fresh fish and chips to London's jet set for 40 years.

Other recommendations include the **Golden Fish Bar** (102–104 Farringdon Rd., EC1, tel 020 7837 3574), in the old City, in business since the mid-19th century; **Rock & Sole Plaice** (47 Endell St., WC2, tel 020 7836 3785), in Covent Garden, a popular haunt of Londoners and tourists alike for more than 100 years; **J Sheekey** (32–34 St. Martins Ct., WC2, tel 020 7240 2565, www.j-sheekey.co.uk), another popular, century-old Covent Garden purveyor of the tried and true (with modern choices as well); and the **Golden Hind** (73 Marylebone Ln., W1, tel 020 7486 3644), a local favorite since 1914, tucked away in the quiet Marylebone neighborhood north of Oxford Street.

Henry VIII added on to Cardinal Wolsey's Hampton Court Palace.

Tower (1078–1097), kernel of the Tower of London, is an important example of Norman military architecture. Built of Caen stone, the walls are 12 feet thick, and the square plan contains three rooms on each floor; the cupolas on the corner towers are 14th-century additions. A masterpiece of Norman ecclesiastical architecture is the White Tower's St. John's Chapel: tiny, simple, and with two massive arches.

In London the best surviving Norman church is St. Bartholomew the Great, built in 1123 as part of the priory and hospital, and now the City's only surviving 12th-century monastic church.

Medieval Architecture: Medieval London's walls, with towers and seven double gateways, are still identifiable by street names such as Aldersgate, Aldgate, and Bishopsgate. They surrounded a city made up of flimsy wooden houses, livery company halls, and about 140 churches. The circular Temple Church in Inner Temple, begun in 1160 and enlarged in 1220, is one of London's earliest buildings constructed in the Gothic style, seen in the pointed arcade arches.

Surviving secular medieval buildings include the labyrinth of Inner and Middle Temples dating from 1350 and Lincoln's Inn from 1400. Richard II's Westminster Hall, with its spectacular hammerbeam roof, was started in 1394, while City merchants built their Guildhall between 1411 and 1440. Archbishop Morton built the redbrick gatehouse of his Lambeth Palace around 1495.

The most impressive of the 20 medieval religious houses in London was Westminster Abbey, the royal abbey church of St. Peter, together with its monks' cloisters. In 1245, Henry III demolished it and began building a lavish Gothic church. Four monastic houses stood just north of the City: St. Bartholomew's Priory, Charterhouse Monastery, St. John of Jerusalem's Priory, and Clerkenwell Nunnery. St. John's great gateway evokes their grandeur.

Tudor Buildings: Some of the most glorious buildings seen in London today were built as expressions of the capital's growing world status under the Tudor sovereigns, who ruled from 1485 to 1603. Henry VII added his soaring, lacelike chapel to Westminster Abbey in the early 1500s. The fine fan-vaulting and large windows typical of this period give it a spiritually uplifting airiness. A rare, surviving domestic building, Charterhouse Priory's heavy Washhouse court, built between 1500 and 1535, contrasts sharply.

A major catalyst for this growth was Henry VIII's Dissolution of the Monasteries (1536–1540), which released large swaths of land for building by royals, aristocrats, and developers. While the monarchs concentrated on their palaces and parks, aristocrats and bishops built along the Strand, which was the riverfront that stretched between the City and Westminster. These buildings survive only in street names—Bridewell, Savoy, Northumberland.

The Old Hall of Lincoln's Inn, built in 1492 as housing for the lawyers who resided there, gives an idea of how most of Tudor London must have looked. There is also Camden's Staple Inn, a group of 16th-century domestic houses built in 1586: The half-timbering, horizontal strips of windows, high gables, and overhanging upper floors are typical of the period, although brick houses with chimneys and glass windows were growing in number.

> While the monarchs concentrated on their palaces and parks, aristocrats and bishops built along the Strand.

The Tudor monarchs realized the importance of an outward show of power. Henry VII began the royal wave of secular building with Richmond Palace and Baynard's Castle at Blackfriars, both completed in 1501. When Henry VIII came to the throne in 1509, he inherited these palaces, plus the Tower of London, Eltham Palace, and others—a total of 16 residences within a day's ride of the capital.

At Greenwich, Henry built tennis courts, a tiltyard (medieval knights' competition area), and a large royal armory that could compete with Continental products. With the fall of Cardinal Wolsey, he seized Whitehall Palace and added entertainment areas and riverside State apartments, painting the brickwork red, white, and black. At Wolsey's already vast Hampton Court Palace, he built a great hall, chapel, kitchens, and service courts. Henry also seized the former leper hospital of St. James's. It is in these last two that Tudor palace-building can best be seen today.

While advances were made in domestic housing, overpopulation in the City led to multiple occupancy of houses, poor hygiene, more fires, poverty, and an increase in fatal illnesses—smallpox, tuberculosis, and bubonic plague. A royal proclamation in 1580 forbade the building of any new houses or the subdivision of any existing ones.

Stuart & Georgian London: Inigo Jones gave Stuart London its first Palladian buildings—Queen's House at Greenwich, built in 1616, Banqueting House at White-hall in 1619, Queen's Chapel by St. James's Palace in 1623–1627, St. Paul's Covent Garden in 1631–1638, and London's first square, Covent Garden Piazza, in 1631.

The Great Fire of 1666 provided the impetus for further change. In 1667 the first Building Act was passed: All structural walls were to be of brick or stone, and the only projections allowed were balconies. There were also rules governing foundations, timbers being near chimneys, house heights, street widths, and other requirements. The aim was to raise building and safety standards and to control town planning. The result was that plain, flat-fronted terraces and squares would be built over the fields as London expanded, creating the classic character of residential Georgian London.

> **The post-Fire architectural hero was Sir Christopher Wren . . .[who] rebuilt St. Paul's Cathedral.**

The post-Fire architectural hero was Sir Christopher Wren. He rebuilt St. Paul's Cathedral, beginning in 1675, designed 51 churches to surround it, and worked for the king and queen at Kensington and Hampton Court Palaces, and at both Chelsea and Greenwich Hospitals.

The 18th-century Enlightenment attracted a plethora of fine classical architects to London. Nicholas Hawksmoor's Christ Church in Spitalfields, completed in 1714, and James Gibbs's St. Martin-in-the-Fields, of 1721, were two of many new churches. Impressive public buildings included William Kent's Treasury of 1733, William Chambers's Somerset House of 1776, and Robert Smirke's British Museum of 1823. Meanwhile, Lord Burlington's Chiswick House of 1725, and Robert Adam's remodel-ing of Syon, Osterley, and Kenwood mansions in the 1760s, introduced new lightness and elegance to classical buildings. Finally, the Prince Regent employed John Nash from 1816 to 1828 to create the great sweep of Regent Street and Regent's Park, all coated in gleaming, white stucco.

Victorian & Edwardian Architecture: As the London of Queen Victoria transformed itself into the huge capital of an empire, sweeping changes took place in many spheres. In architecture, classicism was challenged by a Gothic revival, and by a return to a redbrick, vernacular style inspired by Christopher Wren.

Nineteenth-century developers followed the lead of Georgian builders, whose planning centered on garden squares. Thomas Cubitt's Belgravia by Buckingham Palace was the grandest. Other developments included west London's Cadogan and Ladbroke estates, and the Islington squares. Bedford Park, begun in 1875, and Hampstead Garden Suburb, begun in 1906, broke new ground in suburbia.

There was a proliferation of public buildings aimed at bringing education to the gen-eral public, among them William Wilkins's National Gallery of 1832 and the glasshouses of Kew. The South Kensington buildings stimulated by the Great Exhibition of 1851 included Alfred Waterhouse's Natural History Museum and Richard Norman Shaw's Royal Geographical Society, both of 1873, and Sir Aston Webb's Victoria & Albert

Museum of 1899. Westminster changed radically: The Houses of Parliament suffered a disastrous fire in 1834 and A. W. N. Pugin and Charles Barry designed the new Houses of Parliament in elaborate Victorian neo-Gothic.

London's vastly increased size necessitated improvements in its infrastructure. New communications demanded new types of building: Sir George Gilbert Scott designed the Gothic St. Pancras railway station and adjacent hotel of 1868–1874. Wide Shaftesbury Avenue was one of several new roads that sliced through slums.

London's Buildings, 1900–Today

London's population today is only slightly higher than what it was in 1900 when, at around 7 million, it was the world's most populated city—New York had 4 million people, Paris 2.7 million.

The graceful curves of the Nelson Stair at Somerset House

Trafalgar Square's Fourth Plinth

While Trafalgar Square has always been synonymous with the towering statue of Horatio, Lord Nelson, more contemporary art has also been on show in recent years.

Behold the Fourth Plinth. Although the rest of Trafalgar Square was completed in the 1840s, the plinth (a statue base) in the northwest corner of the square remained vacant after funding ran out.

That changed in the 1990s when three artists were commissioned to create works that, one after the other, would temporarily call the plinth their home. The program proved so popular that the Fourth Plinth is now formally being used to display innovative contemporary art.

Works in recent years have included a 20-foot-long (6 m) ship in a bottle (appropriately featuring Admiral Nelson's ship, H.M.S. *Victory*) by Yinka Shonibare, and Anthony Gormley's "One and Other," where everyday Brits occupied the plinth for one hour. This went on every hour, 24 hours a day, for 100 days.

A display in the basement of nearby St. Martin-in-the-Fields church shows all the shortlisted entries for the artwork to be featured next. The Fourth Plinth even has its own website *(www.london.gov.uk/fourth plinth)*, where you can keep abreast of the latest proposed new displays (and vote for your favorite).

In the 1920s and '30s, crowding, smog, and dirt generated a middle-class exodus to the suburbs, hastened after World War II. Garden suburbs were seen as the idyllic solution to the ills of city life. Nevertheless, the city's population and boundaries continued to grow, and in the 1930s peaked at about 9 million.

After World War II damage, postwar construction focused on much-needed housing, including the City's large Barbican Estate, begun in 1959. In the public sector, Robert Matthew's Royal Festival Hall was built for the 1951 Festival of Britain and marked the start of the South Bank Arts Complex.

The twentieth century saw several interesting theaters added to London's many. They include the Savoy of 1929, Sir Denys Lasdun's Royal National Theatre of 1967–1977, and the re-created Shakespeare's Globe, opened in 1997 (the last two offer tours).

In the 1960s, undistinguished development, coupled with plans to destroy Covent Garden Market, St. John's Wood, and other areas, stimulated the conservation movement and the call for a change of style. Buildings by Frederick Gibberd, James Stirling, Richard Rogers, Terry Farrell, and Nicholas Grimshaw have introduced new ideas. In the 1980s, the Docklands revival began, the commercial "Big Bang" led to City rebuilding, and new life was injected into the riverside. More than 30 major London millennium building projects kick-started the 21st century. The new City Hall, Portcullis House, and 30 St. Mary Axe keep London ever changing. And eyes will focus on the Lower Lea Valley, in the far eastern reaches of the East End, where the firm Foreign Office Architects will be realizing their master plan for the 2012 Olympic Games.

Plaques & Statues

Thousands of Britain's heroes and villains people London's streets and squares with their memorials.

Some are grand: Nelson's statue stands on a tall column and is set in a square named after his great battle, Trafalgar. Others are remarkably modest: The architect of a great sweep of central London, John Nash, has merely a bust in the colonnade of All Souls Church, Langham Place, which he designed. A few have several memorials: The achievements of Prince Albert were recognized in the splendid Albert Memorial in Kensington Gardens, in Charles Bacon's equestrian statue at Holborn Circus, on the facade of the Victoria & Albert Museum, and elsewhere too. But it is the Duke of Wellington—neither king nor prince but one of Britain's greatest generals—who has three equestrian statues: inside St. Paul's Cathedral, in front of the City's Royal Exchange, and in front of Apsley House at Hyde Park Corner.

Twentieth-century paintings hang on transparent dividers at the National Portrait Gallery.

Great Museums

London has more than 300 permanent museums and galleries, large and small, general and specialist. Some are custom-built; others are collectors' homes; all exist thanks to remarkable people.

The British Museum, the capital's first great national public collection, is one example. Sir Hans Sloane died in 1753, leaving his extensive library and collections of fossils, coins, minerals, and more to the nation—subject to a £20,000 ($32,000) payment to his daughters. The museum opened in Montague House on January 15, 1759, and moved into Robert Smirke's new building in 1838.

The National Gallery, founded in 1824, exists thanks to the gift of 38 paintings by financier John Julius Angerstein. Other national collections include the National Portrait Gallery, the National Maritime Museum, the Science Museum, and the Victoria & Albert Museum, which holds the national collection of decorative and fine arts. The Tate Gallery is now divided into two sections, British art in Tate Britain on Millbank, and international modern art in Tate Modern in the refitted Bankside Power Station.

More personal collections include the Dulwich Picture Gallery, opened in 1814 as

J. M. W. Turner's "The Fighting Temeraire" (1839) hangs in the National Gallery.

the country's first public art gallery, and the Iveagh Bequest and Suffolk Collection in Kenwood House in Hampstead. In the house-museums the stamp of the collector's personality is even stronger, lingering on in his or her residence, whether it is the grand Ham House, Osterley Park, Apsley House, the Wallace Collection, or the more intimate Sir John Soane's Museum, Dr. Johnson's House, and Leighton House. Palaces fulfill this role, too, especially Kensington and Hampton Court.

Finally, there are the specialist collections: the Design Museum; the Museum of London and Museum in Docklands, which tell the capital's own story; and Julius Wernher's treasures in Greenwich's lovely Ranger's House.

Artists in London

Artists from the world famous to the quietly anonymous have recorded almost every important event, building, and person of London's history since the 16th century: What the Globe Theatre and Old St. Paul's Cathedral looked like, the extravagance of the Lord Mayor's rich pageant, the formal opening of St. Katharine Dock.

Hans Holbein painted portraits of grandees, while Wenceslaus Hollar, from Prague, worked for the Earl of Arundel drawing the best and most detailed views of 17th-century London that exist, working on the roof of the earl's Strand mansion. Later, patronage reached a peak under Charles I, who employed Sir Anthony Van Dyck for nine prolific years, and also commissioned Sir Peter Paul Rubens to paint the ceiling of Banqueting House. Thomas Rowlandson and William Hogarth caricatured the city's seamier side. In contrast, Canaletto, Claude Monet, Joseph Mallord, J. M. W. Turner, James Whistler, and André Derain all eulogized the Thames.

A considerable number of paintings by artists working in London are to be found in

Hampton Court and Buckingham Palaces, as well as in some museums and galleries.

The Museum of London has 20,000 paintings, prints, drawings, and other exhibits, usually chosen for their image rather than their artist. One is a picture by Abraham Hondius of the Thames frozen over in 1677. In another work, Henry Moore records Londoners taking refuge in Underground stations during World War II.

Holbein the Younger came to London in 1526, and later entered the service of Henry VIII. At Henry's Bridewell Palace on Fleet Street, he painted his remarkable double portrait, "The Ambassadors," now in the National Gallery. Here, too, are pictures by Van Dyck and Thomas Gainsborough, who first came to London in 1740. Next door, the National Portrait Gallery has plenty of personalities painted in their home city, such as John Hayl's portrait of the diarist Samuel Pepys and Tom Phillips's of the theater director Sir Peter Hall. The Imperial War Museum has a rich collection of 20th-century pictures by artists such as Paul Nash, Stanley Spencer, and David Bomberg. Among the smaller museums, Sir John Soane's stacks up the Hogarth series, and Kenwood House has paintings by Sir Joshua Reynolds, who lived in London from the 1740s.

Occasionally, a London artist's home survives as a house-museum. Lord Leighton's splendid indulgence is in Holland Park, Linley Sambourne's overstuffed home is preserved in Kensington, and Hogarth's country cottage hides between a noisy roundabout and elegant Chiswick House.

Tate Britain has plenty of London artists' work on view. Turner, a Londoner by birth, studied at the Royal Academy and always returned to London after his European tours. Tate Britain's Clore Gallery houses his works, while the main buildings may at any time have on display John Constable's "The Opening of Waterloo Bridge," Charles Ginner's "Piccadilly Circus," and works by R. B. Kitaj, Peter Blake, Howard Hodgkin, and younger artists such as Rachel Whiteread, Damien Hirst, and Fiona Rae.

Today London is seething with artists from all over the world; one estimate puts 10,000 working in the East End alone. Howard Hodgkin, Lucian Freud, Richard Hamilton, Gilbert & George, and Maggie Hambling are among the older generation of artists living in London. Hambling's sculpture of Oscar Wilde was set in Leicester Square in 1998.

The annual Turner Prize is the most prestigious contemporary art award and a yardstick for the way art is moving. Hodgkin was an early winner; Damien Hirst (famous for his pickled and chopped-up animals) and Rachel Whiteread (who represents inside spaces as dense matter) have both won it; and 1998's winner, Chris Ofili, marked a return to representational two-dimensional painting. Others to look out for include Jenny Saville, who paints the best flesh since Rubens, and 2005 winner Simon Starling.

Artists . . . have recorded almost every important event, building, and person of London's history since the 16th century.

To see new movements in the art world, visit shows at the Whitechapel Art Gallery, recently reopened after doubling its exhibition space. Near here, the new galleries in the Old Truman Brewery building in Brick Lane and others in Hoxton Square show the cutting edge of contemporary art. In the West End, shows at the Photographers Gallery and Anthony d'Offay are always worth seeing—others are listed in the *London Galleries Guide* (free from most commercial galleries). Farther west, the Serpentine Gallery in Kensington Gardens is a wild card in conservative Kensington.

Literary London

Throughout its 2,000-year history, Londoners and visitors have documented the city in diaries, chronicles, poetry, and fiction. Reading some of these is one way of getting beneath the surface of London, of evoking its atmosphere at different historical periods. Many are now reprinted, either in their entirety or in anthologies.

The earliest known description is by the Roman historian Tacitus. Loyally he wrote that during Boudicca's revenge "the enemy massacred, hanged, burned and crucified with an energy that suggested ... retribution would soon be visited upon them." From a later age, detailed descriptions of the city include the remarkable one of Elizabethan London by retired tailor and self-taught historian John Stow, in *A Survey of London*, published in 1598.

Meanwhile, the first English-language poem about London, *To the City of London* (circa 1501), once attributed to Scottish poet William Dunbar, ends with the accolade "London, thou art the flower of cities all."

Some remarkable diaries survive from the 17th and 18th centuries. The little known John Manningham described Elizabeth I's calm death in his diary: "At about three o'clock her Majesty departed this life, mildly like a lamb, easily like a ripe apple from a tree." Samuel Pepys's diary of 1660–1669 is better known. In it, the details of his daily life hopping on boats to move from the City to Whitehall Palace, or playing music and going to church, vividly conjure up the Stuart Restoration, and are as interesting as his spectacular account of the Great Fire of 1666. In the same way, John Evelyn, whose diary spans the years from 1640 to 1706, is as keen to describe William and Mary's new Kensington Palace as the beaching of a whale at Greenwich or Cromwell's funeral—"the joyfullest funeral that I ever saw." The Scot James Boswell kept his *London Journal* in 1762–1763, in which he is depressed by the "tumultuous scene" in Parliament, enjoys a friendship with the popular actor-manager David Garrick, and is, like Pepys, indiscreet on the subject of love.

Oscar Wilde found success as a playwright in Victorian London.

Diaries were kept by many 19th-century Londoners, from schoolboy John Thomas Pocock to Queen Victoria, and by visitors, from the Frenchmen Gustave Doré and Blanchard Jerrold to American Nathaniel Hawthorne.

London life comes alive in the great Victorian novels. Thackeray's *Vanity Fair* paints social London during the Regency period, when Knightsbridge was almost in open country. In contrast, Charles Dickens's novels sum up deprivation and squalor. In *Sketches by Boz*, St. Giles slums are described as "wretched houses with broken windows patched with rags and paper ... filth everywhere—a gutter before the houses and a drain behind them."

London's Antiquarian Bookstores

London is a bibliophile's kind of town. An excellent array of antiquarian booksellers could keep you browsing for days on end.

Charing Cross Road, north of Trafalgar Square, is home to a slew of secondhand, rare, and collectible booksellers, including **Quinto Books** (72 Charing Cross Rd., WC2, tel 020 7379 7669, quintobookshop.co.uk); **Francis Edwards Antiquarian Booksellers** (www.francisedwards.co.uk), established in 1855 and sharing the same premises as Quinto; and **Henry Pordes Bookshop** (58–60 Charing Cross Rd., WC2, tel 020 7836 903, www.henrypordesbooks.com). **Cecil Court,** a charming pedestrianized

alley off the east side of Charing Cross Road, contains several more. Check www .cecilcourt.co.uk for a complete list.

Fans of the 1970 Helene Hanff book (and 1987 movie) 84 Charing Cross Road might be disappointed to learn that Marks & Co., the bookstore featured in the memoir, is no longer in business. The store was on the east side of Charing Cross Road, just north of Cambridge Circus. A restaurant now occupies the site, but a plaque notes the shop's location.

The website www.inprint.co.uk/thebook guide/shops lists antiquarian bookshops in London (and elsewhere).

To get a flavor of the variety of London lives in the 20th century would require a dip into, perhaps, Beatrice Webb's diary, Bertrand Russell's autobiography, and Arnold Bennett's journals. George Orwell's journal, Laurie Lee's autobiography, Raymond Chandler's letters, Sir Winston Churchill's copious writings, John Betjeman's poems, and Martin Amis's novels make an equally diverse set.

But it is William Wordsworth's radiant celebration of the city in his sonnet "Upon Westminster," written in 1802 after he crossed Westminster Bridge in the dawn coach, that still encapsulates the romance of London beginning with: "Earth has not anything to show more fair; . . . This City now doth, like a garment, wear/The beauty of the morning; silent, bare,/Ships, towers, domes, theaters, and temples lie/. . .All bright and glittering in the smokeless air."

Few contemporary authors can match the outpouring of quality prose about London written down the centuries. Martin Amis is an exception, seen in his novels *Money* and *London Fields,* as is Michael Moorcock, whose many books set in London include *Mother London.* Peter Ackroyd writes both biography (on Dickens, for instance, and on London itself) and novels. His *Hawksmoor* is set in Spitalfields, *The House of Doctor Dee* concerns an Elizabethan alchemist, and *The Lambs of London* is set in 19th-century Holborn. Monica Ali's acclaimed 2003 novel, *Brick Lane,* explores the life of a young bride in Londons' Bengali community. But perhaps it is Iain Sinclair who touches the raw nerve of London today, setting many of his books in the City and Docklands. His novels include *Lud Heat* about the founder of London.

Performing Arts

Up to a thousand concerts are given in London every week. There are also operas, plays, musicals, and ballets performed in theaters, rooms, gardens, churches—almost any kind of space.

London has always offered plentiful and innovative entertainment, bewildering visitors with its sheer quantity of plays and shows available. In 1599, Thomas Platter, a visitor from Basel, remarked that "every day at two o'clock in the afternoon . . . two and sometimes three comedies are performed at separate places, wherewith folk make merry together, and whichever does best gets the greatest audience."

The Elizabethan stage was, at this period, in its infancy, mixing traditions of secular plays performed in the yards of inns with dancing, singing, and the baiting of bears and bulls. The Puritan City fathers banned theater from the City in 1574. Two years later, James Burbage built London's first permanent playhouse at Shoreditch City. In 1587 the Rose was the first of four theaters to open at Southwark, which soon became London's entertainment center. Here Burbage opened his Globe in 1599. More than 2,000 people would cram into the circular, tiered, wooden theaters to watch plays by Shakespeare, Ben Jonson, and Thomas Dekker, although use of the open-air venues depended upon good weather.

> **From the 1840s onward, London witnessed an explosion in theater, music halls, and entertainment of all kinds.**

With Charles II's restoration, theater returned to the city. Plays were an almost daily event at Whitehall Palace. The King granted two men permission to produce public plays: Thomas Killigrew, who opened the Theatre Royal, Drury Lane, in 1663, and William D'Avenant, whose theater at Lincoln's Inn Fields had the first proscenium arch and facilities to set scenery during a play.

Throughout the 18th century, there were only two legitimate theaters and companies inside the city, Drury Lane and the Opera House in Covent Garden; the many others were illegal. London theater later suffered its second persecution, when Henry Fielding's crude satires at the old Theatre Royal in the Haymarket caused the Lord Chamberlain to introduce powers of censorship in 1737, lifted only in 1968.

Despite strict censorship, theater and entertainment flourished. David Garrick was the actor-manager who revived classical theater and treated Shakespeare with a new respect. He demanded that actors learn their parts, improved production, and transformed audience behavior, which had often been raucous—people would walk across the stage to chat with friends during performances. In 1728 the first performance of John Gay's *Beggar's Opera* marked the arrival of English opera. Meanwhile, 18th-century London was full of musical activity, both amateur and professional. Concert rooms and theaters were opened to cater to the increased demand for concerts, opera, and masquerades: Mozart appeared at the Hanover Square Rooms, J. S. Bach and Haydn conducted their own compositions, and Handel composed operas, concerts, and chamber works.

From the 1840s onward, London witnessed an explosion in theater, music halls, and entertainment of all kinds. The music halls grew out of informal sing-alongs held in taverns. By the end of the century, huge halls were being built. The lavish, newly renovated Hackney Empire flourishes in north London. The Coliseum, opened in 1904, had a stage large enough to hold a chariot race, with an audience capacity of 2,558, still London's largest. These variety theaters attracted a new audience, the middle-class visitor to London. Gradually, the vulgarity was tempered, so that Sarah Bernhardt played at the Coliseum, Sir Thomas Beecham conducted excerpts from *Tannhäuser* at the Palladium, and one music hall even put a cricket match on stage.

In theater, the great actor-managers dominated. Herbert Beerbohm Tree built Her Majesty's Theatre and staged *A Midsummer Night's Dream,* with real rabbits hopping about the Athenian woods set, and, in 1895, Oscar Wilde's *An Ideal Husband.* Sir Henry Irving made Ellen Terry his leading lady at the Lyceum, which he managed for 24 years from 1879. Richard D'Oyly Carte staged Gilbert and Sullivan operettas, including *The Mikado,* at his Savoy Theatre with such success that the profits financed the building of his deluxe Savoy Hotel next door.

Landmark events in London theaterland included Richard Wagner conducting *The Ring* at the Royal Opera House in 1867 and Anna Pavlova making her London ballet debut at the Palace Theatre in 1910. This theater, restored by Andrew Lloyd Webber, is

The cast of *Thriller Live* strikes a pose at London's Lyric Theatre.

where his *Jesus Christ Superstar,* written with Tim Rice, became London's longest-running musical until it was eclipsed by another of his productions, *Cats (now closed).*

Meanwhile, Harley Granville-Barker dazzled Londoners at the Royal Court in Chelsea, where he staged 32 plays from 1904 to 1907, including the first performances of George Bernard Shaw's *Candida.* More recently, Sir Peter Hall was the first director of the National Theatre when it finally opened in 1976, the realization of an idea put forward by Garrick.

Today, some of London's most interesting theater is found in the "Off–West End" and "fringe" venues. The Royal Court, Almeida, Hampstead, Old Vic, Young Vic, and Donmar Warehouse theaters stage many of London's most innovative productions. Avant-garde fringe theaters, often housed in pubs, warehouses, and small upstairs rooms, are dotted across the capital. Ones at the forefront include the King's Head, Riverside Studios, The Bush, BAC, and Tricycle; others, often more offbeat, include the Etcetera Theatre, Old Red Lion, and The Finborough (for more information see the Entertainment section on pp. 263–264).

Back in the mainstream, the three auditoriums of the state-funded National Theatre and Shakespeare's Globe show traditional and contemporary plays, and some musicals, in repertory. This enables visitors to see a number of productions in any week. The traditional Victorian and Edwardian theaters of the West End stage more conventional productions and long-running musicals. These include *Les Misérables* and Andrew Lloyd Webber's *Phantom of the Opera.* The rebuilt Sadler's Wells Theatre focuses on ballet and some opera and stage productions. Currently, opera is staged in several renovated or restored theaters: Royal Opera House, Coliseum, Savoy Theatre, Sadler's Wells, and Hackney Empire. ■

EXPERIENCE: Explore the London of Film

London is a living movie set—only Hollywood and New York have had more films set within their borders. Notable movies filmed in the city include *Bridget Jones's Diary, The Da Vinci Code,* and many scenes in the popular *Harry Potter* series.

A host of companies offer regular walking and bus tours of famous London film sites. Try **Celebrity Planet** *(tel 020 7193 8770, www.celebrityplanet.com, $$$$);* **Brit Movie Tours** *(tel 0844 2471 007, www .britmovietours.com, $$$$);* and **The Great Movie Tour** *(e-mail: davinci.gawwy@ hotmail.co.uk for reservations, www .greatmovietour.co.uk, $$$$).*

Also worth considering is a unique Hollywood on the Thames boat tour run by **Thames Luxury Charters** *(tel 020 8780 1562, www.thamesluxurycharters.co.uk, $$$$).*

Tours depart twice a day from Butler's Wharf Pier to a variety of TV and film locations set on the river or its banks.

True film buffs should plan a visit to the **BFI,** the British Film Institute *(www.bfi.org .uk; see p. 263).* This repository of all things related to British film holds special events and exhibitions and includes the Mediatheque, a screening room where you can request a free private viewing of any of nearly 2,000 film and television titles from the BFI archive.

A few hundred yards west of the BFI on the South Bank brings you to the **London Film Museum** *(County Hall, SE1, tel 020 7202 7040, www.londonfilmmuseum .com, $$$$),* a 2008 museum that celebrates British cinema and includes an exhibit featuring "London on Film."

Twisting and turning past London's history—custom houses, quays, palaces, parliamentary buildings, and the Tower of London

The Thames

Looking toward the South Bank of the Thames at twilight

The Thames

The Thames is narrow as it runs northward from Hampton Court Palace, passing in great curves through the once rural villages of Twickenham, Richmond, Kew, Chiswick, and Barnes—now swallowed up by the mass of Greater London. Then it swings eastward into the city center. The last eight of London's 34 Thames bridges cluster close together and beyond the final one, Tower Bridge, the waters of the widening river slip slowly round the Isle of Dogs peninsula and through the great metal fins of the Thames Barrier.

Along the Thames stand buildings that testify to the river's role in history. For centuries, the river was the main highway for Londoners, and a facade within view of it was prestigious, as it still is. St. Paul's Cathedral, the Tower of London, and Westminster's Houses of Parliament are all close to the Thames.

Kings and queens, accompanied by boatloads of courtiers and musicians, would be rowed up and down the Thames between their riverside palaces at Greenwich, the Tower of London, Whitehall, Westminster, Richmond, and Hampton Court. Aristocrats often chose rural locations upstream from the city, for their homes—Ham House, Syon House, and Marble Hill House are the most impressive survivors. And there are several riverside parks: Greenwich downstream, and Battersea, Kew, Richmond, and Hampton Court's Home and Bushy Parks upstream.

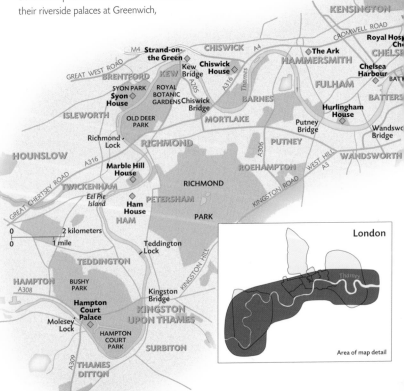

Vauxhall Bridge is among 34 that span the Thames.

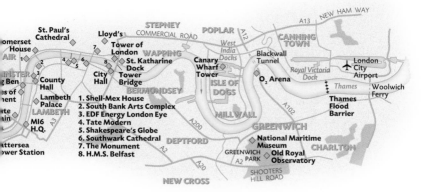

1. Shell-Mex House
2. South Bank Arts Complex
3. EDF Energy London Eye
4. Tate Modern
5. Shakespeare's Globe
6. Southwark Cathedral
7. The Monument
8. H.M.S. Belfast

NOT TO BE MISSED:

An early morning or late afternoon walk along the Thames embankments **49**

Cruising east on the Thames past the rejuvenated Docklands district and on to Greenwich **52–53**

Combining a land and sea sightseeing excursion on the fun-for-all-ages Duck tour **53**

Taking a boat ride to the grand country estates in Richmond and beyond **54**

Today, energetic riverfront building marks the rediscovery of the Thames. The redevelopment of the Docklands, in particular the Isle of Dogs, has been infectious. Riverside buildings that have lost their original purpose, such as Bankside Power Station and County Hall, breathe again as they are put to new uses. Dramatic modern buildings are being added, including City Hall at Southwark.

Forgotten harbors, such as St. Katharine and Chelsea, have been redeveloped. River taxis beat rush-hour roadblocks, and the Millennium Bridge spans the Thames from St. Paul's to Bankside. As for strolling, the newly designated riverside walk has brought Londoners close to their river again. ∎

The Historical Port

Once the biggest port in the world, London no longer sees laden ships coming and going up the Thames. And the boats riding it now, for pleasure or transport, are few compared to those of the past, when much of Britain's wealth flowed in and out of the river.

Canaletto's "The Thames on Lord Mayor's Day," circa 1747

The Roman port flourished on what is now Cornhill, with a wooden bridge, warehouses, and quays. The Anglo-Saxons traded with France and the Rhineland, then ventured farther to the Baltic and Middle East. In Tudor times, merchants built up the port to the point where about 40,000 people lived off the river, from bargemen and boatbuilders to stevedores and porters—and 2,000 boats ferried people up and down the river highway. Trade soared in the 17th and 18th centuries, and London became the world's largest port. In 1802 the new enclosed docks relieved the Thames of its shipping jam. By 1900, a million people worked in the port, but when the port moved to Tilbury in 1965, London's river fell silent.

Amid all the bustle of trading, London's river pageantry was always impressive. Henry VIII's ostentatious minister, Cardinal Wolsey, would dress in crimson satin to be rowed in his barge from Westminster to Greenwich to visit the king. The best shows on the Thames were those staged by the Lord Mayor. From 1422 to 1846, each year Livery Company barges escorted the Lord Mayor elect to Westminster, to seek the sovereign's approval.

By the mid-19th century, the river was little more than an open sewer, slowly carrying the industrial and domestic effluent of London out to sea. But after Queen Victoria's lawyers won back the Crown's river rights from the City Fathers in 1857, engineer Joseph Bazalgette designed London's first city-wide sewerage system. He also found a solution to the Thames's poor state of hygiene and the frequent winter freeze-ups that threw London into chaos. Inspired by Wren's suggestion of a river wall, he devised a land-reclamation scheme that narrowed the Thames and made the water flow faster. This embankment had a road on top to relieve the congested city, public gardens, and a tall river wall to combat floods.

Thames Revival

When the docks moved and industry was no longer allowed to dispose of its waste straight into the river, London's river-water quality improved dramatically. Today, more than 100 species of fish now live in the city stretch, including perch, sea stars, mussels, and eco-fragile salmon. With cleaner water, overhauled bridges, and new riverside buildings, Londoners have rediscovered their riverscape.

The revival began in the 1980s. The government's Docklands project was born in 1981. The aim was to reshape the 8.5 square miles of disused docklands with houses and offices. Soon individual developments were under way the length of London's riverbank. Old warehouses were converted to apartments. New office blocks arose, reflected in the waters of the old docks, which have been kept for their recreational potential.

Up at Hammersmith, architect Richard Rogers converted an oil depot into offices and apartments in 1987, creating a new working community. Nearby, Ralph Erskine's fun-shaped The Ark, of 1991, is a brave attempt at an ecologically sound office building.

Chelsea Harbour, where coal barges unloaded their cargo until 1960, was developed in 1986–1987 into a luxurious riverside community. On the opposite bank, a simple concrete-and-glass building by Norman Foster houses his own architectural practice.

In central London, Farrell's Embankment Place, built in 1987–1990 as an office block dramatically suspended over Charing Cross railway station, was the first of several major riverside projects. Michael Hopkins's severe Portcullis House at Westminster and Lifschutz Davidson's remodeling of Hungerford Bridge followed upstream; and a string of South Bank transformations and creations appeared, from County Hall to the Oxo Tower.

Downstream from here is the dynamic revival of Somerset House, the new Thames span of the Millennium Bridge, and the remodeling of Bankside Power Station into the new Tate Modern. Beyond lie Foster's elliptical City Hall and the converted warehouses of Shad Thames and Docklands.

Frost Fairs

Climate change is not a topic unique to our times. From the 14th to the 19th centuries, a "little ice age" held northern Europe in its grip. During these centuries, the Thames froze over more than a dozen times, allowing the citizens of London to set up Frost Fairs—winter festivals on the iced-over river that featured sports, entertainment, and plenty of food and drink.

Another reason for the freeze-overs was the Thames's slow-moving waters— the banks were wider then, and old London Bridge's many arches further slowed the river. A 19th-century government project to build embankments and remove some of the arches sped up the river's flow, ending freeze-ups.

The first organized Frost Fair took place in the 17th century. Vendors roasted and sold mutton and oxen; booths were set up for souvenirs and snacks; swings, sideshows, puppet shows, and merry-go-rounds were built; and people played hockey and (English) football.

Never a people to forgo a chance to set up shop, entrepreneurial Londoners were adept at cashing in on the festive atmosphere of the fairs. Admission fees were charged for most events, and a popular contemporary rhyme alerts us to the pricing patterns: "What you can buy for threepence on the shore, will cost you fourpence on the Thames, or more." Frost Fairs continued until 1813, the last time the Thames froze over.

Two Thames Boat Trips

Taking a pleasure boat trip on the Thames is a delightful way to appreciate how this great river was the backbone of the capital's development. From Westminster pier, you can take a short, urban journey downstream past the City of Westminster and the City of London, or a longer rural journey upstream, gliding through increasingly green areas of outer London.

A tour boat approaches Tower Bridge.

Down the Thames: Westminster to Greenwich

Starting from Westminster pier, some boats swing around beneath Westminster Bridge for a view of the Houses of Parliament before moving downstream, with County Hall on the right. Bazalgette's Victoria Embankment, left, has the Portcullis House, castle-like Whitehall Court, and the National Liberal Club, built in the 1880s. Behind Whitehall Stairs—there were once hundreds of river stairways like this giving access to the river—stood Whitehall Palace.

Under Hungerford Railway Bridge, Farrell's new offices are suspended above older Charing Cross Station, to the left. The South Bank Arts Complex is right, Charing Cross Pier and Embankment Gardens left, where the Duke of Buckingham's watergate survives to evoke the Strand's past glories. From here, Victorians took steamboats on day trips down to seaside towns on the Thames estuary. On the skyline you see the Shell-Mex House of 1932, with clock, and Macmurdo's 1903–1904 bedroom wing of the Savoy Hotel. Monet painted his views of Waterloo Bridge from one room. At Victoria Embankment the misnamed Cleopatra's

Needle—London's oldest monument, dating from 1450 B.C.—is an obelisk of pink granite from Heliopolis in Egypt.

Under Waterloo Bridge, the National Theatre is to the right. Somerset House is to your left, then Inner Temple Gardens and the riverside, cast-iron griffins marking the boundary of the City. After Blackfriars Bridge, you can see Millennium Bridge and, on your left, St. Paul's and the City's vast, egg-shaped 30 St. Mary Axe. Bankside Power Station, now Tate Modern, is on the right, with the new Shakespeare's Globe beyond.

Southwark Bridge and Cannon Street Railway Bridge come next, then the Doric column of the Monument, to the left, commemorating the Great Fire, the modern London Bridge marking Roman London's beginnings, Hays Galleria, H.M.S. *Belfast,* and the curved glass of City Hall.

The medieval Tower of London is on the left and Tower Bridge spans the river beside it. The revived Docklands line the widening river as it sweeps through the Pool of London, until recently filled with ships. To the right are the areas of Shad Thames, Bermondsey, Rotherhithe, and Deptford. To the left are the districts of Wapping, Shadwell, and Limehouse. The soaring towers of Canary Wharf, on the Isle of Dogs peninsula, face across the Thames to Greenwich. Beyond soars the O_2 Arena, the massive sports and concert venue on Greenwich Peninsula. Farther downstream, the shining fins of the Thames

EXPERIENCE: Taking to the Thames

No trip to London would be complete without taking to the water in some fashion. Tourist and commuter services launch from both banks of the Thames.

River Bus services, generally catering to commuters, are a fun way to move about the city: **Thames Clippers** (tel 0870 781 5049, www.thamesclippers.com, $$$$) runs frequent commuter boats from Woolwich Pier in the east to Waterloo in the west, with convenient stops. **Thames Executive Charters River Taxi** (tel 0134 282 0600, www.thamesexecutivecharters.com/rivertaxi .html, $$–$$$$) provides service farther west, past Chelsea to Putnam. Check out **London Transport** (tel 020 7222 1234, www.tfl.gov.uk) for additional information.

Many operators offer leisure tours along the Thames. Most run sightseeing cruises, while others specialize in brunch, dinner, jazz, and other themed tours. Options include **The London Eye River Cruise** (tel 0871 781 3000, www .londoneye.com, $$$$); the **Westminster Passenger Service Association** (tel 020 8940 3891, www.thamesriverboats.co.uk, $$$$), which runs the only scheduled service upriver to Kew and Hampton Court; **Crown River Cruises** (tel 020 7936 2033, www.crownriver.com, $$$$); **City Cruises** (tel 020 7740 0400, www.citycruises.com); and **Thames River Services** (tel 020 7930 4097, www.thamesriverservices.co.uk.)

Thrill seekers might like the **London RIB** (tel 020 7928 8933, www.londonrib voyages.com, $$$$$), a speedboat; while the **London Duck** (Chicheley St., tel 020 7928 3132, www.londonducktours.co.uk, $$$$), ideal for families, offers a land and river tour in an amphibious WWII landing craft.

Flood Barrier, a series of gates, straddle the river at Woolwich.

Up the Thames: Westminster to Hampton Court

From Westminster pier, the boats pass under Westminster Bridge. The Houses of Parliament and Victoria Tower Gardens are on the right, with Lambeth Palace and the floating fire station on the left. After Lambeth Bridge, Bazalgette's embankments support Tate Britain on the right.

INSIDER TIP:

Held on a September weekend each year, the Thames Festival (www.thamesfestival .org) features art, food, music, and fireworks.

—LARRY PORGES
National Geographic Books editor

Beyond Vauxhall Bridge and Farrell's MI6 headquarters, energy from Battersea Power Station, left, is used to heat Dolphin Square's apartments, right. After Chelsea Bridge the banks look more rural: Battersea Park, with its Peace Pagoda, on the left, and, on the right, the gardens of the Royal Hospital Chelsea, the site of the Chelsea Flower Show. Albert Bridge springs from the core of old Chelsea village, right. After Battersea Bridge, familiar from Whistler's paintings, is Chelsea Harbour. Turner painted sunsets from the tower of riverside

St. Mary's church, Battersea.

Round a great bend in the river, Hurlingham House, right, built in 1760, and its gardens are now a private sports club. Bazalgette's Putney Bridge replaced the 1729 wooden one, which was the Thames's second longest span but outside London when it was built. Bishops Park is on the right, boathouses for avid rowers on the left—the Oxford and Cambridge Boat Race starts here. The offices of British architects Sir Richard Rogers and Ralph Erskine's The Ark are visible on the right, before you reach castellated Hammersmith Bridge.

Chiswick's Malls, on the right, are lined with handsome houses; pretty Barnes village is to the left. After Duke's Meadows, right, comes Chiswick and its elegant bridge, then Kew railway and road bridges, with Strand-on-the-Green's charming cottages on the right. The Royal Botanic Gardens (see p. 192) at Kew follow, left, with their riverside palace, and on the opposite side gleaming Syon House (see p. 195). After Richmond Half-Tide Weir and Footbridge come Twickenham and Richmond Bridges. Here stand the remains of Richmond Palace, behind the riverside Asgill House, built in 1758. Richmond Park and Ham House follow, left, with Marble Hill House on the right.

Teddington Lock and Weir mark the end of the tidal stretch of the Thames. After Kingston Bridge and the great sweep past Home Park, Tijou's grand river gates announce Hampton Court Palace (see p. 197). ∎

Churches by Christopher Wren and skyscrapers in a maze of narrow lanes that date from the capital's origins

The City

The Lord Mayor's coach, Museum of London

The City

Much of the City's 2,000 years of busy history can be traced on the map. The two defendable hills that attracted the Romans to this spot are still clear to see: Ludgate, on which St. Paul's Cathedral now stands, and Cornhill. Here, 40 miles up the Thames from the sea, the river could be forded and the gravel riverbed bridged. The north bank was firm, and streams from Highgate and Hampstead provided fresh water—the Walbrook ran through the new settlement, the Fleet formed the western boundary.

The Romans' basilica and forum stood on Cornhill, where Lombard Street now runs; the remains of one of their temples, dedicated in the middle of the third century A.D. to Mithras, the god of a mystery cult, can be seen on Queen Victoria Street (see sidebar p. 69). Around A.D. 200, the Romans encased their 330-acre city with a tall, thick, tapering wall of Kentish ragstone, 3 miles long and pierced by seven gates. Today, chunks of wall, with medieval repairs, survive in the Barbican Centre, the Tower of London, Noble Street, and elsewhere. The gateways survive in place-names only: Aldgate, the poet Geoffrey Chaucer's home (1374–1386); Bishopsgate, whose road led all the way to Hadrian's Wall in the north of England;

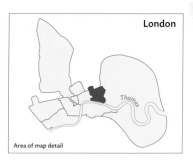

London

Area of map detail

Moorgate, beyond which lay marshy land; Cripplegate, which led to a medieval suburb and to Islington village; and Aldersgate, which led to the monasteries of Clerkenwell and to Smithfield market.

When medieval London burst out of the walls, it crept westward toward its rival, Westminster. The City boundaries barely changed. Even today, the City's nickname, "the Square Mile," is a roughly accurate description of the Roman settlement.

Then two dramatic events occurred. Plague was endemic to London, but in April, 1665, what was to be the worst outbreak since the Black Death of 1348–1350 began, killing an estimated 110,000 before the cold weather brought it to a halt.

The next year, on September 2, fire broke out at about 1 a.m. at Thomas Farrinor's bakery on Pudding Lane. By morning, 300 houses and part of London Bridge were alight. The strong east wind fanned the fire as it gobbled up the pitch-coated, wooden buildings. Over the next two days, the flames ate up Lombard Street, Cheapside, St. Paul's Cathedral, and

NOT TO BE MISSED:

Touring glorious St. Paul's Cathedral, including climbing up to the dome for spectacular views of London 60–63

A lunchtime concert in one of Wren's City churches 61

Visiting the City's art collection in the Guildhall Art Gallery 64–65

A stroll along the atmospheric lanes around St. Bartholomew church and Cloth Fair 67

Viewing London's history at the Museum of London's extensive collections and exhibits 68–69

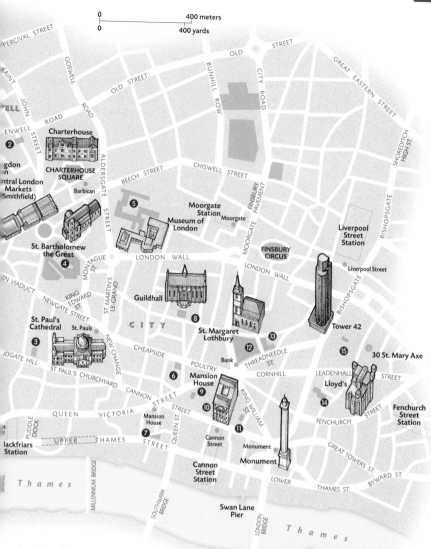

Inner Temple. On September 5, the fire was checked, but not before four-fifths of the City—including 13,000 houses, 87 churches, and 44 livery halls—had been burned.

While embers were still glowing, Charles II pledged that the city would be rebuilt. Sir Christopher Wren's dream of a city of avenues radiating from a new St. Paul's was impractical, partly because the guilds would not give up their land. Instead, fireproof, brick houses were built following the medieval street plan. ■

1 St. James's 2 St. John's Gate
3 St. Martin within Ludgate 4 St. Bartholomew's Hospital 5 The Barbican
6 St. Mary-le-Bow 7 St. James Garlickhythe 8 St. Lawrence Jewry 9 Temple of Mithras 10 St. Stephen Walbrook
11 St. Mary Abchurch 12 Bank of England & Museum 13 Stock Exchange 14 Leadenhall Market 15 St. Helen Bishopsgate

Wren's City Churches

The double disaster of the Great Plague of 1665 and the Great Fire of 1666 changed the City forever. The wealthy left, sparking the development of the elite residential area of St. James's. The rebuilt City was safer, with wider streets and better-constructed houses. Markets, shops, and other suppliers moved west, toward their customers. Sir Christopher Wren's new cathedral and churches gave a cohesive architectural character to the City that can still be felt today.

Wren's 51 City churches, built from 1670 onward, made a huge impact. Today, 23 churches remain—19 were destroyed in World War II bombing, and nine have been lost at other times.

Their designs vary considerably. They include the domed and centralized **St. Mary-at-Hill** (*Lovat Lane, EC3, tel 020 7626 4184, www .stmary-at-hill.org*) and **St. Stephen**

St. Bride's on Fleet Street is one of Wren's grander post-Fire structures.

Walbrook (*39 Walbrook, EC4, tel 020 7626 9000, www.ststephen walbrook.net*), the grandly baroque **St. Bride's** (*Fleet St., EC4, tel 020 7427 0133, www.stbrides.com*), and **St. Lawrence Jewry** (*Guildhall Yard, EC4, tel 020 7600 9478, www .slj.btik.com*), whose facade is based on Wren's great model for St. Paul's Cathedral. **St. Magnus the Martyr** (*Lower Thames St., EC3, tel 020 7626 4481, www.stmagnus martyr.org.uk*) is a good one to visit for its classic design and sumptuous interior, described in T. S. Eliot's *The Waste Land* (1922) as "inexplicable splendour of Ionian white and gold." He refers to the colonnades supporting the tunnel vaulting of the nave, which leads to the finely carved original reredos. Among the baroque statues and gilded sword rests, do not miss two other original features: the font and the organ case. The steeple, added in 1705, is one of Wren's best; his other notable ones surviving today are on St. Bride's and St. Mary-le-Bow.

Some of Wren's interiors have their original—or another, older or ruined church's—fittings. **St. Margaret Lothbury** (*Lothbury, EC2, tel 020 7726 4878, www.stml.org .uk*) fulfills both criteria. Outside, Wren has perched his obelisk tower on a domed base. Inside, the rectangular nave's magnificent furnishings include Wren's design for the finely carved tester and screen, whose barleystick columns and soaring eagle were originally built for All Hallows-the-Great (demolished in 1876).

Almost every Wren church has something special about it. For the interior of his very pretty **St. Mary Abchurch** (*Abchurch Lane, EC4, tel 020 7626 0306*), Wren gathered a team of talented friends, and their work remains almost unaltered. Beneath William Snow's paintings on the dome, some of the City's finest 17th-century wood carving survives, all retaining its original oxblood stain. There are William Emmett's door cases, font cover, and rails, Christopher Kempster's font, William Gray's pulpit, and—the church's glory—Grinling Gibbons's reredos, the City's only authenticated piece by him.

INSIDER TIP:

Stay at the Andaz [see p. 243] on Liverpool Street and ask to see the Grecian-style Masonic Temple that lies beneath it.

—SIMON HORSFORD
Sunday Telegraph *travel writer*

St. Margaret Pattens

(*Eastcheap, EC3, tel 020 7623 6630, www.stmargaretpattens.org*), so-called because wooden clogs or pattens were made nearby in the 13th century, also has a special interior. Here are some of London's few remaining canopied

St. Bride's

St. Bride's, tucked off the south side of Fleet Street, near Ludgate Hill, has more than one claim to fame. In addition to being a handsome example of one of Sir Christopher Wren's post–Fire churches, and containing ancient Roman ruins in its basement, St. Bride's also holds itself dear to wedding planners around the world. Whether apocryphal or not, the story goes that an 18th-century London baker, William Rich, based the shape of his daughter's wedding cake on the multitiered steeple of the church. The design apparently caught on, earning the 225-foot (69 m) spire the moniker "wedding-cake steeple" and locking cakesmiths into the pattern for centuries to come.

pews, and the one carved with "CW 1686" is thought to have been Wren's own. There is also a punishment bench for the parish miscreants, and, in the side chapel, hooks on which gentlemen hung their wigs on hot days. Wren's slender lead steeple rises above another fine interior, that of **St. Martin-within-Ludgate** (*Ludgate Hill, EC4, tel 020 7248 6054, Ludgate, www.stmartin-within-ludgate.org.uk*). The altarpiece, pulpit, font, and organ case are magnificent examples of late 17th-century carving.

Finally, a visit to **St. Mary Aldermary** (*Queen Victoria St., EC4, tel 020 7248 9902, www.stmaryaldermary.co.uk, by appt.*) takes you to Wren's only Gothic-style church. The fan vaulting, the only work of its kind made in the City in the 17th century, was probably Wren's interpretation of the pre-Fire church. ∎

St. Paul's Cathedral

This is the cathedral church of the London diocese—a church for Londoners, while Westminster Abbey serves the nation. St. Paul's was founded by King Aethelbert of Kent for the missionary monk, Mellitus. This, the fifth church on the site, is England's only baroque cathedral, the only one with a dome, and the only one built between the Reformation and the 19th century. It was also the first to be constructed entirely by a single architect, Sir Christopher Wren.

Sir Christopher Wren's vision of St. Paul's Cathedral included a massive dome.

St. Paul's Cathedral

- 🗺 Map p. 57
- ✉ Ludgate Hill, EC4
- ☎ 020 7236 4128
  Visit inquiries:
  020 7246 8357
- 🕓 Closed Sun. except for services & for special events
- 💲 $$$$
- 🚇 Tube: St. Paul's, Mansion House, or Blackfriars
  Rail: City Thameslink

www.stpauls.co.uk

The foundation stone was laid on June 21, 1675. Boatloads of Portland stone from Dorset were delivered to the nearest wharves, and the bulk of the cathedral was built by 1679. Wren's son put the last stone on the lantern supporting the triple-layered dome in 1708, and the cathedral was completed in January 1711. The entire building is in the throes of a 15-year, £40 million ($64 million) restoration and cleaning of stonework, statues, and mosaics to commemorate the 300th anniversary of the cathedral's consecration in 2010. Renovation work is expected to continue through 2011.

Exterior

Before going in, stand well back on Ludgate Hill and look at St. Paul's in its entirety. The building is arranged in four volumes: the dome and crossing, the nave and choir, the transepts, and the west end. The dome rests on a wide drum—which provides an open terrace—and is made of an inner brick dome, an intermediate brick cone that supports the lantern, and an outer wooden casing covered in lead. The grand facade has a pediment relief of the Conversion of St. Paul. Pilasters and pediments give the building baroque movement.

Interior

Standing just inside the building, you get a good first view looking straight down the length of the nave and choir to the modern towering altar. This stunning setting has contributed to memorials such as the funerals of Admiral Lord Nelson in 1806 and Winston Churchill in 1965; to celebrations such as Queen Victoria's Diamond Jubilee in 1897, the Queen's Silver Jubilee in 1977, and the marriage of Prince Charles and Lady Diana Spencer in 1981.

Dome & Crossing: The crossing is irresistible. Sit beneath it and rest as you look up at the dome. It is supported on eight huge arches. Corinthian columns rise up to the dome, where the grisaille frescoes of the life of St. Paul by Sir John Thornhill, painted 1716–1719, are the only original decorations. The mosaics in the spandrels—the prophets by Alfred Stevens and the evangelists by G. F. Watts—were added in the 19th century, after a visit by Queen Victoria, who criticized the building as dreary and uncolorful.

Wren's several designs for St. Paul's are on display in the **crypt,** reached from the south transept. After the 1666 fire, Wren was appointed Surveyor General in 1669 and was already designing new City churches when he produced his first model for St. Paul's in 1670. This was judged to be too modest; his Great Model of 1673–1674 showed his ideal design of a Greek cross. When this was rejected by the clergy as unsuitable for the bishop's processions, Wren made a third design, with a small dome and long nave. Once the clergy had approved it and he had received the King's Warrant to go ahead in 1675, he enlarged the dome, removed the spire, raised the nave walls, and chopped off three bays—thus returning as closely as he dared to his Great Model design. All the foundations were laid out at the start so that no changes could be forced upon him at a later stage.

There is much more in the crypt, including the Oculus (a multiscreen presentation on the cathedral's history) and Wren's own tomb, inscribed *Lector, si monumentum requiris, circumspice* (Reader, if you seek his monument, look around you), words repeated on the floor beneath

---

EXPERIENCE:
Hear Music in Wren's Churches

Take a respite from your day's travels with classical music recitals and choral services in the tranquil settings of Wren's City of London churches.

St. Paul's Cathedral's 50-voice choir sings hour-long Evensong services at 5:00 p.m. from Tuesday to Saturday and at 3:15 p.m. on Sundays.

Meanwhile, **St. Lawrence Jewry** (see p. 58) hosts organ recitals at 1:00 p.m. every Tuesday and classical piano concerts at the same time on Mondays. There are also organ recitals at **St. Stephen Walbrook** (see p. 58) at 12:30 p.m. on Fridays and **St. Margaret Lothbury** (see p. 58) at 1:10 p.m. on Thursdays.

John Donne

A poet, lawyer, Member of Parliament, and preacher, John Donne (1572–1631) had a career both impressive and eclectic, rising to be dean of St. Paul's Cathedral in 1621, a position he held for the last ten years of his life.

He was admitted to the bar in 1592 at Lincoln's Inn where, for centuries, a somber tradition was in place: Whenever a senior member of the bar died, the chapel bells would ring out. Messengers were sent to find out who had passed away. This practice became the subject of Donne's most famous work, "Meditation 17" of his *Devotions Upon Emergent Occasions*, which he wrote in 1624 as he recovered from a near-fatal illness:

"Any man's death diminishes me, because I am involved in mankind; and therefore never send to know for whom the bell tolls; it tolls for thee." Donne is buried in St. Paul's Cathedral.

the dome. Adm. Nelson and the Duke of Wellington lie here, and near Wren lie the artists Joshua Reynolds, J. M. W. Turner, and John Singer Sargent.

The monuments in the nave are a roll call of British heroes of the 19th and 20th centuries. Francis Bird's font of 1727 stands in the west transept and Jean Tijou's screens close off the Sanctuary; the **American Memorial Chapel** is behind the altar; and Wren's original high altar is kept in the **Lady Chapel.** Near it is the monument to the poet John Donne (1571–1631), who was dean of St. Paul's and the greatest preacher of his day (see sidebar above). In the south aisle is Holman Hunt's painting "The Light of the World," the artist's copy of his original version (in Keble College, Oxford).

Galleries

Part of the massive building's restoration project includes the re-opening of the **Triforium,** a level above the main floor, which features a 300-year-old library and the Trophy Room containing Sir Christopher Wren's sketches, yardstick, and death mask, as well as a huge model of the church. The Triforium can currently be visited only as part of the highly recommended guided tour; there's no timetable yet for

West Portico

when it will open to the public. drum. From here, you can see how
The 560 steps leading to the the second story of the screen
other galleries begin with a gentle around the building is blind,
climb to the **Whispering Gallery.** with nothing behind it. Finally, a
Unless you arrive early, there will spiral staircase leads up to the
not be enough peace and quiet **Golden Gallery,** narrow and
for the whispers to carry round not for the fainthearted, but
the gallery. Steeper steps, with giving stupendous views of
views of the cone supporting the City, the twisting
the lantern, lead to the Thames, and Parlia-
wide outside **Stone** ment's many
Gallery, resting spires at West-
on the dome's minster. ■

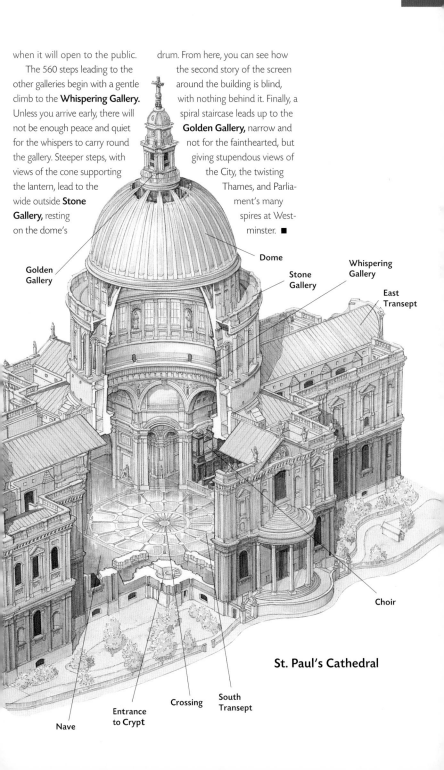

Golden
Gallery

Dome

Stone
Gallery

Whispering
Gallery

East
Transept

Choir

St. Paul's Cathedral

Nave

Entrance
to Crypt

Crossing

South
Transept

A City Walk

This walk gives a good idea of the dense, medieval compactness of the City and its range of fine buildings of all periods. Go on a weekday for liveliness, on weekends for quiet.

From Monument Tube station, walk down Monument Street to the **Monument** ❶ *(www .themonument.info, $)*, which commemorates the Great Fire of London. Turn right onto Fish Street Hill. At the bottom is Wren's glorious church **St. Magnus the Martyr** (see p. 58) on Lower Thames Street. Farther east, walk up St. Mary at Hill, veering right onto St. Dunstan's Lane, to the remains of **St. Dunstan-in-the-East**—a Wren tower of 1697 and a garden.

Beyond St. Margaret Pattens (see p. 59), turn left at Fenchurch Street, then right onto Lime Street to find the arches of Leadenhall Market, the City's food market, opened in 1881. Continue on Lime Street past Richard Rogers's colorful **Lloyd's building** ❷ of 1978–1986. Cross Leadenhall onto St. Mary Axe to inspect the vast egg-shaped building at **No. 30** ❸ (nicknamed "the Gherkin") before turning left to find peace in medieval **St. Helen's Bishopsgate.** Cross Bishopsgate to find Richard Seifert's 600-foot-tall (183 m) **Tower 42.**

Turn left down Old Broad Street, cut through Finch Lane, and proceed across Cornhill and into the narrow court opposite to find **St. Michael Cornhill,** where Wren and Hawksmoor added to the medieval tower. Now go right, onto Lombard Street, whose banking signs evoke medieval origins. Hawksmoor's **St. Mary Woolnoth** ❹ of 1716–1727 faces onto Mansion House Square, the core of financial London: the **Mansion House** of 1739–1753, the Lord Mayor's official residence, and the

Bank of England. Walk around the **Bank of England museum** on Bartholomew Lane, close to **St. Margaret Lothbury** (see p. 58).

Lothbury runs into Gresham Street, where **St. Lawrence Jewry** (see p. 58) stands in front of the **Guildhall** ❺ on Aldermanbury, the seat of the City's government. The medieval crypt is open to the public. You can also visit the magnificent hall, and also the **Guildhall Art Gallery** *(Guildhall Yard, EC2, tel 020 7332*

NOT TO BE MISSED:

Guildhall and Art Gallery • Museum of London • St. Paul's Cathedral

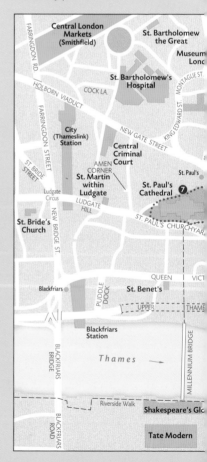

3700, www.guildhall-art-gallery.org.uk), whose new building displays the City's art collection and incorporates a section of Roman London's amphitheater (see sidebar p. 69). Farther along Gresham Street, the Goldsmiths' Company has its hall on Foster Lane (exhibitions open to the public). Haberdashers' Hall is on Staining Lane, and there is a chunk of Roman wall on Noble Street. A bridge across London Wall road leads to the **Museum of London ❻** (see p. 68).

Now walk down St. Martin's-le-Grand to **St. Paul's Cathedral ❼** (see p. 60). South of the cathedral, steps lead down to Millennium Bridge. But to continue the walk, go east of the cathedral, along Watling Street, to Bow Lane,

with **St. Mary-le-Bow** at the top. Up Queen Victoria Street is the Roman **Temple of Mithras ❽** (see sidebar p. 69). St. Stephen Walbrook stands behind Mansion House, off Bucklersbury, while **St. Mary Abchurch ❾** (see p. 59) is set in a square down St. Swithin's Lane. Cannon Street leads to Monument station.

◪	Inside front cover F4
►	Monument Tube station
⟷	3.75 miles (6 km)
◔	3 hours if just walking, a day with visits
►	Monument Tube station

Smithfield & Clerkenwell

These two early overspills from the crowded medieval City survived as a north London backwater while fashionable London moved west. Today, Clerkenwell has more medieval buildings than any other district; and London's only wholesale food market, Smithfield Meat Market, has been glamorously restored.

The Smithfield Meat Market is a carnivore's dream.

**Smithfield &
Clerkenwell**
🔼 Map pp. 56–57

**Smithfield Meat
Market**
🔼 Map p. 57
🕐 Closed Sat.–Sun.
🚇 Tube: Barbican,
Farringdon
Rail: City
Thameslink

**www.smithfield
market.com**

The 12th-century horse market on "Smooth field" (Smithfield) grew into a full-scale livestock market—the scene of terrific noise, brawls, and blood from slaughtered animals. It was moved to Islington in 1855 when the sale and slaughter of live animals was banned; only the magnificent **Smithfield Meat Market,** built in 1851–1866, survives.

The original open space was the scene of major events, including the Bartholomew Fair, England's international cloth fair, held annually from 1133 to 1855. Around the edges, seek out the medieval St. Bartholomew the Great (see opposite), Cloth Fair (see sidebar opposite), and beautiful St. Etheldreda Church, tucked into Ely Place and built in 1300.

Charterhouse Square is northeast of the market, with cobbles, gates, 18th-century houses, and, at the back, the substantial remains of **Charterhouse Monastery's** *(www.thecharterhouse.org, tours weekly April–Aug. by appt.)* cloisters and washhouse, once used by Carthusian monks. In St. John's Square, off St. John Street, stands the grand **St. John's Gate** of 1504. With the church's crypt and chancel, it was part of the Priory of St. John of Jerusalem *(tel 020 4070 4005, www.sja.org.uk)* and now houses a small museum *($$).*

Clerkenwell was a refuge for monks and for craftsmen fleeing restrictions imposed by the City's guilds. The village center was the Green, a focus for the jewelers, milliners, and metalworkers who are now returning to this area. Little of St. Mary's Nunnery survives, but James Carr's **St. James's Church** *(Clerkenwell Close, EC1, tel 020 7251 1190, www.jc-church.org),* built in 1788–1791 to replace the nunnery, has a fine organ. ∎

St. Bartholomew the Great

Medieval piety and pilgrimages had a profound effect on London. Henry I's court jester Rahere, having been cured of malaria caught during his pilgrimage to Rome, became an Augustinian monk and, in 1123, founded St. Bartholomew's Hospital and Priory. Both were funded by tolls from the annual Bartholomew Fair. What remains of this foundation today is London's oldest church, its only 12th-century monastic church, and its best piece of Romanesque building.

The Priory

The evocative priory church of St. Bartholomew the Great, built in 1123, was restored in 1880–1890 by Sir Aston Webb. It is reached through a 13th-century stone arch, originally the entrance to the nave. The half-timbered Tudor gatehouse is post-Dissolution (1559). The path to the church's door runs past what was once the ten-bay nave, and the cloisters were on the right.

Inside, Rahere's choir, ambulatory, and Lady Chapel survive, showing the magnificence of medieval London's wealthy religious houses. The honey-colored walls, squat columns, unmolded arches, and simple decoration create an atmosphere for contemplation far from the city's bustle.

Rahere was buried here in 1143; his tomb (of a later date) is beside the altar. William Bolton, one of the last priors, gave the Tudor Window in 1515. Soon after, Sir Richard Rich acquired the dissolved priory, destroyed most of it, and lived in the Lady Chapel, which is found through Webb's wrought-iron screen. It later became a printer's office—Benjamin Franklin worked here as a young man in 1725.

The Hospital

St. Bartholomew's *(West Smith-field, EC1, tel 020 3465 5798, www.bartsandthelondon.nhs .uk)* was London's first hospital, built on land given by King Henry I. After the Dissolution, the hospital became secular. It acquired buildings by James Gibbs in 1730–1759, and two murals by Hogarth. Inigo Jones, the architect, was born nearby in 1573 and baptized in the hospital church. There is an interesting museum on site *(closed Sat.–Mon.)* accessible via the Henry VIII Gate on Giltspur Street. ■

St. Bartholomew the Great

- ⬛ Map p. 57
- ✉ West Smithfield, EC1
- ☎ 020 7606 5171
- 🕐 Closed Sat. p.m. & Mon.
- 🚇 Tube: Barbican

www.greatstbarts .com

Cloth Fair

The tiny lanes and alleys around Cloth Fair, next to St. Bartholomew the Great, are among the most atmospheric in London. A walk around this neighborhood, especially on a misty evening, can transport you back to the medieval days when the city's cloth-iers hosted an annual fair in the area.

Cloth Fair, the little street that gives the area its name, wends its way from West Smithfield (and the 21st century), passing 17th-century houses, jettied upper stories, faux gaslights, and the stone exterior wall of St. Bartholomew. Two interesting pubs are the Victorian **Rising Sun** *(38 Cloth Fair, EC1, tel 020 7726 6671)* and the **Hand & Shears** *(1 Middle St., EC1, tel 020 7600 0257)*, in business since 1537.

Museum of London

London's local museum holds an astounding collection. Its agenda is to tell the story of the capital of Britain from prehistoric times to the present. Treasures range from a wealthy Roman's floor mosaic to an 18th-century doll house and dresses made of Spitalfields silk. London's glories, atrocities, and failures are all represented here in nine permanent galleries. Above all, the impression is one of Londoners speaking to us across the centuries.

The Layout

The museum, impressively renovated and expanded, is housed in a building designed in 1975 by Powell and Moya. Opened in 1976, the core collection is an amalgamation of the Guildhall Museum, founded in 1826 for City-related objects, and the London Museum at Kensington Palace, which since 1912 has focused on London's cultural history, especially costume. London's frantic rebuilding during the 1980s and '90s, and developers' willingness to halt work while archaeologists excavated, extended the collection beyond manageable limits. Only a portion is on display; more can be seen in the Museum of London in Docklands (see p. 214).

Five of the nine permanent galleries were reorganized and reopened in 2010 to tell the story of modern London (from 1666 to the present). Rooms are arranged chronologically, with maps, models, and music putting the objects into context. It is always worth visiting the temporary exhibitions and displays of new acquisitions.

Your Visit

A rewarding first visit might well take a visual overview of the whole of London's history, dipping into one or two thematic rooms.

On the Upper Level, the **Roman rooms** startle with their sophistication. The detailed models of the port and the forum become even more impressive when you view the nearby

Fashion on display at the Museum of London

EXPERIENCE: Discovering Roman London

Remnants of the old Roman city wall and other ancient ruins are scattered around and under the City of London's streets. The **Museum of London** offers excellent walking tours, often with working archaeologists, to these sites and many other hidden gems. Check out *www .museumoflondon.org.uk*.

One of the most impressive sections of Roman wall (with bonus Norman and medieval add-ons) can be found somewhat incongruously at the back of the parking lot fronting the Grange City Hotel, on Cooper's Row, just north of the Tower Hill Tube stop.

In 1954, British construction workers digging a building foundation on Walbrook unearthed another Roman ruin, the third-century A.D. **Temple of Mithras,** dedicated to the Persian god of light and sun. The ancient temple was uprooted and moved nearby so that building construction could continue—today it is accessible up a small flight of stairs on Queen Victoria Street. Its current position, above ground level, is misleading; Mithraic temples were built underground, with a low ceiling, to mimic the cave in which Mithras is said to have killed a sacred bull and brought life to the world.

---

re-created rooms. There are mosaic floors, kitchens equipped with herbs and spices, an elegant dining room, and some fine sculptures from the Temple of Mithras (see sidebar above).

Coins and imported pottery in the **Saxon galleries,** together with weapons left by Viking raiders, prove London by no means ground to a halt when the Romans left. The **medieval galleries** bring alive another London—pilgrims' badges, Black Death crosses, a merchant's chest. The grandeur of **Tudor London** is apparent in tantalizing snippets from Henry VIII's Nonsuch Palace and a model of pre-1666 St. Paul's, while the era's darker side is explored with gruesome information on superstitions, food, and water supplies. "War, Fire, and Plague" brings Elizabethan London to life, while **Stuart London** chronicles the instability of civil war, with one monarch executed and another restored to the throne. There are

memorial medallions to Charles I, a hoard of jewelry from Cheapside, Oliver Cromwell's death mask, and an enthralling sight-and-sound diorama that lets you witness the Great Fire of 1666.

Downstairs, the Georgian era is recalled in **"The Expanding City"** through 18th-century newspapers, trade cards, and ceramics. The 19th-century galleries are a deluge of transport, building, public utilities, and entertainment displays. In the **"Victorian Walk,"** a re-created street of well-stocked shops—including a barbershop, pub, tailor, and pawnbroker—charmingly evokes the London of 1900.

London continued to grow in the 20th century. Reflecting this, the **"People's City"** section showcases an art deco elevator from Selfridges, the story of the British suffragette movement, and a Ford Model T. Do not miss the Lord Mayor's coach, still used for his November procession, at the end of the **"World City"** gallery. ■

Museum of London

- Map p. 57
- London Wall, EC2
- 020 7001 9844
- Charge for some special exhibitions
- Tube: Barbican, St. Paul's, Moorgate, or Bank

www.museumof london.org.uk

Islington

Up the hill from the City, Islington has long been associated with fun. Some aristocrats set up house here after the dissolution of the monasteries in the 16th century, but it was as an 18th-century spa that Islington's character was established. Although Georgian houses were soon surrounded by a patchwork of Victorian squares, Islington is still synonymous with entertainment—theaters, markets, restaurants, pubs—and has a strong community spirit of its own.

Camden Passage
- ✉ Off Upper Street, N1
- ☎ 020 7359 0190
- 🕐 Shops: closed Mon. Stalls: open Wed. & Sat. Book market: open Thurs.
- 🚇 Tube: Angel

www.camdenpassage islington.co.uk

London Canal Museum
- ✉ 12–13 New Wharf Rd.
- ☎ (020) 7713 0836
- 🚇 Tube: King's Cross

www.canalmuseum org.uk

Two contrasting markets capture the spirit of Islington: traditional **Chapel Market,** on a street of the same name just northwest of the Angel Tube stop, where locals buy their food (the market is renowned for its fish) and other goods; and sophisticated, international **Camden Passage** (see sidebar below), saved from developers in the 1960s. Duncan Street and Charlton Place lead from Camden Passage to the grand Georgian houses of Duncan Terrace. The successful Tudor merchant Hugh Middleton has his statue on Islington Green, opposite the Royal Agricultural Hall of 1861–1862, now London's Business Design Centre.

Upper Street, reputed to have

INSIDER TIP:

Take time for the often overlooked, charming little London Canal Museum, north of King's Cross just east of Islington.

—DEREK LAMBERTON
National Geographic contributor

more restaurants than any other European street, has the landmark **St. Mary's Church** (*tel 020 7226 3400, www.stmarysislington.co.uk*) of 1751–1754, with a fine steeple. Three of Islington's theaters are close by: the King's Head pub-theater (*tel 020 7226 8561, www .kingsheadtheatre.org*); the Little Angel Theatre for children (*tel 020 7226 1787, www.littleangeltheatre .com*), near handsome Cross Street; and the avant-garde Almeida Theatre (*tel 020 7359 4404, www .almeida.co.uk*) on Almeida Street.

Canonbury, to the northeast, is a delight to walk through: rows of late Georgian terraces, now desirable houses. Canonbury Square, with the grand Canonbury House of 1780, leads to Compton Terrace and Alwyne Villas. Barnsbury, to the west, has a string of Victorian squares, the next wave of building for City business people. ■

Camden Passage

One of the densest concentrations of antique dealers in Britain crams into this narrow Islington lane, paved with York flagstones. Serious specialist shops line the passage, devoted to clocks, old clothes, prints, and other subjects. Arcades have been squeezed in wherever possible, and you can find art nouveau objects, Staffordshire figures, Bakelite, enamelware, and more. Go early on Wednesday or Saturday, when stalls fill every inch, goods are piled on the ground, and every last fish fork has its price.

The grandeur of Westminster Abbey, the Houses of Parliament, and Buckingham Palace, offset by chapels and parks

Westminster

The Changing of the Guard at Buckingham Palace

Westminster

Westminster, the nation's political and royal hub, has a totally different atmosphere from that of the commercial City. Lying 2 miles (3.2 km) upstream from it, London's second city was born a thousand years later, on a very different type of riverbank and for different reasons. This is an area of palaces and large open spaces, of public buildings and public spectacle rather than secret deals; of unfenced royal estates instead of a protected, walled port.

Origins of Westminster

Westminster was born beside the Thames, on boggy land watered by the River Tyburn. This unlikely spot is believed to be where Sebert, king of the East Saxons, founded the Church of St. Peter, possibly in A.D. 604.

Whatever its cloudy origins, Westminster quickly received royal blessings. Saxon kings gave land and relics; St. Dunstan, Bishop of London, contributed a dozen monks in 960; but it was Edward the Confessor who put it firmly on the map. His dream, inspired by royal foundations on the Continent, was to build a new palace, an extensive monastery, and an abbey church fit for royal burial. William the Conqueror and all subsequent sovereigns have reinforced Westminster's royal, religious, and political role in England's life.

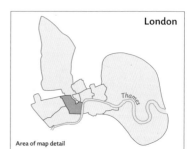

Westminster Today

The riverside Palace of Westminster, better known as the Houses of Parliament, has long dominated the day-to-day life of the area. Westminster Bridge, beside Parliament, was opened in 1750 and rebuilt in 1852–1862. Today, it is a departure point for pleasure boats on the river (see p. 52).

Parliament's offices have spilled into neighboring buildings, most recently into Michael Hopkins's fortresslike gray-black Portcullis House. Members of Parliament (MPs) have worshipped at the parish church of Westminster, St. Margaret's, in preference to the much grander abbey ever since the Puritan Speaker of the House of Commons worshipped there on Palm Sunday, 1614.

NOT TO BE MISSED:

Poets' Corner, Henry VII's chapel, and the peaceful cloisters at Westminster Abbey 74–77

The fascinating Churchill War Rooms and Churchill Museum in Whitehall 79

Sitting in on a heated Parliamentary debate in the House of Commons 79

Seeing the Changing of the Guard 89

The Wallace Collection's impressive displays of art and armor 94

London

Thames

Area of map detail

Parliament's bureaucratic offices on Whitehall—a street lined with grand, sometimes pompous buildings—would have obliterated all memory of the glorious Whitehall Palace, had Inigo Jones's Banqueting House and John Vardy's Horse Guards not survived.

The abbey is Westminster's second focus and it is the abbey's magnificent building, and its role in Britain's history, that attracts visitors today. The Archbishop of Canterbury's London palace is across the river from Westminster.

As London grew increasingly polluted, the monarchs left Whitehall Palace for Kensington Palace and Hampton Court, but they always kept Court at St. James's Palace. When George III bought Buckingham House in 1761, he brought the London life of the sovereign back into Westminster. Buckingham Palace has remained the monarch's London home to this day, though St. James's Palace is the official Court residence. ■

❶ U.S. Embassy ❷ Royal Mews ❸ Queen's Gallery ❹ Queen Victoria Memorial ❺ Spencer House ❻ Lancaster House ❼ Clarence House ❽ Queen's Chapel ❾ Marlborough House ❿ Queen Anne's Gate ⓫ Churchill War Rooms & Churchill Museum ⓬ Central Methodist Hall ⓭ St. Margaret's ⓮ Cenotaph ⓯ Westminster Hall

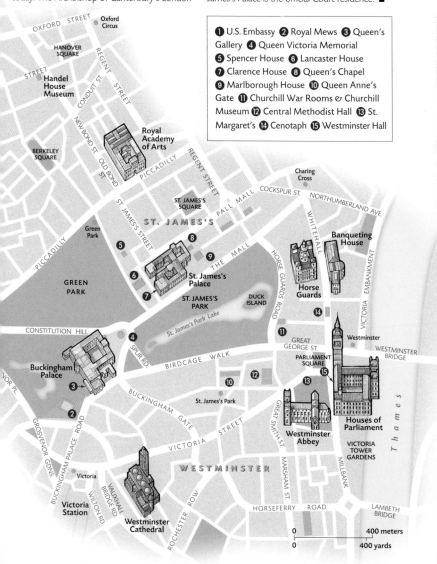

Westminster Abbey

It is always worth pausing in front of a great building before entering, and this is particularly true of Westminster Abbey. Today, it takes a leap of the imagination to envisage the impact on medieval London of this soaring church—it is the tallest Gothic church in the country—and of its extensive abbey buildings and grounds.

Complete with crown, Elizabeth I's effigy lies in state in Westminster Abbey's Lady Chapel. Her half sister, Mary Tudor, is buried with her in the tomb.

This is not the original abbey church. No evidence has been found of the first church built on this spot, dedicated to St. Peter. Edward the Confessor's, begun in 1050, is gone too. So is the Norman church of 1110–1150, which was gradually demolished to make way for Henry III's church. Today's abbey is largely the result of Henry's devout and expensive building program, begun in 1245. It was he who built the Gothic chancel, transepts, and crossing, and the first five bays of the nave, using soft stone from Reigate in Surrey. Henry was close to the French Court and his architect, Henry of Reynes, may very well have been French. Several basic elements are clearly French-inspired: the polygonal apse with its radiating chapels, the first of its kind to be built in Britain; its amazing height; and its lavish decoration.

Imagine just the chancel, pinned on to the Norman nave. That is how it was for a century. Then, in 1375, Richard II had the Norman nave pulled down so Henry Yevele could begin the new one. The nave was completed in the 1390s, and the great west window was added in the prevailing perpendicular style. The west towers, designed by Nicholas Hawksmoor, were not added until the 18th century.

Henry VII used the leanest possible perpendicular style when he added his chapel to the east end in 1503–1512. It is well worth viewing from the outside. The great outer piers carrying the buttresses that support the weight of the roof—and so enable the windows to be huge—are folded and paneled.

The Interior

The first impression is one of extreme richness, in decoration and in monuments. But it was not always so. Imagine the interior empty of all monuments, with a delicate chancel screen whose function was to divide the monks from the worshippers. Today's rich but heavy Gothic Revival screen, made in 1839, is by Edward Blore; he also designed the elaborate choir stalls, in place by 1848. When pilgrims flocked to see the Confessor's shrine and the cloisters were filled with Benedictine monks, multicolored light would have streamed through the stained-glass windows onto the whitewashed interior walls, and only the carved decoration would have been seen.

When Henry VIII dissolved the monasteries, he took the rich Abbey of Westminster for himself in 1534, closed it in 1540, and later sold off two-thirds of its extensive lands. There was a brief reprieve under Mary I, then Elizabeth I sealed the abbey's fate and it became the Collegiate Church of St. Peter at Westminster.

Your Visit

So rich are the abbey's monuments that you should either join a tour or make a list of priorities, allowing time out to rest. Try to arrive early to attend a service in St. Faith's Chapel, or come in the afternoon to join Evensong.

Visitors are directed through the abbey on a one-way clockwise circuit. Entrance is through the **Great North Door,** underneath James Thornhill's beautiful stained-glass rose window in the north transept. At the crossing

INSIDER TIP:

Evensong at Westminster Abbey, with young choristers from the Choir School, is sublime.

—MARY LAMBERTON
National Geographic contributor

see Sir George Gilbert Scott's high altar of 1868, incorporating Salviati's mosaic of the Last Supper. It is here that the monarch is crowned; for Elizabeth II's coronation in 1952, nine processions lasted over four hours in a service based on King Edgar's coronation at Bath in 973.

Henry VII's Chapel (also called The Lady Chapel) is arrestingly beautiful. London's finest late perpendicular building,

Westminster Abbey

Map p. 73
Broad Sanctuary, SW1
020 7222 5152 or 020 7654 4900
Closed Sun. except for services. Last admission 3:30 p.m., except 6:00 p.m. on Weds.
$$$$$
Cloisters: Free
www.westminster-abbey.org

its centerpiece is the poignant tomb of Henry VII, who lies next to his beloved queen. The huge windows, together with the cobweb-fine fan vaulting, create a delicate, decorative lightness. The statuary, as elsewhere, was at one time brightly painted and gilded; the choir stalls have richly carved misericords; the banners belong to knights of the ancient Order of the Bath, revived by George I in 1725.

The **Royal Tombs** display some of the abbey's most impressive monuments. The ancient tomb of Edward the Confessor is at the heart of the building—though, unless you're part of the verger tour *(times vary, $),* it is off-limits to visitors. Edward's tomb is surrounded by his royal devotees: Henry III, Edward I, Edward III, and Richard II, with Henry V at the entrance. The **Coronation Chair** is found beside his grave.

Where the south transept joins the nave, a door leads to the **Abbey Cloisters,** which give a good idea of the atmosphere in London's medieval monasteries. Surrounding the cloisters

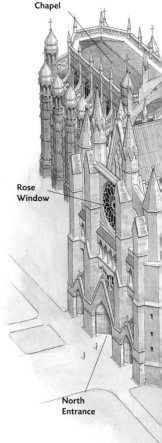

Henry VII's Chapel

Rose Window

North Entrance

are several abbey buildings. The **Chapter House** of 1250–1253 is where the abbot would give daily instructions to his monks, and it was here that Parliament met in the later 13th and 14th centuries. The **Pyx Chamber** of 1065–1090 and the **Undercroft Museum,** once monks' dormitories, now house wax effigies made for funeral processions: Charles II's is the oldest. More buildings lie outside: In **Broad Sanctuary,** an arch leads into Dean's Yard, where Westminster School is found. Look for the College Hall of the 1360s.

Wandering the nave is like

Poets' Corner

Poets' Corner, by no means restricted to memorials to poets, is in the South Transept. Here, with patience, you can find not only Geoffrey Chaucer and Edmund Spenser, but also novelists Jane Austen and George Eliot, composer George Frederick Handel, and actor David Garrick. The walls are decorated with 13th-century wall paintings. Behind lies the quiet, magical St. Faith's Chapel, with a 14th-century wall painting.

e of Edward
onfessor

South Transept

Chapter House

West Towers

High Altar

 h
sept

Choir

Choir Stalls

Nave

West
Window

West Entrance
(Services Only)

Westminster Abbey

being in an overstocked museum of sculptures and reliefs. The monument to Sir Isaac Newton, designed by William Kent in 1731, is straight ahead, at the left side of the screen. Michael Rysbrack sculpted that figure and those of Ben Jonson and John Milton, both in **Poets' Corner.** The portrait of Richard II, from 1390, is just inside the entrance. Next to it the **Tomb of the Unknown Warrior,** an unidentified soldier's body from World War I, is the abbey's most recent burial. ∎

Palace of Westminster

Commonly known as the Houses of Parliament, this Victorian Gothic riverside palace, with its landmark Big Ben clock tower, is London's newest palace, built on the foundations of its oldest. On October 16, 1834, a fire destroyed the rambling old palace, which had been the principal London royal residence from William the Conqueror to Henry VIII. Even after Henry moved to Whitehall Palace in 1530, Westminster remained the seat of government—as it does today.

The Palace of Westminster, housing Parliament, dates primarily from the 19th century.

Palace of Westminster

- Map p. 73
- Parliament Square, SW1
- 020 7219 3000
- Tours in summer recess: $$$
- Tube: Westminster

www.parliament.uk
& www.explore.parliament.uk

Little survived the 1834 fire: William II's Westminster Hall, the cloisters and crypt of St. Stephen's Chapel, and the 14th-century **Jewel Tower,** possibly built as a giant safe for Edward III's jewels, furs, and gold. A visit to the Jewel Tower, the only old part easily accessible, makes a good start.

There were 97 entries in the competition for the new building—all designs had to be in the fashionable Gothic or Elizabethan Revival styles. Architects Charles Barry and Augustus Welby Pugin won. Their great building had 1,200 rooms, 2 miles (3.2 km) of corridor, 11 courtyards, 100 staircases, and a river facade 320 yards (293 m) long. Almost complete by 1847, this was the symbol of the Mother of Parliaments as the British Empire enjoyed its apogee.

Although parts of the interior can be visited (see sidebar opposite), a look at the exterior can be rewarding. There are two ways of enjoying the river facade:

Churchill War Rooms & Churchill Museum

This maze of underground rooms served as the headquarters for the government's War Cabinet from August 1939 until September 1945. They are decorated and furnished as they were, and it is easy to imagine the secret information arriving, the meetings and planning sessions, the transatlantic telephone calls—and Sir Winston Churchill catching a few hours' sleep in his small bedroom. Beside them, the Churchill Museum illuminates the man and his period. A branch of the Imperial War Museum, this fascinating time capsule is very much recommended.

from nearby Westminster Bridge; or from across the river beside Lambeth Palace.

The view from the river is fairy tale. Pugin, an ardent Gothicist, coated the classicist Barry's order with a riot of decoration. Statues of sovereigns from William the Conqueror to Victoria cover the facade, while gilded pinnacles catch any sunlight. Such sumptuousness was matched on the inside and is today undergoing long-term refurbishment.

On the southern end of the palace is **Victoria Tower,** over which the Union Jack flies. Completed in 1860, the tower houses a copy of every Act of Parliament since 1497. The interior of this end of the building, devoted to the House of Lords, is decorated in red. The Lords' function is to review, question, revise, and amend proposed legislation. Their Peers' Lobby leads to the Central Lobby. To the right is the Members' Lobby, where non-Members (Strangers) can come to meet their Member of Parliament (MP) or watch debates from the Strangers' Gallery. Farther north, the House of Commons (St. Stephen's Hall) is clad in somber green. It is built on the site of the original royal chapel and is where Parliament met from 1547 to 1834. The 19th-century building kept to the chapel layout, as did the rebuilding that took place after World War II bombing: The Speaker's chair is in the center, where the altar had been, the party in government on his/her right, the Opposition on the left.

The clock tower, known by the name of its bell, **Big Ben,** symbolizes British government. If Parliament sits at night, a light shines on top. The tower was completed in 1858, and the clock, with a bell cast in Whitechapel (see p. 211), started in 1859. Its dials are 23 feet (7 m) wide, its hour hand 9 feet (2.7 m) long, and the minute hand 14 feet (4.2 m) long. ∎

Jewel Tower

- ✉ Abingdon Street, SW1
- ☎ 020 7222 2219
- 💲 $
- Ⓜ Tube: Westminster

www.english-heritage.org.uk

Churchill War Rooms & Churchill Museum

- Ⓐ Map p. 73
- ✉ Clive Steps, King Charles Street, SW1
- ☎ 020 7930 6961
- 💲 $$$$
- Ⓜ Tube: Westminster, St. James's Park

www.iwm.org.uk

EXPERIENCE: Visiting the Palace of Westminster

You can get a feel for government in action by attending a debate whenever Parliament is in session (Mon.–Thurs. & some Fridays): Just join the line at the St. Stephen's entrance (the wait is shortest after 5 p.m.). To go on a highly recommended 75-minute guided palace tour (Sat. & Aug.–Sept., $$$$), prepurchase a ticket (tel 0844 847 1672, www.ticketmaster.co.uk/housesofparliament or www.parliament.uk).

A Westminster Walk

This half-day walk is strong on street statuary. It's a good one to do on a day of unsure weather, as there is always a remarkable building for shelter if the clouds burst.

From **Westminster Bridge** ❶, enjoy the river facade of the Palace of Westminster and, downstream, County Hall, home to the London Aquarium. On the north end of the bridge, Thomas Thornycroft's bronze, unveiled in 1902, shows **Queen Boudicca** and her daughters hurtling toward London in their chariot.

Walk past **Big Ben's** clock tower ❷ (see p. 79), then left around the Palace of Westminster, passing first an 1899 statue of Parliamentarian leader Oliver Cromwell (1599–1658), then the Crusader Richard I (*R.* 1189–1199). **St. Margaret's Church, Westminster,** and the **Jewel Tower** ❸ stand across the road. In **Victoria Tower Gardens** find three memorials: to the emancipation of slaves in 1833; to the suffragette Emmeline Pankhurst (1857–1928); and Rodin's sculpture, "The Burghers of Calais."

Cross Lambeth Bridge for **Lambeth Palace** ❹, the intriguing little **Museum of Garden History,** and, in front, the finest viewpoint for

---

NOT TO BE MISSED:

Parliament Square ● **Banqueting House** ● **Downing Street** ● **St. James's Park**

---

the Palace of Westminster. The superb **Imperial War Museum** (see p. 101) is a five-minute walk down Lambeth Road.

Back on the north bank, elegant 18th-century Westminster is found down Dean Bradley Street, in Smith Square, where **St. John's Church** ❺, now a concert hall, often has lunchtime concerts. Walk past the fine houses of Lord North Street and down Cowley and Dean Barton Streets to Great College Street, where an arch on the right leads into Dean's Yard. At the far end, another arch opens into Broad Sanctuary, beside the west door of **Westminster Abbey** (see pp. 74–77). Opposite, the domed Central Methodist Hall of 1905–1911 and the Middlesex Guildhall of the same date stand on either side of Powell Moya and Partners' **Queen Elizabeth II Conference Centre** ❻, opened in 1986.

Parliament Square, down Broad Sanctuary to the right, is a political sculpture court. Statues include those of Abraham Lincoln, statesman Lord Beaconsfield (born Benjamin Disraeli, 1804–1881), and the old, bearlike Sir Winston Churchill. Sir George Gilbert Scott's Foreign Office (Old Treasury), built in 1868–1873, fills the north side of the square.

Past Big Ben again, find two annexes for MPs: new Portcullis House and, on Victoria Embankment road, Richard Norman Shaw's striped 1880s building. Farther along, a section of old Whitehall Palace's terrace can be seen in the gardens. Turn up Horse Guards Avenue

---

EXPERIENCE:
Rent a Deck Chair

After a long day walking the streets of London, there are few sights as appealing as the comfortable canvas deck chairs clustered in several of London's parks from spring through fall. The most well known group stands at the northern tip of **Green Park,** though chairs are also set up in **Kensington Gardens, St. James's Park,** and **Hyde Park** (by both the Serpentine and Speaker's Corner).

But this restorative respite isn't free. Expect to pay up to £2 ($3) to soak up an hour of English sunshine. A beleaguered civic employee has the thankless job of walking around to ask payment from the grumbling patrons.

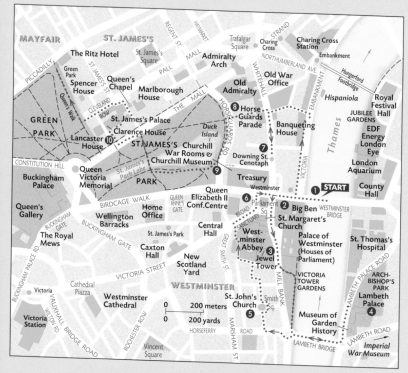

to Whitehall; the **Banqueting House** (see p. 82) stands on the corner. Whitehall has three monuments in the road: Sir Edwin Lutyens's **Cenotaph** and equestrian statues to Field Marshals Earl Haig (1861–1928) and the 2nd Duke of Cambridge (1819–1904).

Across Whitehall and left, **Downing Street** **7** lies behind its great gates on the right. The prime minister's official residence is at No. 10. Back up Whitehall, William Kent and John Vardy's **Horse Guards** was built in 1745–1755. The guard is changed twice daily. Go through to **Horse Guards Parade** **8** to see the building's park facade that forms the backdrop to royal pageantry such as Trooping the Colour.

St. James's Park lies ahead, surrounded by an assortment of buildings. To the left, near the statue of Clive of India (1725–1774), are the **Churchill War Rooms & Churchill Museum** **9** (see p. 79). The bridge over the lake gives fine views toward Whitehall and leads to the

- Inside front cover D3
- Westminster Tube station
- 3 hours
- 3.4 miles (5.5 km)
- Green Park Tube station

Mall. From here look left, up past the Queen Victoria Memorial to Buckingham Palace. **Clarence House** **10**, formerly the Queen Mother's home, is now refurbished as the Prince of Wales's London home (www.princeofwales.gov .uk). Its reception rooms are open to the public (tel 020 7766 7303, www.royalcollection.org.uk) for a month during the summer, usually around August. Marlborough Road runs between them to **St. James's Palace**, whose Queen's Chapel is to the right. Walk around the palace, turning into Cleveland Row, which leads to Green Park, where Queen's Walk goes up past the Ritz Hotel's park facade to Green Park Tube station.

Banqueting House

More a grand room with a basement than a house, this huge, double-cube space, lit by floor-to-ceiling windows on the Whitehall side, has its entire ceiling painted by Peter Paul Rubens and is perhaps London's most beautiful room.

Banqueting House

- 🅰 Map p. 73
- ✉ Whitehall, SW1
- ☎ 0844 482 7777
- 🕐 Closed Sun. & for government functions
- 💲 $$. Recorded tour for rent
- 🚇 Tube: Westminster, Charing Cross, or Embankment

www.hrp.org.uk

James I built it between 1619 and 1622, employing architect Inigo Jones, who was already working on Queen's House at Greenwich (see p. 218). Later Jones would design Queen's Chapel for St. James's Palace and Covent Garden's St. Paul's as well as the Piazza (see p. 124). The king wanted to rebuild the whole of Henry VIII's rambling, brick Whitehall Palace, but this was the only part to be completed. The Banqueting House survived the fire of 1698, when the rest of the palace was destroyed. London's first building to be partly encased in Portland stone, it set a new design tone.

The crypt was for the king's informal parties. The grand room

INSIDER TIP:

Supine mirrors in the center of Banqueting House's great room allow you to comfortably gaze at Rubens's impressive ceiling art.

—LARRY PORGES
National Geographic Books editor

upstairs was for masques, banquets, Court ceremonies, and diplomatic functions. On entering the room, the visitor would see the decoration of two orders, Ionic below and Corinthian above, mirroring the exterior of the building. Ranks of courtiers standing on both sides led the visitor to the enthroned king, ahead. Looking up, he or she would see Rubens's panels, painted in 1634 for Charles I for £3,000 (about $4,800). For these paintings, which honored Charles's father, James I, as the symbol of the union of England and Scotland and celebrated the benefits of wise rule, Charles bestowed a knighthood on Rubens.

Later events were to put Rubens's allegory into question. Charles I was beheaded on a scaffold mounted outside the windows on January 30, 1649; but in 1660, it was here that Charles II celebrated his own restoration to the throne. ∎

Maundy Thursday

British monarchs long observed the Thursday before Easter by washing the feet of paupers, a reference to Jesus' washing his disciples' feet at the Last Supper. You won't find bare toes and suds at a modern Royal Maundy Service, but the queen's attendants sport towels over their clothes, and her fragrant floral bouquet hints at the tradition's malodorous history. At the event, the queen gives elderly citizens purses of special coins; the monarch's age determines the number of recipients. The Banqueting House hosted the service, its name based on the Latin for "command," for centuries, but the venue now changes annually.

Westminster Cathedral

Begin in the Cathedral's piazza, off Victoria Street. Here, the red and white bulk of London's last cathedral rises uninterrupted. The Roman Catholic hierarchy was not reestablished in England and Wales until 1850, 300 years after the Reformation. In 1894, Archbishop Vaughan chose John Bentley to design a cathedral on two conditions: that it had a wide nave for big congregations, and that it looked nothing like nearby (Protestant) Westminster Abbey.

The Blessed Sacrament Chapel of Westminster Cathedral

Bentley had been working in the Gothic style. This would not do, being too similar to the abbey. So he toured Italy, Greece, and Constantinople (Istanbul), and returned to create a church that mixed Byzantine and Romanesque ideas using red brick and white Portland stone.

Climb the **Campanile** for views toward Big Ben, Nelson's Column, and Buckingham Palace. The cross on top of the Campanile contains a relic of the True Cross.

Inside the cathedral, incense perfumes the air, mosaics in chapel domes reflect the lights of votive candles, and a great gold cross hangs above the huge nave. Marble lines the walls, while the domes and apse are held together by bridges supported on columns inspired by Ravenna's seventh-century churches. Eric Gill's **"Stations of the Cross,"** made in 1914–1918, are on the nave piers. To see Bentley's scheme complete, peep into the **Lady Chapel.** ■

Westminster Cathedral

🅰 Map p. 73

✉ Victoria Street, SW1

☎ 020 7798 9055

🕐 Campanile: closed Thurs.– Sun. Dec.– March

💲 Donation; Campanile: $

🚇 Tube/rail: Victoria

www.westminster cathedral.org.uk

St. James's Palace

A visit to St. James's Palace should begin in Friary Court on Marlborough Road, watching the queen's color trooped, as the old guard forms up during the Changing of the Guard ceremony. The original palace, which had four courts, was built in the 1530s by Henry VIII as part of a lavish building program. Despite fires and rebuilding, much of the exterior survives.

St. James's Palace

⚐ Map p. 73

✉ Cleveland Row, Marlborough Gate, SW1

🕐 Palace closed to the public

🚇 Tube: Green Park

The name of one of the courts, Friary Court, betrays the origins of the palace. A medieval Augustinian friary, it became a women's leper hospital dedicated to St. James the Less. Henry VIII bought the hospital and grounds, built the palace, and enclosed 300 acres (121 ha) of land (now St. James's Park).

After the Whitehall Palace fire of 1698, St. James's became the sovereign's principal London residence. After George III's move to Buckingham Palace in 1762, St. James's remained the official royal residence. Today, new sovereigns are proclaimed and make their first speeches here. Foreign ambassadors are appointed to the Court of St. James's, and they ride from here in a glass coach to make their first courtesy call on the queen.

Opposite Friary Court stands **Queen's Chapel** (*Sun. services Easter–July*). Built in 1623 for Charles I's Catholic wife, Henrietta Maria, it was England's first Italian-inspired classical church. Inigo Jones designed it and, as at Banqueting House, made the interior a simple double cube.

Henry's four-story **Gatehouse**, with its clock, octagonal towers, and linenfold-paneled doors, gives an idea of what fairy-tale palaces Tudor Whitehall and Greenwich must have been. It is sometimes possible to peek into Ambassadors Court and, on some Sundays, to visit the **Chapel Royal** (*Sun. services Oct.– Easter*), whose painted roof may have been done by Holbein. The rest was lavishly redecorated in the 1830s.

It was at St. James's Palace that the court custom of having a poet-laureate as an official part of the royal household began. John Dryden was the first; the current laureate is Carol Ann Duffy. ∎

The Tudor Gatehouse of St. James's Palace

Buckingham Palace

The Duke of Buckingham's relatively modest mansion, built in 1705, is now lost behind successive additions of regal rooms, splendid art, and an imposing facade. Outside the railings, people gather on momentous occasions to cheer the queen and the royal family, who come out onto the balcony between the great central columns. The sovereign's London home is a focal point of the capital.

A detachment of the Queen's Guard marches in front of Buckingham Palace.

The View

The best view of Buckingham Palace is from the Mall, near Sir Aston Webb's "Queen Victoria Memorial," created in 1901–1913. Thomas Brock's marble statue of the queen looks up the Mall, surrounded by allegorical figures of such Victorian virtues as Charity, Truth, Progress, and Manufacture; a gold-leaf Victory figure soars above. The circular **Memorial Gardens** that surround it, symbolizing the Empire, have gates given by Canada, South Africa, and Australia.

Straight ahead, across the parade ground where the Changing of the Guard ceremony takes place, the palace's Portland stone facade seen today was constructed by Sir Aston Webb in just three months in 1913. Before that, Buckingham Palace and its surroundings had been far less imposing. John Sheffield, Duke of Buckingham, built a country house here in 1705. After George III bought it in 1761 for his wife, Queen Charlotte of

Buckingham Palace

🅰 Map p. 73

✉ The Mall, SW1

☎ 020 7766 7300

Tickets for the State Rooms also available at ticket office opposite the palace. Royal Mews: 020 7766 7302.

🕐 Open Aug.–Sept.

💲 $$$$$

🚇 Tube: Green Park, Victoria, or St. James's Park

www.royal collection.org.uk

Mecklenburgh-Strelitz, Sir William Chambers remodeled it, retaining its private character; ceremonial functions continued to take place at St. James's Palace.

The Building

It was George IV who began aggrandizing the house in 1826. He instructed John Nash to transform it into an appropriately grand palace where he could hold court and official ceremonies. The elderly Nash, hampered by inadequate funds and the need to incorporate the old building, added a string of new rooms along the garden side, with State Rooms up on the first floor. Nash's Bath stone garden facade is particularly delightful in its light, French neoclassical style, but his Mall facade was obscured by Edward Blore's east wing, added in 1847–1850 to provide more space for Queen Victoria—nurseries, bedrooms, kitchens, and a huge ballroom 123 feet (37 m) long.

The Interior

In all, the palace has 600 rooms, including 19 State Rooms, 52 royal and guest bedrooms, 188 staff bedrooms, and 78 bathrooms. More than 400 people work here, and each year more than 40,000 are entertained here. Used for state ceremonies, official entertaining, and royal garden parties, it is one of the world's few remaining working royal palaces.

While the queen keeps a mere dozen rooms overlooking Green Park for herself, visitors can enjoy the scale and lavish furnishings of the State Rooms. George IV's taste for opulence is displayed in sculpted panels, elaborate ceilings, and bright colors. The Blue, White, and Green Drawing Rooms, the

The Palace's White Drawing Room is open to the public in August and September.

Royal Parks

London's nine royal parks were once private possessions of the sovereign, used for hunting and other pastimes. Gradually, under pressure, they were opened to the public, beginning with St. James's Park in the 1660s.

The parks have various origins. Henry VIII took Hyde Park in exchange for land in Berkshire. Primrose Hill was an exchange with Eton College. Richmond Park was a series of farms bought by Charles I. William and Mary added Kensington Gardens to Nottingham House.

Today, an informal atmosphere is preserved, though park law and regulations are enforced by a parks security force. Gardeners maintain a labor-intensive but impressive style—40,000 tulips are planted annually in front of Buckingham Palace, 250,000 more at Hampton Court. Naturalists look after the animals, trees, and lakes. You can walk through nearly 2 miles (3.2 km) of parkland—from Westminster to Notting Hill—through St. James's, Green, and Hyde Parks to Kensington Gardens.

Music Room, and the Throne Room are some of the grandest.

The palace is a treasure house of art; the Royal Collection is one of the world's finest. When George V and Queen Mary came to the throne in 1910, they employed Sir Aston Webb to improve the exterior while they arranged the contents. Queen Mary's organized approach resulted in furniture being reassembled from all over the royal residences and restored.

The Tour

Today, it is possible to visit some of the **State Rooms**, a move initiated to raise funds after Windsor Castle's 1992 fire (see p. 223). Visitors enter Buckingham Palace through the **Ambassadors Entrance,** where Nash's facade is visible past the Grand Quadrangle. Go up the grand Carrara marble double staircase to see the **Green Drawing Room** and the **Throne Room.** Next is the **Picture Gallery,** where 50 major paintings from the Royal Collection hang in the 165-foot-long (50 m), top-lit room. The **Silk Tapestry Room** leads into the **East Gallery,** then past the **ballroom** (where knighthoods are bestowed) to the rooms overlooking the 30 acres (12 ha) of gardens. The **State Dining Room** is first, then the **Blue Drawing Room,** the **Music Room** with its great bow window, and the **White Drawing Room.** You leave down the Ministers' Stair, past the portraits and sculptures of the **Marble Hall,** and out to the gardens.

Other Palace Areas

You can see more of the Royal Collection at the newly rebuilt and enlarged **Queen's Gallery.** Here, changing exhibitions display a selection of the queen's own art, one of the world's finest private collections. At the nearby **Royal Mews** on Buckingham Palace Road, Nash's stables and coach house still contain the painted State Coach of 1761 and the horses that pull it today. ■

Royal London

London is full of contradictions. Although a democratically elected government sits at Westminster, with the sovereign merely a figurehead, the royal presence is strongly felt. At a time when the very existence of a royal family is under question, the capital is littered with royal reminders.

Queen Elizabeth II rides out during her official birthday celebration in 2005.

It was Edward the Confessor, King of England 1042–1066, who first made Westminster his capital. Queen Elizabeth II traces her blood-descent back to Egbert of Wessex, king of the English from 829. London's palaces, pageantry, statues, and symbols result from this history.

Homes & Gardens

The choice of royal homes to visit in London begins with Buckingham Palace (see pp. 85–87), followed by Clarence House (see p. 81), both lived in today. Then there are Whitehall Palace's surviving Banqueting House (see p. 82), Westminster's Jewel Tower (see p. 80), Kensington Palace (see pp. 158–159), and the fortress-palace, the Tower of London (see pp. 204–207). Farther afield, magnificent Hampton Court Palace (see pp. 197–200) lies upriver, beyond Kew Palace (see p. 192) and Marble Hill House (see p. 194). Greenwich (see pp. 215–218) is downstream, while the riches of Windsor Castle (see pp. 222–223) are a 40-minute train ride away. On Sundays, the Chapels Royal at St. James's, Hampton Court, the

By Appointment

More than 800 shops in Britain have a royal coat of arms above the door. This indicates that the business holds a royal warrant to supply "By Appointment" to the queen, Duke of Edinburgh, or the Prince of Wales. Dating from the Middle Ages, the tradition remains strong today. The highest concentration of these suppliers, who use the position to promote their goods' quality, is in St. James's and Mayfair.

Tower, and the Queen's Chapel are occasionally open to worshippers. St. James's Palace, Westminster Hall, and Marlborough House can be enjoyed just from the outside, but only tantalizing fragments remain of Richmond, Rotherhithe, and other lost palaces.

The royal parks were once royal hunting grounds. Garden lovers should not miss Queen Mary's Rose Garden in Regent's Park, the Tudor and Dutch gardens at Hampton Court, the Rose Garden in Hyde Park, or the Royal Botanical Gardens at Kew.

Pageantry

Despite some scaling down of royal pageantry, there is still plenty to see.

The colorful Changing of the Guard takes place at Buckingham and St. James's Palaces at 11:00 a.m. every day from May to July, and on alternate days the rest of the year. (Arrive early if you want a good view.) You can also watch the mounted Queen's Life Guard change guard at Horse Guards Parade at 11:00 a.m. Monday to Friday, and at 10:00 a.m. on Sundays.

The Ceremony of the Keys is the ritual locking of the Tower of London's gates that has been performed nightly without fail for more than 700 years. The ceremony, led by the Chief Yeoman Warder, takes place at exactly 9:53 p.m. and lasts for seven minutes. For tickets, write six to eight weeks ahead of time to the Ceremony of the Keys Office (HM Tower of London, Waterloo Block, London EC3N 4AB) with the full names and addresses of those wishing to attend, several proposed dates, and a self-addressed stamped envelope. Visit www.hrp.org.uk for complete information.

Another colorful bit of public pageantry is the annual Trooping the Colour ceremony in June that marks the official celebration of the queen's birthday (though her actual birthday is April 21). The queen proceeds in a carriage from Buckingham Palace to Horse Guards Parade, where she inspects her troops. The event began in the early 1700s, when it was a practical event for soldiers to be shown the flags ("colors") of their battalions so that they could easily recognize and rally behind them in battle. It's free to watch the procession; check www.royal.gov.uk for information on getting seats.

Other annual events include Beating the Retreat in the summer, and the State Opening of Parliament in November. The queen still follows the Court Year, and entertains visiting heads of state in April, July, and November.

A formal procession attends the State Opening of Parliament each November.

St. James's, Mayfair & Piccadilly

The heart of aristocratic London has enjoyed a reputation for exclusiveness since its development by the aristocrats themselves, when they moved westward from the City and leased land to speculative builders.

St. James's

Today, St. James's Square, laid out by Henry Jermyn in the 1660s, is home to the discerning bibliophiles' refuge, the **London Library** (*tel 020 7930 7705, www.londonlibrary.co.uk*) at No. 14. Founded by Thomas Carlyle in 1841, the library is a private collection of nearly 1,000,000 titles, some dating back to the 16th century. A London residence is required for library membership, but temporary four-month subscriptions are available for overseas visitors—for a somewhat hefty fee.

Christie's (*tel 020 7839 9060, www.christies.com*), the international art auctioneers founded in 1766, is on nearby King Street. Auctions take place daily; visit the website to register as a bidder or to view the catalog. Christie's is surrounded by art dealers who break from their shops to lunch at their clubs (see sidebar p. 92) or shop on Jermyn Street (see sidebar opposite). Guests of the Ritz, Stafford, and Duke's hotels echo the luxurious lifestyle once enjoyed in such mansions as **Spencer House,** painstakingly restored by Lord Rothschild.

Mayfair

Essentially a development of six great estates, Mayfair's residential grandeur is enhanced by deluxe hotels: the Dorchester, Claridges, and the Connaught. The Mayfair home

Burlington Arcade in Piccadilly

of composer George Frideric Handel from 1723 to 1759 is now **Handel House Museum** (*25 Brook St., W1, tel 020 7495 1685, www.handelhouse.org*). **Sotheby's** (*34–35 New Bond St., W1*), Mayfair's art focus, is worth a visit if only for the fascinating sculpture sitting inconspicuously atop its doors. Bought from Sotheby's by a collector in the 1880s for £40 ($64), it's London's oldest statue: a 1320 b.c. depiction of the Egyptian lion-goddess Sekhmet. The piece was never picked up and has been the auction house's symbol and guardian ever since.

INSIDER TIP:

In business for more than a century, the chocolatier Prestat, in Princes Arcade, Piccadilly, makes some of the best truffles you'll ever eat.

—JANE SUNDERLAND
National Geographic contributor

Sotheby's is on the most stylish shopping strip, New and Old Bond Streets, where Asprey's, Versace, Gucci, Prada, Rolex, Tiffany, Cartier, and the Fine Art Society create dazzling shop windows to lure spenders. Savile Row runs parallel to New Bond Street to the east and is the place to go—as it has been for centuries—for custom-made suits.

EXPERIENCE:
Take Home a Custom-Made Shirt

Jermyn Street is known for its bespoke (an English term denoting "custom-made") shirtmakers serving the discerning male dresser since the 18th century.

The process begins by selecting a fabric, which can be a more daunting proposition than it sounds—**Turnbull & Asser** (*71–72 Jermyn St., SW1, tel 020 7808 3000, www.turnbullandasser.co.uk*), for example, has more than 1,000 options on hand. Then comes the fitting, the off-site cutting and stitching, and your one-shirt test period. The entire process can take up to six weeks, but it can be done by mail once the original fitting is complete. There's usually a six-shirt minimum per order; expect to spend up to £200 ($320) per shirt. Other shirtsmiths include **Harvie & Hudson** (*77 & 96–97 Jermyn St., SW1, tel 020 7930 3949, www.harvieandhudson.com*) and **Hilditch & Key** (*37 & 73 Jermyn St., SW1, tel 020 7734 4707 www.hilditchandkey.co.uk*).

Piccadilly

Dividing Mayfair and St. James's, Piccadilly runs from Piccadilly Circus to Hyde Park Corner. The Duke of Wellington's **Apsley House** at Hyde Park Corner is a rare survivor of Mayfair's mansions, with Adam fireplaces and pictures by Goya and Rubens. Quality pleasures line the street's core: the Ritz hotel and Hatchard's bookshop on one side; the **Royal Academy of Arts** and Burlington Arcade on the other.

The academy was founded in 1768, with George III as its patron and Sir Joshua Reynolds its first

Spencer House

🗺	Map p. 73
✉	27 St. James's Place, SW1
☎	020 7499 8620
🕐	Open Sun. only. Closed Jan. & Aug.
$	$$$
🚇	Tube: Green Park

www.spencerhouse.co.uk

Gentlemen's Clubs

The 18th-century coffeehouses and gambling clubs of Mayfair and St. James's developed into somber gentlemen's clubs. Large clubhouses along Pall Mall and St. James's Street became homes-away-from-home for members who tended to share the same interests. On Pall Mall, the **Athenaeum** *(tel 020 7930 4843, www.athenaeumclub.co.uk)* is known for academics and bishops, while the **Reform Club** *(tel 020 7930 9374,* *www.reformclub.com)* attracts liberal thinkers (it was the first to give full membership to women). On St. James's Street, the **Carlton** *(tel 020 7493 1164, www.carltonclub.co.uk)* is for Tories, **Brooks's** *(tel 020 7493 4411)* is more liberal, and **White's** *(tel 020 7493 6671)* is for the very grand. Several of the clubs enjoy reciprocal membership arrangements with private clubs in the United States.

Apsley House

- Map p. 72
- Wellington Museum, Apsley House, 149 Piccadilly, SW1
- 020 7499 5676
- Closed Mon.
- $$
- Tube: Hyde Park Corner

www.english-heritage.org.uk

Royal Academy of Arts

- Map p. 73
- Burlington House, Piccadilly, W1
- 020 7300 8000
- Open daily during exhibitions
- Cost varies with the exhibition
- Tube: Green Park, Piccadilly Circus

www.royalacademy.org.uk

president. Gainsborough was a founding member; Constable and Turner were students. The tradition of newly elected Academicians presenting one work to the academy began early, and is the origin of the annual Summer Exhibitions.

At the show in 1855, Queen Victoria bought Frederick, Lord Leighton's painting, "Cimabue's Madonna," thus securing the young artist's reputation. Even today, international exhibitions make way for the great Summer Exhibition, when Royal Academicians exhibit their work alongside amateur and professional artists who enter in competition.

Burlington Arcade runs alongside the academy. Samuel Ware's covered shopping arcade, completed in 1819, was a Continental idea welcomed by fashionable, often rain-drenched London. Piccadilly, Royal Opera, Princes, and Royal Arcades are all in this area, each containing boutiques. ∎

Shoppers take a break in the boutique-filled Burlington Arcade.

EXPERIENCE: Enjoying a Cuppa (Tea)

Never mind that tea wasn't introduced to Britain until the mid-17th century or that coffee actually preceded it to the scepter'd isle: The image of an English afternoon tea is practically synonymous with refined British culture.

A visit to London wouldn't be complete without enjoying an afternoon tea. Nearly all services offer an eclectic choice of teas—ranging from Indian black teas (Indian and Chinese) to English or Irish Breakfast, Earl Grey, and Lapsang Suchong. These fine brews are accompanied by sandwiches, then scones with clotted cream and jam, and pastries to finish.

A traditional British afternoon tea includes not only tea, but finger foods such as small sandwiches and pastries.

Hotel Teas

Most major hotels in the city offer an afternoon tea. The experience won't come cheap; the hotel teas below average about £35–£40 ($56–$64) per person. Dress is usually smart casual (i.e., no shorts or sandals) and reservations are highly recommended.

Tea in the **Ritz**'s Palm Court *(150 Piccadilly, W1, tel 020 7493 8181 and toll-free from the U.S. 877-748-9536, www.theritzlondon.com)* is the classic experience. Men need to wear a tie and jacket, and photos are not allowed (so refrain if you see David Beckham at the next table). Reserve at least one month in advance for a weekday and four months in advance for a weekend. It is best to book the last sitting, so you do not have to rush.

The **Dorchester** *(Park Lane, W1, tel 020 7629 8888, www.thedorchester.com)* offers many timed seatings in two separate restaurants. **Brown's Hotel** *(Albemarle St., W1, tel 020 7518 4155, www .brownshotel.com)* has two tea sommeliers in their English Tea Room. Other excellent afternoon teas are served at the Park Room at **Grosvenor House** *(Park Lane, W1, reservations 020 7399 8452, www .marriott.co.uk)*; **Claridge's Hotel** *(Brook St., W1, tel 020 7629 8860, www.claridges. co.uk)*; the **Lanesborough Hotel** *(Hyde Park Corner, SW1, tel 020 7259 5599, www.lanesborough.com)*; and the **Landmark Hotel** *(222 Marylebone Rd., NW1, tel 020 7631 8000 www.landmark london.co.uk)*.

Department Stores

Harrods *(87–135 Brompton Rd., SW1, tel 020 7225 6800, www.harrods.com)* began in 1849 as a tea merchant, so it would be fitting to visit the beautiful Georgian Restaurant for a traditional tea. Nearby, the Fifth Floor Restaurant at **Harvey Nichols** *(109–125 Knightsbridge, SW1, tel 020 7235 5250, www .harveynichols.com)* is less expensive than other options at £22.50 ($36). In Mayfair, the St. James's Restaurant at **Fortnum & Mason** *(181 Piccadilly, W1, 0845 300 1707, www.fortnumandmason.com)* offers a variety of tea services, including a signature Estate High Tea.

Wallace Collection

One of the capital's finest private art collections is found at Hertford House, a palatial 18th-century mansion just north of Mayfair and Oxford Street in Manchester Square.

The Wallace Collection includes a first-class assembly of paintings.

Wallace Collection

- Map p. 72
- Hertford House, Manchester Square, W1
- 020 7935 0687
- Tube: Bond Street, Marble Arch

www.wallace collection.org

The house was built for the Duke of Manchester in 1777. But it was four generations of the art-loving Hertford family who created the collection. The 1st Marquess supplied Canalettos and the 2nd Gainsboroughs. The 3rd added Sèvres porcelain and Dutch canvases, and the 4th bought Fragonards, Watteaus, and Bouchers, plus furniture, and installed the Parisian staircase. As a postscript, the 4th Marquess's illegitimate son and inheritor, Richard Wallace, renovated the house and added his Italian majolica and Renaissance armor, bronzes, and gold. His widow gave both house and collection to the nation.

Hertford House is a joy to visit; Rick Mather's glazed roof spans the inner courtyard and the Wallace Restaurant. The lower ground floor houses two galleries, a lecture theater, studio, and visitors' library *(by appt. only)*.

When you enter, climb the opulent double staircase; do not miss the Boucher paintings. On the next floor, treats include a roomful of Venetian paintings by Canaletto and his pupil, Guardi, and another room of Dutch pictures by Ruisdael, Hobbema, and Wijnants. The finest collection of French paintings outside France includes Fragonard's "The Swing" (1767). Frans Hals's 1624 "The Laughing Cavalier" is among the familiar paintings in the 100-foot (30 m) Long Gallery. Downstairs, enjoy English paintings, medieval and Renaissance works, and ornate clocks. Also here are Limoges enamels, Venetian glass, and the amazing armor collection. ∎

Great views and great entertainment: museums, concert halls, theaters, and restaurants

South Bank

Sea life surrounds visitors at the London Aquarium.

South Bank

The serious core of London—Westminster and the City—sits on the north bank of the Thames; the south bank is a solid strip of entertainment. Here, museums for design, modern art, war, and underwater life are interspersed with theaters, concert halls, restaurants, and a fine cathedral. The seeds for development were sown when Puritan City government banned theaters from the City in 1574 and they went over the river, making Southwark a refuge for actor-managers. Today, bridges old and new, plus the Jubilee Tube line, make access to this vibrant area easy.

This stretch of the Thames between Tower and Westminster Bridges sits directly opposite the City and Westminster, filling the space inside the river's broad curve. Here, South-wark developed early as a dormitory town for Roman London directly opposite, linked

by the one bridge across the tidal Thames. Over the centuries, as London expanded, the south bank developed—and the bridges multiplied to six for road traffic, three for rail, and one for pedestrians. A revival of the south bank is now close to completion. A nearly continuous river

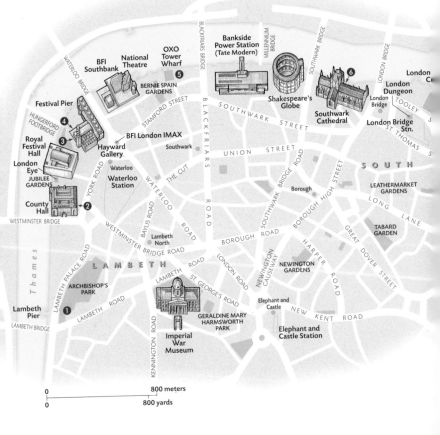

walkway provides stunning views of City and Westminster landmarks.

The Jubilee Line extension, which runs along the south bank from Westminster to the O$_2$ Arena, opened in 1999. Its Bermondsey station is a short walk from Cherry Garden Pier. Nearby, the Angel pub is where Captain Cook planned his trips and James McNeill Whistler painted London views.

Westward at St. Saviour's Dock is Mill Street, where New Concordia Wharf became the Docklands' first residential conversion in 1980—a model project that showed meticulous

❶ Lambeth Palace ❷ Sea Life London Aquarium ❸ Purcell Room ❹ Queen Elizabeth Hall ❺ OXO Tower ❻ Clink Exhibition ❼ Hays Galleria ❽ H.M.S. *Belfast* ❾ City Hall ❿ Bramah Tea and Coffee Museum ⓫ Design Museum

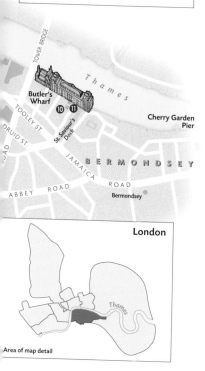

Area of map detail

respect for the building. Here, too, is Piers Gough's dramatic China Wharf and Michael Squire Associates' Vogan's Mill. Beyond Butler's Wharf and Tower Bridge is London Bridge City. Here, Goodhart-Rendel's striking art deco St. Olaf's House and Hay's Wharf have been restored. H.M.S. *Belfast* (see p. 106), moored in the Thames nearby, is a World War II cruiser.

Southwark occupies the area between London and Blackfriars Bridges. Its great cathedral is almost smothered by railway lines. In contrast the riverside beyond is open, a fine setting for the rebuilt Globe Theatre and its Museum, which evoke memories of Tudor entertainment. Here, too, is Tate Modern at Bankside.

West of Blackfriars Bridge and the OXO Tower, the South Bank Arts Complex now fills the riverside. In the heart of this major entertainment area is Nicholas Grimshaw's heroic, 400-yard-long (365 m), curved and glazed Waterloo International Terminal (1991–1993), used by Eurostar trains until 2007, when they began to terminate at St. Pancras instead. Finally, the Sea Life London Aquarium fills the basement of the County Hall building. Beyond it, steps lead onto Westminster Bridge, one of the best viewpoints for the Houses of Parliament across the river. ■

South Bank Arts Complex

Built for the 1951 Festival of Britain, this is now Western Europe's largest arts complex. Events run from morning until late at night and range from informal jazz to highest Shakespearean tragedy. From the north bank the buildings are best reached along the splendidly wide river walk, a pleasant stroll in summer after crossing Waterloo or Westminster Bridges, or the elegant new pedestrian section of Hungerford Bridge.

The London Eye provides unmatched views of the city on the Thames.

Southbank Centre

- Map p. 96
- South Bank, SE1
- 020 7960 4200
  Ticket office:
  0844 875 0073
- Free–$$$$$,
  depending on the
  event
- Tube: Waterloo,
  Westminster,
  Embankment,
  Charing Cross,
  then walk across
  Hungerford Bridge

www.southbankcentre.co.uk

The 1951 Festival of Britain, a government-sponsored extravaganza, was held to cheer up the British people during postwar austerity. It was also a showcase for the better world Londoners had fought for. A new generation of architects built a miniature wonderland showing off Britain's modern achievements in science, art, and sociology. There was a Dome of Discovery, itself destined to inspire the Millennium Dome (now the O$_2$ Arena), as well as sculptures by Reg Butler and Henry Moore, and the Festival Hall.

Now called the **Royal Festival Hall,** this concert hall built in 1951 by Robert Matthew and J. L. Martin was extended in 1962 and is the only building to survive from the festival. The 2,600-seat hall replaced Queen's Hall, which had been bombed during the war, and has recently been entirely renovated. With its Le Corbusier inspiration, its clean lines, and its egglike auditorium nestling in a forest of columns and glazed galleries, this was London's first modern public building.

In 1964–1967, the **Queen Elizabeth Hall** and the **Purcell Room,** smaller concert halls, were built, together with the now

EXPERIENCE: The BFI London Film Festival

If you happen to visit London in October, treat yourself to some of the film industry's latest offerings at the **BFI London Film Festival** *(bfi.org.uk/lff)*. Running for two weeks, the festival brings a sampling of the world's best new films to more than a dozen venues across the city. The festival has been running since 1955 and includes special events, lectures, and on-stage interviews with directors and other industry insiders in addition to the eclectic film lineup itself.

You can obtain tickets though the festival's website; via telephone at 020 7928 3232; in person at the BFI Southbank Box Office; or at each individual theater on the day of the film.

The exact dates vary from year to year, so check the festival website for this year's particulars.

refurbished **Hayward Gallery,** whose rooftop neon sculpture changes with the wind. The upper level, often windy walkways, anonymous entrances, and blank concrete walls are not inviting—but compensation is found in the glorious music and art inside.

The **British Film Institute** (BFI; see sidebar p. 46), built 1956–1958, is tucked beneath Waterloo Bridge, where second-hand bookstalls are set up daily on the towpath beneath the bridge arches. The BFI's huge program ranges from old classics to the latest avant-garde foreign films. It also runs the huge annual London Film Festival (see sidebar above).

Sir Denys Lasdun's **National Theatre,** known by Londoners as the "National" or the "NT," was the culmination of an old dream. Back in the 18th century, actor-manager David Garrick suggested a national theater. The campaign was taken up by H. Granville-Barker, George Bernard Shaw, Laurence Olivier, and others, and the theater finally opened in 1977. It has three auditoriums. The Olivier's open stage lends itself to epic productions; the smaller Lyttelton has a conventional layout; and the flexible little Cottesloe has a shell that can be made into any shape at all. Foyer spaces are also used for music, the theaters for pre-performance talks, and the backstage tour is one of London's best. The nighttime panorama from the terraces is breathtaking—stretching from St. Paul's to Westminster.

The distinctive circular **BFI London IMAX Cinema** *(tel 0870 787 2525, www.bfi.org.uk/showing/imax)* shows films on the largest screen in Britain. Digital sound and larger-than-life images offer fun for the whole family.

The **London Eye** opened in 2000 opposite the Houses of Parliament and quickly established itself as one of the capital's best run attractions. Passengers ride a complete circle in one of 32 enclosed capsules. Breathtaking views are enjoyed morning to late evening, weather permitting.

The embankment between the London Eye and the Southbank Centre is a popular tourist hang-out that attracts an array of food vendors and street entertainers. ∎

British Film Institute (BFI)
- Map p. 96
- South Bank, SE1
- 020 7928 3232
- $$
- Same as Southbank Centre

www.bfi.org.uk

National Theatre
- Map p. 96
- South Bank, SE1
- Information & backstage tours: 020 7452 3400 Box office: 020 7452 3000
- Closed Sun.
- Free–$$$$$, depending on the event
- Same as Southbank Centre

www.nationaltheatre.org.uk

EDF Energy London Eye
- South Bank, SE1
- 0871 781 3000
- $$$$. Book a timed ticket in advance to beat the lines.
- Tube: Waterloo, Westminster

www.londoneye.com

Sea Life London Aquarium

Down in the bowels of County Hall lurks the capital's biggest, darkest, and most fascinating maze; its glass walls are windows onto softly lit underwater habitats from around the world. Thousands of fish live here, from shoals of tiny, turquoise fish, zipping along in formation, to smoothhound sharks. After a visit, the desire to slow down the destruction and pollution of the world's waters takes on a new urgency.

London Aquarium

⚠ Map p. 96

✉ County Hall, Riverside Building, Westminster Bridge Road, SE1

☎ 020 7967 8000

$ $$$$

🚇 Tube: Westminster, Waterloo

www.london aquarium.co.uk

First opened in 1997, the London Aquarium was purchased in 2008 by Merlin Entertainments, the owner of such mega-popular London sites as the London Eye and Madame Tussauds. After an extensive £5 million ($8 million) refurbishment, the aquarium reopened to visitors in 2009 as one of Sea Life's network of 30 sea sanctuaries in 11 countries.

The new layout offers a one-way route over three floors, exhibiting nearly 600 species in more than 60 displays. The one-way system ensures you won't miss anything important, but it also can cause bottlenecks at popular displays.

The aquarium's tanks are arranged along 14 themed zones, with touchpools and plenty of clear descriptions about the contents of each tank. They start with displays of sea creatures from the depths of the Atlantic Ocean and move on to illustrate life in a tidal zone, a Pacific Ocean shipwreck, coral reefs, rain forests, the Antarctic, and even the Thames River. The coup de grâce is the Shark Walk, which takes you over a huge tank that is home to more than 40 sharks representing 14 different species.

Free talks by the resident aquarists and interactive feedings add to the fascination. What is needed is time: To stand watching one tank for several minutes is much more rewarding than rushing from one to another. ■

London's Other Aquariums

While the London Aquarium is the granddaddy of the genre, two other good aquariums in London are also well worth visiting:

Take the train from London Bridge to Forest Hill to visit the **Horniman Museum & Gardens** (100 London Rd., Forest Hill, SE23, tel 020 8699 1872, www.horniman.ac.uk), home to a well-regarded aquarium with displays of jellyfish, seahorses, and coral and tropical fish. Entrance to the museum and gardens is free, except for the aquarium, which costs £6 ($10; children under 16 free).

The aquarium at the **London Zoo** (Outer Circle, Regent's Park, NW1, tel 020 7722 3333, www.zsl.org) was the world's first, established in 1853. The very term "aquarium" was coined here, shortening the "aquatic vivarium" name then in use. The current building dates from 1924 and highlights coral reefs, Amazonian fish, and conservation and breeding programs for endangered species (including Thames fish and eels). Admission to the aquarium is included in the zoo entrance fee ($$$$$).

Imperial War Museum

Britain's national museum of 20th-century war is not only about tanks and guns. In fact, they form just a tiny fraction of a large and fascinating collection that covers every aspect of war, civil or military, allied or enemy, military or political, social or cultural.

The museum opened in 1920 in the former Bedlam Asylum, which moved to this building in 1812–1815 and where Charlie Chaplin's mother lived for some time. In addition to the wide-ranging displays, special exhibitions draw on the museum's 10,000 or so quality posters and paintings. The museum continues to send official war artists to places of conflict around the world.

Fighter planes and a giant V2 rocket stand in the hall, contrasting with the displays that graphically demonstrate the human damage of war, such as an impressive but harrowing account of the liberation of Belsen in 1945. This is part of the **Holocaust Exhibition** (recommended for people over 14 years old), which examines the persecution and murder of European Jews and other groups from 1933 to 1945. The exhibition begins on the third floor and exits on the second, next to the gallery that features a very difficult-to-watch film, *Crimes Against Humanity,* chronicling the impact of 20th-century war on civilians.

The **Secret War Gallery,** upstairs, justifies the money and expertise spent on government spying, artificial intelligence, and undercover espionage, with accounts of Special Air Services (SAS) operations in the Gulf Wars.

The Imperial War Museum focuses on 20th-century wars, including the weaponry of World War II.

Other galleries contain original WWI uniforms and firearms, and German straw overboots for protection against the Soviet Union's cold.

The gallery focusing on conflicts since 1945 has a slice of the Berlin Wall and General Schwarzkopf's Gulf War uniform. The walk-through of World War I trenches and the Blitz Experience, portraying London's bomb-strewn streets, are especially evocative. In 2010, the **Lord Ashcroft Gallery** opened, displaying Victoria Crosses (for members of the military) and George Crosses (for civilians) and telling the stories of heroism that earned them. ■

Imperial War Museum

🏛 Map p. 96

✉ Lambeth Road, SE1

☎ 020 7416 5000

🚇 Tube: Lambeth North, then 5-minute walk, or Elephant & Castle

www.iwm.org.uk

Southwark Cathedral

Medieval Southwark's liberal reputation was encouraged by its priory church, St. Mary Overie, which belonged to the diocese of Winchester, in Hampshire. Prostitutes, known as Winchester Geese, were rife, and assorted rough entertainment included bull- and bearbaiting and gambling. The arrival of the theaters sealed the area's position as the Tudor and Stuart entertainment center. All this is evoked in the Clink Exhibition (see sidebar below), on the site of Clink Prison, which began as a dungeon for disobedient clerics beneath the bishop's palace.

Southwark Cathedral

- Map p. 96
- Southwark Cathedral, SE1
- 020 7367 6700 Tours: 020 7367 6734
- Donation
- Tube/Rail: London Bridge

www.southwark.anglican.org/cathedral

Today, after new warehouses, railways, and a new bridge have destroyed much of the Southwark of the 19th century, renovation work has restored the cathedral and its surrounding cobbled streets and old warehouses.

The cathedral began as the Augustinian Priory of St. Mary Overie, founded in 1106. In 1212 the priory burned down; of the Gothic church, only the choir and retrochoir survived. The choir was then renovated (a fine Tudor stone screen was added), but after the Reformation it was used as a bakery and pigsty. In the 19th century, it lost its east-end chapel to the London Bridge approach,

and was substantially restored—the tower and retrochoir in 1822, the nave in 1838 and again in 1890 by Sir Arthur Blomfield. In 1905 the church of St. Mary was made a cathedral.

You need sharp eyes to pick out the mixture of French and English Gothic style. Attentive eyes may note the 14th-century crossing tower with its later (1689) pinnacles, the Norman north transept and 19th-century south transept window, and the Harvard Memorial Chapel's 12th-century walls and 1907 interior. The cathedral's memorials include the painted tomb of poet John Gower, a contemporary of Chaucer. ∎

Ghoulish London

The area south of London Bridge seems to have proclaimed itself London's theme park for the macabre.

It all started in 1974 with the **London Dungeon** (28–34 Tooley St., SE1, tel 020 7403 7221, www.thedungeons.com, $$$$$), which has rides and realistic depictions of medieval torture, disease, poverty, and despair . . . perfect for a family holiday. Live actors lead shows that inform, entertain, and occasionally torment.

West of Southwark Cathedral you'll find the **Clink Prison Museum** (1 Clink St., SE1, tel 020 7403 0900, www.clink.co.uk,

$$$), located on the site of the old jail. Less a scare show than a real educational museum, it nonetheless uses live actors and a creepy atmosphere to grab its visitors' attention.

For a look at some real-life terror, visit the **Old Operating Theatre and Herb Garret** (9a St. Thomas St., SE1, tel 020 7188 2679, www.thegarret.org.uk, $$), just off Borough High Street. This operating theater for women was in use from 1822 until 1862. The theater and its medical museum depict the nature of surgery in the bad old days before anesthesia or proper hygiene.

Shakespeare's Globe Theatre

When American actor Sam Wanamaker came to London in 1949, he began searching for the site of the original Globe Theatre, first built in 1599, closed in 1642, and later destroyed. In 1970 Wanamaker began to re-create what he believed was the most important public theater ever built. Although he died in 1993, as did the theater's architect, Theo Crosby, in the following year, the project to reconstruct the Elizabethan theater continued to completion.

A standing audience surrounds actors performing *Henry VIII* at the Globe Theatre.

The site of the theater, 200 yards (183 m) from the original location, was cleared in 1987. Pentagram Design used contemporary illustrations and archaeological evidence, together with traditional materials and techniques, to re-create the Tudor theater: a polygonal building of 20 three-story wooden bays. Audience capacity is 1,401, including 500 standing places. In 1994 the theater's walls were constructed as Britain's largest lime plastering project, and thatching began of the first new thatched building in central London since the Great Fire of 1666. On May 27, 1997, the theater opened for its first season of 17th-century plays with Shakespeare's *Henry V* and *The Winter's Tale*, Middleton's *A Chaste Maid in Cheapside*, and Beaumont & Fletcher's *The Maid's Tragedy*. It has all been hugely successful, apart from the difficulty of hearing the actors if it is raining. Actors report experiencing a new closeness with their audience.

Each season has brought the acting company more acclaim. Shakespeare addicts should reserve time for the hands-on challenges in the exhibition, too. ∎

Shakespeare's Globe Theatre

- Map p. 96
- New Globe Walk, Bankside, SE1
- Theater: 020 7902 1400 Exhibition: 020 7902 1500
- No performances Oct.–April
- Exhibition: $$$
- Tube: Southwark, London Bridge Rail: London Bridge

www.shakespeares globe.org

Tate Modern

As if to put the final stamp of approval on the revived South Bank, the Tate's collection of international modern art opened in May 2000 in the Sir Giles Gilbert Scott's Bankside Power Station. Now a major London landmark, Tate Modern is revitalizing its surroundings, and has generated the first new Thames bridge in a century—the Millennium Bridge, which opened in June 2000.

Tate Modern features modern art such as "Ishi's Light" by Anish Kapoor.

Tate Modern

 Map p. 96

 Bankside, SE1

☎ 020 7887 8888

🚇 Tube: Southwark, London Bridge, or Mansion House and walk across the Millennium Bridge

www.tate.org.uk

Both building and site are sensational. Scott's cathedral-like, brick power station stands on a wide riverside terrace looking across to St. Paul's Cathedral. Wren lived nearby, and his favorite view of his masterpiece was from here. Completed in 1963 to replace an older power station on the same site, the Bankside structure's most valuable asset is the Turbine Hall, about 100 feet (30 m) high and 500 feet (152 m) long, running the width of the building.

Herzog & de Meuron, a Swiss architectural firm, won the international competition (there were 148 entries) to make the transformation. They have been praised for their use of space and light and for their originality. Visitors enter the building on a ramp and descend into the Turbine Hall, which is a "covered street." They then proceed through a series of top- and side-lit galleries into the other areas of the building. There are activity spaces, an information center, an auditorium, shops, and education programs. Four eating areas include pleasant garden and riverside outlooks; one rooftop bar-restaurant has spectacular views over London. The ground-floor café opens for breakfast.

The Collection

In 1916 the Tate was given the responsibility of forming a collection of international modern art, encompassing painting and sculpture from 1900 and after. The recent growth of the collection, together with a huge increase in its popularity, meant the Millbank site was too small. Tate outposts opened in Liverpool in 1987 and St. Ives in Cornwall in 1993. Then the modern collection gained its own vast space.

As the number of works has doubled since 1950, the collection is now acknowledged as one of the world's four most important

INSIDER TIP:

Tate Modern's Level 7 restaurant offers amazing views spanning the Thames.

—AIMÉE TAYLOR
Tate information assistant

collections of modern art, competing with New York's MoMA and Solomon R. Guggenheim Museum, and Paris's Musée National d'Art Moderne.

Movements especially well represented include surrealism, abstract expressionism, pop art, and conceptual art. Many masterpieces by influential artists seen only rarely are regularly

---

EXPERIENCE:
Take the Ferry from Tate to Tate

Art fans can shuttle back and forth between Tate Modern and Tate Britain on the Tate Boat service run by **Thames Clippers** (tel 0870 781 5049, www.thames clippers.com, $$). Boats depart every 40 minutes from both Bankside Pier (at Tate Modern) and Millbank Pier, home of Tate Britain (see p. 186). Getting there is half the fun: The 20-minute ride between the museums presents superb views of St. Paul's, the City, Somerset House, and Westminster on the north bank, and the arts venues of the south bank.

---

rotated among the four suites of permanent galleries (on levels 3 and 5). These include Salvador Dalí's "The Metamorphosis of Narcissus" (1937), Pablo Picasso's "The Three Dancers" (1925), and Andy Warhol's "Camouflage" (1986) and "Self-Portrait Strangulation" (1978).

The same is true for major British artists. There is now more opportunity to see great works such as Francis Bacon's "Study for Portrait on Folding Bed" (1963), Henry Moore's "Helmet Head No. 1" (1950), and Stanley Spencer's "The Centurion's Servant" (1914).

In addition, a special suite of galleries holds three major loan exhibitions a year. The 2009 rehang of the permanent galleries explores four distinct themes: "States of Flux," "Poetry and Dream," "Energy and Process," and "Material Gestures." The clear captions help in appreciating a complex period in art. ∎

Butler's Wharf

London's principal wharves were the "legal quays" on the north bank, while the south bank's "suffrance wharves" eased the volume of 19th-century shipping. After the docks closed, Londoners treated these testimonies to their city's wealth in different ways.

Design Museum

- Map p. 97
- Butler's Wharf, Shad Thames, SE1
- 020 7403 6933
- $$
- Tube: Bermondsey, London Bridge or Tower Hill and walk across the river Rail: London Bridge

www.designmuseum.org

Two vistas reveal the dramatic differences. One is from Butler's Wharf to the unforgiving Guoman Hotel, out of sympathy with St. Katharine Dock and the riverside in scale, shape, and materials. The other is of Butler's Wharf from the north bank. Here, the sensitive mixture of renovated warehouse building and interesting, well-proportioned new structures maintains London's riverside history while equipping it to be a lively neighborhood for the 21st century.

The hero of Butler's Wharf is Sir Terence Conran. As a small boy, he came here with his father, a dealer in gum copal resin, and watched the freighters unloading. He saw Bermondsey's decline, then boldly stepped in to revive this spot. In 1984, his company, Conran Roche, acquired the south bank site and its 17 historic buildings. The flour, grain, and rice warehouses had closed, as had those for rubber, tapioca, tea, and coffee.

Conran opened up the quayside and converted the central, massive Butler's Wharf Building (1871–1873) into apartments, shops, and a string of restaurants. His pet project was the newly built **Design Museum,** opened in 1989 to display provocative and classic examples and thus stimulate design awareness. Its restaurant offers panoramic views.

Atmospheric **Shad Thames** street, a historic remnant of an old Victorian warehouse district, runs west from just behind the Fashion Museum toward Tower Bridge.

Designer Zandra Rhodes is the energy behind the **Fashion & Textile Museum** *(83 Bermondsey St., tel 020 7407 8664, www.ftm london.org),* which displays Rhodes's own collection and contemporary designers.

As if to confirm Conran's revival, the first mayor of London, Ken Livingstone, chose this area, just west of Tower Bridge, for **City Hall** *(The Queen's Walk, SE1, www.london.gov.uk),* his egg-shaped headquarters designed by Foster and Partners. ■

H.M.S. *Belfast*

Docked near London Bridge, the H.M.S. *Belfast (Morgan's Lane, Tooley Street, SE1, tel 020 7940 6300, www.hmsbelfast.iwm .org.uk, $$$)* was one of the most powerful light cruisers ever built. In 1944, the warship—now an official branch of the Imperial War Museum—was among the first to open fire against the Germans on D-Day. In 1971 the ship's decks opened to the public. Wear comfortable shoes—tours include climbing ladders.

Two major national galleries, theaters, restaurants, first-run cinemas, and state-of-the-art amusements

Trafalgar Square & Soho

Bright lights at Piccadilly Circus

Trafalgar Square & Soho

This small area of uncompromisingly urban London, cut off from the river and parks, has few great public buildings. It is, nevertheless, a microcosm of the capital's passive and active reaction to Londoners' demands for change over the centuries.

In Tudor times, farms, fields, and woods—the possessions of various monasteries—lay north of royal Westminster. To improve his hunting around Whitehall Palace, whose stables until the 19th century covered much of today's Trafalgar Square, Henry VIII appropriated the land that later became Soho. The focus for London's commercial entertainment was established.

Shaftesbury Avenue, completed in 1886, divides Soho into two distinct halves. The narrow streets to the north have in the 20th century been home to newly arrived Greeks, mainland Italians, and Sicilians, creating a slightly exotic and friendly Continental atmosphere. Today, many of the seedy clubs have been turned into chic bars and restaurants, and there are plans to pedestrianize some of the narrow streets. To the south, a handful of streets makes up Tong Yan Kai (Chinese Street), as one of London's newest immigrant populations calls it.

The Chinese, fleeing poverty in Hong Kong, arrived here from the 1950s onward and quickly created an atmospheric Chinatown. Tucked down Leicester Place is Notre-Dame-de-France—once a theater but converted in 1865 by art nouveau pioneer Auguste Boileau. In 1960, Jean Cocteau added some frescoes.

Moving farther south, 19th-century Leicester Square had transformed from residential square to entertainment center by the 1950s, with Turkish baths and a full-scale circus. And when the picture palaces arrived from America, several great halls offered their clients the cheap but gloriously escapist Hollywood dreams. Nightclubs soon abounded, where Noël Coward, Gloria Swanson, and Marlene Dietrich encouraged the inter-war fashionable set to dance fast and forget the looming clouds of social change and the onset of another war. Today, cinemas still dominate the square.

Trafalgar Square, to the southeast, makes an uneasy transfer from entertainment center to more somber London districts. James Gibbs's St. Martin-in-the-Fields, 1721, was the blueprint for colonial churches, especially in America. It stands on the corner

NOT TO BE MISSED:

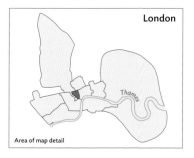

London

Thames

Area of map detail

of the 19th-century square, conceived as a vast crossroads for routes to Buckingham Palace, the Houses of Parliament, Whitehall, and the City. The square's walls are Smirke's porticoed Canada House, Baker's fine South Africa House, and William Wilkins's National Gallery, which was built in 1832–1838; the Sainsbury Wing was added in 1988–1991. In the center of the square, Horatio, Viscount Nelson, the hero of the Battle of Trafalgar in 1805, looks down on a timeless London scene of visitors, statues, fountains, and hundreds of pigeons. ■

0   300 meters
0   300 yards

❶ Criterion Theatre ❷ Lyric Theatre ❸ Apollo Theatre ❹ Gielgud Theatre ❺ Queen's Theatre ❻ House of St. Barnabas ❼ Chinatown ❽ Notre-Dame-de-France ❾ Canada House ❿ South Africa House

National Gallery

This is one of the world's most impressive national galleries. Indeed, the National Gallery's collection of more than 2,300 paintings is a succession of masterpieces that tells the story of European painting from the 13th to the early 20th centuries. Because the collection is relatively small and the rooms compact, the visitor can stroll through all the galleries, pick out some highlights, and choose areas to return to on another day for an in-depth look.

Thousands of European paintings from past centuries crowd the walls of the National Gallery.

It was George IV who, observing the enlightened progress of public art galleries in Paris and elsewhere, suggested to a government reluctant to fund the arts that there should be a National Gallery of England. Fortunately, prompted by the promised gift of a fine collection, it stumped up £57,000 ($91,200) in 1824 to pay for the 38 pictures left by John Julius Angerstein, a Russian-born financier living in London. At first, his pictures were exhibited in his Pall Mall house; then in 1838 they were moved into William Wilkins's building overlooking Trafalgar Square. Exhibition space increased in more recent years with the building of the North Wing in 1975 and the 1991 opening of the Sainsbury Wing extension.

Overview

At least 85 percent of the paintings in the impressive

collection—unless on loan or in restoration—are on display. If a room is closed, its contents will usually be displayed elsewhere; simply ask. The 66 galleries are divided into four sections: 13th- to 15th-century paintings in the Sainsbury Wing; 16th-century in the West Wing; 17th-century paintings in the North Wing; and 18th- to early 20th-century painting in the East Wing. (Ground floor computer terminals enable visitors to create tours of their favorite pictures and print them out.) More recent 20th-century art is displayed at Bankside's Tate Modern (see p. 104), while most of the British paintings are at Tate Britain (see p. 186) in Pimlico.

13th- to 15th-Century Paintings (Rooms 51–66)

The place to start is the Sainsbury Wing. The gallery's earliest Renaissance paintings are hung here, a mixture of northern and southern European works. One of the earliest is Giotto's "The Pentecost" (1306–1312), in Room 51. With his murals in Florence and Padua, this work marks the beginning of a new artistic era, one in which painting became realistic, three-dimensional and dramatic. Rooms 52–56 illustrate this further, notably with "The Wilton Diptych" (1395–1399), possibly commissioned by Richard II of England for his private devotions; Paolo Uccello's "Battle of San Romano" (circa 1440), showing a Florentine victory

over the Sienese; and Rogier van der Weyden's almost surreal naturalistic "The Magdalen Reading" (before 1438). As for portraits, there are the groundbreaking heads by Robert Campin and Jan van Eyck's "The Arnolfini Portrait" (both from the 1430s).

INSIDER TIP:

The National Gallery is at its quietest on Monday mornings, the best time to visit popular exhibitions.

—ELOISE MAXWELL
National Gallery press assistant

Rooms 57–60 contain more complex technical challenges, such as Carlo Crivelli's "The Annunciation, with Saint Emidius" (1486), with its deep perspective and political overtones, and "A Muse (Calliope?)" circa 1455–1460, by Cosimo Tura, an Italian who had absorbed the northern precision technique. Botticelli's "Venus and Mars" (1480–1490) is one of the Florentine artist's few secular works, still decorative, but achieving a wonderfully translucent gown for Venus.

Rooms 61–66, at the end of this section, contain a number of familiar Renaissance paintings. From the Veneto, there is Andrea Mantegna's "The Agony in the Garden" (circa 1460) and his brother-in-law Giovanni Bellini's picture of the same subject,

National Gallery

- Map p. 109
- Trafalgar Square, WC2
- 020 7747 2885
- Charge for some special exhibitions
- Tube: Charing Cross, Embankment, Leicester Square

www.nationalgallery.org.uk

painted five years later. Portraits grow in number and refinement in this section—for instance, Giovanni Bellini's "The Doge Leonardo Loredan" (circa 1501). Finally, don't miss the two sedate Piero della Francesca panels, "The Baptism of Christ" from the 1450s and "Nativity" (1470–1475).

Georges-Pierre Seurat's "Bathers at Asnières" (1884)

16th-Century Paintings (Rooms 2–14)

The High Renaissance artists represented here include Raphael, Michelangelo, Bronzino, and Correggio. All were influenced by Leonardo da Vinci. Inspired by Bellini, Venetian artists such as Titian explored color and worked increasingly in oil paints on canvas. Subject matter broadened to include bigger portraits, mythological compositions, still lifes, and landscapes. The age of collectors began and the artist's skills were valued as much as his subject matter.

Two Italian artists featured in Room 2 demonstrate these changes: Correggio in "The School of Love" (1525) and Parmigianino in his "Madonna and Child with Saints" (both circa 1520).

Room 2 also contains Leonardo da Vinci's large, fragile drawing of "The Virgin and Child with Saint Anne and Saint John the Baptist" (circa 1499–1500) and his "Virgin of the Rocks" (circa 1508).

The Holbeins in Room 4 include "The Ambassadors" (1533), an early portrait of two full-length figures. Room 8 contains paintings by some of the leading artists of 1500–1550: Michelangelo's "The Entombment," Sebastiano del Piombo's "The Raising of Lazarus," Bronzino's "An Allegory with Venus and Cupid," and three paintings by the young Raphael: "Saint Catherine of Alexandria" (1507); "The Ansidei Altarpiece" (1505); and "Madonna of the Pinks" (1506-1507), which already display the influence of ancient Greco-Roman art, as well as the High Renaissance search for ideal beauty. Venetian color dominates in Rooms 9 and 10, with Titian's "Bacchus and Ariadne" (1520–1523) and "The Vendramin Family" (1543–1547) and Paolo Veronese's "The Family of Darius before Alexander" (1565–1570).

17th-Century Paintings (rooms 15–32, 37)

The richness of 17th-century painting fills the next 19 rooms. Landscape had become a favorite subject of collectors

Take a break and rest your feet at the National Gallery Café, a good place to stop for afternoon tea and cakes.

—ELOISE MAXWELL
National Gallery press assistant

and patrons, and northern artists such as Cuyp, Ruisdael, and Rubens produced some of the most sublime canvases. Under the influence of northern artists, Italians reduced the size of pictures, while Italy's classical art and southern light inspired such northerners as Poussin, Claude, and Rubens. Van Dyck, Velázquez, and Rembrandt took the portrait tradition a step further, and the most innovative painting schools were the Spanish and Dutch, typified by Velázquez and Rembrandt.

Claude Lorrain's landscapes in Rooms 15 and 19, such as "Seaport with the Embarkation of the Queen of Sheba" (1648), were hugely influential in 18th-century English painting and landscape gardening. The Turner pictures in Room 15 are proof of this. French paintings in Rooms 18 and 19 include Philippe de Champaigne's magnificent 1637 portrait of Cardinal Richelieu and Nicholas Poussin's golden-lit "The Adoration of the Golden Calf" (1634). The Dutch pictures in Rooms 21–28 include Aelbert Cuyp's pastoral "River Landscape with Horseman and Peasants" (circa 1660); a collection of Rembrandts, such as "Self-Portrait at the Age of 34"

EXPERIENCE: Dig Deeper into the Gallery

The National Gallery offers a bevy of excellent free programs for both adults and families.

Children under 5 can join the **Magic Carpet Storytelling** program on offer at 10:30 a.m. and 11:30 a.m. every Sunday. This storytelling session takes place in front of a gallery painting. For families with children aged 5 to 11, there are free art workshops at 11:00 a.m. and 2:00 p.m. on Sundays. These hands-on sessions, led by artists, offer children—with inspiration from the collection—the chance to create drawings on their own. No reservations are required for either the storytelling or the art workshops, but space is limited. The entrance to the programs is from the Education Centre foyer, accessible via Orange Street at the back of the museum.

For adults, a popular program that may inspire the inner Gainsborough is **Talk & Draw** at 1:00 p.m. every Friday. After a short, in-gallery talk on a painting, you'll try your hand at reproducing the artwork. No experience is necessary, and all materials are provided.

At 1 p.m. each day, Tuesday through Saturday, you can join a 35-minute **gallery lecture** on a collection piece. Or, if time is short, at 4 p.m. every weekday you can join a quick **"ten-minute talk"** that provides insight into one selected painting.

Music lovers shouldn't miss the opportunity to hear a Royal Academy of Music mini-concert, performed at 6:00 p.m. each Friday evening. Enjoy beautiful music in a sublime setting in Room 18.

Dulwich Picture Gallery

Before the National Gallery came into existence, Sir John Soane's custom-designed neoclassical gallery, opened in 1814, was England's first public art museum. Located about 15 minutes by train from Victoria or London Bridge Stations, it owes its astounding collection to the failure of the British government to accept the offer of 400 pictures collected by the art dealer Noel Desenfans. The collection was intended for the projected National Gallery of Poland in Warsaw, but when the Polish king was forced to abdicate in 1795, Desenfans offered it to Britain. Unbelievably, the government refused the offer. Desenfans then gave the paintings to Sir Francis Bourgeois, who later bequeathed them to Dulwich College, already the owners of a good art collection. Wandering the dozen top-lit rooms today, you can enjoy in peace what might have been exhibited in Trafalgar Square: Rembrandt's "Girl at a Window," sketches by Rubens, and several Gainsboroughs.

Dulwich Picture Gallery

- ✉ College Road, SE21
- ☎ 020 8693 5254
- 🕐 Closed Mon.
- 💲 $$. Free on Fri.
- 🚇 Regular trains from Victoria and London Bridge Stations to North Dulwich or West Dulwich

www.dulwichpicture gallery.org.uk

(1640) and "Belshazzar's Feast" (1636–1638); and Vermeer's especially intimate "A Young Woman Standing at a Virginal" (1670). Equally stunning is Room 29, a collection of Rubens canvases that range from the allegorical "Peace and War" (1629–1630) to his powerful "Samson and Delilah" of 1609. Royal portraits reach new grandeur in rooms 30–31 with Velázquez's "Philip IV of Spain in Brown and Silver" (1631–1632) and Van Dyck's "Equestrian Portrait of Charles I" (1637–1638).

18th- to Early 20th-Century Paintings (Rooms 33–36, 38–46)

The subject matter of 18th- and 19th-century painting is both colorful and accessible—beach scenes, flowerpots, the writing of a letter. It retains many traditional genres, such as portrait, landscape, still life, domestic scenes, and narrative.

In Room 33, French painter Jean-Siméon Chardin sustained domestic intimacy in his "The House of Cards" (1736–1777). British paintings fill Rooms 34–36. Portraits are especially strong, and include Sir Joshua Reynolds's "Lady Cockburn and Her Three Eldest Sons" (1773), Thomas Gainsborough's "The Morning Walk" (1785), and Sir Thomas Lawrence's aging, delicate Queen Charlotte, painted four years later. Turner's "Fighting Temeraire" (1838–1839) takes landscape painting into new territory. Spanish portraits in Rooms 30 and 39 include Francisco de Goya's "The Duke of Wellington" (1812–1814), and French paintings in Room 41 feature Ingres's sumptuous "Madame Moitessier" (1856). Lyrical Impressionist paintings fill Rooms 43 and 44, including Claude Monet's "The Beach at Trouville" (1870), Pierre-Auguste Renoir's "The Skiff" (1875), and Georges-Pierre Seurat's "Bathers at Asnières" (1884). The collection ends in Rooms 45 and 46 with such works as Vincent van Gogh's "Sunflowers" (1888). ∎

National Portrait Gallery

This is where you can put faces to familiar names, from a Tudor king to the inventor of the steam engine or a favorite novelist. Here you can see the faces of the personalities who have influenced all facets of British history. From top to bottom, this is a chronological parade of the brilliant, talented, or high-achieving, of the beautiful and ugly, of the good and devious. Each is fascinating, and the clear labeling helps explain the significance of those people who may not be so familiar. Seen all in one visit, even casually, the collection makes an excellent, visual skip through the island's history.

Founded in 1856 in the Victorian spirit of idealism, heroism, and didactic hopes of education by example, the collection's aim was to assemble and display portraits of the British great and good as an inspiration to others. The portraits moved around London until they came to rest here in 1896, in Ewan Christian's building behind the National Gallery.

At first, a person had to be dead to be eligible for inclusion here, allowing time to assess his or her worthiness. Today, that rule has been broken, and living inspirations include athletes, actors, businesspeople, playwrights, artists, and scientists; visitors renting the audio/visual guide can hear some of these contemporary sitters and artists talking frankly about their portraits. More than 10,000 portraits are in the collection, although only about 10 percent of that number are on display at any one time. Even allowing for the fact that some people have more than one image, that is still a considerable number of significant people, and a wide enough selection for visitors to find their ideal hero.

Your Visit

Because the portraits are arranged chronologically, with the earliest at the top of the building, the best way to visit the gallery is to start on the second floor and walk down. Here in Rooms 1–20, personalities run through the 16th to 19th centuries. On the first floor in Rooms 21–32, you'll find

National Portrait Gallery

🅰 Map p. 109

✉ St. Martin's Place, WC2

☎ 020 7306 0055

💲 Charge for some special exhibitions

🚇 Tube: Charing Cross, Leicester Square

www.npg.org.uk

Stuart Pearson Wright's portrait of writer J. K. Rowling

portraits of people who lived in the 19th and 20th centuries; members of the current royal family are either in Room 32 or on the ground floor. The rest of the ground floor is a daring selection of recent and contemporary contributors to British society, both painted and photographed. Special exhibitions in the Wolfson Gallery, also on the ground floor, include the annual BP Portrait Award in summer and, in the Photography Gallery, the annual wintertime Taylor Wessing Photographic Portrait Prize.

The gallery's Ondaatje wing extension opened in 2000 and includes an atmospheric new Tudor room, a downstairs theater, and the rooftop Portrait Restaurant with spectacular panoramic views across London.

Second Floor: Here are a few stars to look out for. The Tudor Galleries open with Rowland Lockey's (copied partly from Holbein) great portrait of Sir Thomas More and his family in their Chelsea home.

Seek out William Scrots's anamorphic portrait, "Edward VI" (1546), meaning that it has been painted to be viewed from a sharp angle to correct the perspective. Elizabeth I portraits include one by Marcus Gheeraerts the Younger to mark her visit to Ditchley Park, near Oxford—her feet are planted on Oxfordshire. The portrait of Shakespeare is the only known contemporary portrait of the playwright, and was the gallery's first acquisition. Do not miss the case of exquisite miniatures of Tudor aristocracy—including Catherine of Aragon,

EXPERIENCE: Make Your Own Brass Rubbing

There was a time when a visit to any church or abbey in London would include the sight of men, women, boys, and girls on their knees, rubbing wax on construction paper pulled tight over raised brass tomb reliefs to create a semi-magical pictorial representation of the artwork underneath.

But the realization that this was damaging the medieval and Victorian reliefs has stopped this practice, so today one of the only spots in London where you can discover the simple and engaging craft of brass rubbing is the **London Brass Rubbing Centre** (Trafalgar Square, tel 020 7766 1122, www.smitf.org, $$–$$$$$), located in the basement crypt of St. Martin-in-the-Fields church, just across from the National Portrait Gallery.

While the brasses are replicas, the range of subjects is impressive. With some time and just a little skill, you can take home a monochromatic or multi-colored depiction of a regal lord or lady, William Shakespeare, a Celtic circle, St. George and the dragon, or Zodiac signs.

A small rubbing can be created in about 20 minutes, though a quality medium- or large-size image can take an hour or two to make. For those with the desire for a great souvenir but not the time or artistic inclination, ready-rubbed drawings can be purchased at the center's shop.

Near the Tower of London, **All Hallows by the Tower** (tel 020 7481 2928, www.ahbtt.org.uk, $$) also offers replica brasses for rubbing (Mon.–Fri., 2–4 p.m.).

Mary, Queen of Scots, and Robert Dudley, Earl of Leicester—by Nicholas Hilliard and others. "Star players" in the English Civil War (Oliver Cromwell) and Restoration (Charles II) hang near the diarist Samuel Pepys, who is painted in a rented Indian outfit and holding a music score he composed.

Britain's dynamic 18th century produced a host of exceptional figures. You can find Jonathan Swift, Sir Christopher Wren, Sir Joshua Reynolds, and Dr. Johnson, not forgetting explorer Capt. James Cook and Adm. Lord Nelson. The Romantic poets John Keats, Samuel Taylor Coleridge, and a contemplative William Wordsworth are here, too, as well as Patrick Miller, designer of the first steam-propelled boat, and other heroes of the industrial revolution. Lawrence's portrait of George IV nicely captures that king's decadent elegance.

First Floor: Victorian and Edwardian personalities start with early Victorians such as the Brontë sisters, who were painted by their brother, Patrick Branwell. Heroes of the empire include linguist and explorer Sir Richard Burton, painted by Leighton. Prince Albert, Queen Victoria's consort, epitomizes 19th-century cultural-scientific advances, whereas William Morris, Thomas Carlyle, and Benjamin Disraeli are proponents of later Victorian culture. For the Edwardian arts, you can discover what Rudyard Kipling, G. B. Shaw, and Edward Elgar looked like.

Architect Piers Gough has refurbished Rooms 30–31; the vista down this great space is retained by hanging the early 20th-century portraits on glass panels. Near here, a splendid picture by John Lavery of George V, Queen Mary, and their family at Buckingham Palace in 1913 is usually on display.

A double portrait of newsman Jon Snow by John Keane

Ground Floor: These rooms are some of the most exciting, for they contain images of living people. In addition to the annual BP Portrait Award exhibition, special exhibits and rotating selections of contemporary paintings and photographs are on display here, as well as new acquisitions not yet integrated into the permanent collection. A half-flight up from the ground floor brings you to the IT Gallery, where touch-screen computers allow searches of the entire collection for specific portraits. ∎

Soho

Until Westminster Council began its crackdown in June 1986, Soho was one of London's raunchiest areas. It appeared to the outsider never to sleep. The maze of narrow streets, passages, and courts were the haunts of prostitutes; seedy bars lurked on the corners; basements housed peep shows, striptease clubs, and pornographic bookshops. Collectively, it was known as the Vice, and the council decided to do away with it. As each lease expired, its renewal was refused and the property sold off, usually to become a restaurant, office, or flat.

Madame JoJo's *(8–10 Brewer Street, W1, tel 020 7734 3040, www.madamejojos.com),* a longtime survivor, offers "kitsch cabaret" and burlesque, while the numerous new residents, restaurants, and sleek bars have helped maintain some of Soho's round-the-clock liveliness. It is a good area to wander.

Sidewalk diners enjoy a cappuccino in Soho.

Piccadilly Circus

Piccadilly Circus is the hub of Soho's amusements. It was laid out by Nash in 1819 as part of the Prince Regent's dream to link Carlton House and Regent's Park (see p. 147). This busy intersection of streets, with Eros in its center, was transformed when Shaftesbury Avenue was built in the 1880s. When the Eros statue was added in 1893, its nudity outraged Victorian sensibilities, but it quickly became a symbol for London.

Alfred Gilbert's aluminum figure in fact portrays not Eros the god of love, but the Angel of Christian Charity. It commemorates Antony Ashley Cooper, 7th Earl of Shaftesbury, 1801–1885, a philanthropist and statesman who fought hard to improve conditions for factory and colliery workers, chimney sweeps, and the insane.

Such was the significance of Piccadilly Circus that London's first illuminated advertisements blazed here in the 1890s. More theaters arrived, including one right beside Eros, the basement Criterion. This theater, and its street-level restaurant, are decorated with Thomas Verity's beautiful mosaics and tiles, well worth a look.

To the east of Piccadilly Circus, travelers of the world meet in lively, pedestrianized **Leicester Square.**

Shaftesbury Avenue

The backbone of London's commercial theaterland, Shaftesbury Avenue was driven through the Soho slums, necessitating the rehousing of 3,000 people.

EXPERIENCE: Having a Pint in a Historic Pub

A visit to London wouldn't be complete without having a traditional ale in one or two of the city's renowned and historic watering holes.

Historic Pubs

London is a city brimming with history and many surviving pubs have served as silent witnesses. In Soho, French expatriates during World War II gathered at the **French House** *(49 Dean St., W1, tel 020 7437 2799, www .frenchhousesoho.com)*, a bohemian enclave—Charles DeGaulle is said to have planned resistance strategies from the upstairs bar. South of the Thames, the Tudor **George Inn** *(77 Borough High St., SE1, tel 020 7407 2056, www.nationaltrust. org.uk/main/w-george inn)* is London's last remaining two-storied coaching inn. Bougainvillea and half-timbering set the mood.

In Smithfield, the **Hand & Shears** *(1 Middle St., EC1, tel 020 7600 0257)* stands on the site of a 12th-century alehouse. Condemned prisoners from Newgate Gaol were known to stop there for their last drink. In nearby Clerkenwell, the **Jerusalem Tavern** *(55 Britton St., EC1, tel 020 7490 4281, www.st petersbrewery.co.uk)* has been in business since the 14th century; the current building dates from 1720 and offers traditional craft beers from the St. Peter's Brewery.

The **White Hart** *(191 Drury La., WC2, tel 020 7242 2317, www.whiteheartdrury lane.co.uk)* in Holborn is

The City's Black Friar pub, on Queen Victoria Street, built in 1875

believed to have been originally licensed in 1216 (the year after the Magna Carta was signed). **Ye Olde Cheshire Cheese** *(145 Fleet St., EC4, tel 020 7353 6170)*, north of Inner Temple, dates from 1667 and was a favorite of Dickens. And, hidden down an alleyway off Hatton Garden in Holborn, **Ye Olde Mitre** *(1 Ely Ct., EC1, tel 020 7405 4751, www.yeoldemitre .co.uk, closed weekends)* was mentioned by Shakespeare in both *Richard II* and *Richard III*. The current structure was built in 1772.

Victorian Gin Palaces

These extravagant 19th-century pubs—no longer serving just gin—often have beautiful frosted and etched glass and mirrors, ornate furnishings, rich wood paneling, and interesting features such as snugs (small, semi-private bar-parlors designed for ladies—and for flirting) and snob screens (frosted-glass bricks that divide the snugs from the perceived riffraff tending the bar).

Some worthy examples: the **Argyll Arms** *(18 Argyll St., W1, tel 020 7734 6117, www.nicholsonspubs.co.uk)*, off Oxford Circus; Holborn's 1872 **Princess Louise** *(208 High Holborn, WC1, tel 020 7405 8816)*; in Little Venice, the **Prince Alfred** *(5a Formosa St., W9, tel 020 7286 3287, www.theprincealfred .com)* with tiny doors to stoop under as you venture from snug to snug; and, just up the street from the Prince Alfred, the **Warrington Hotel** *(93 Warrington Crescent, W9, tel 020 7592 7960, www.gordonramsay.com)*, a grand 1857 pub now owned by chef Gordon Ramsey.

Opened to traffic in 1886, it quickly attracted theatrical impresarios who built theaters suitable for staging fashionable musical farces. Today, a modern impresario, Andrew Lloyd Webber, has bought and restored to glory the **Palace Theatre,** originally designed by Collcutt and Holloway in 1888–1891.

A cluster of theaters down the street begins with **Queen's Theatre** of 1907, subsequently rebuilt, and the **Gielgud Theatre,** built in 1906. The French Renaissance **Apollo** rose five years earlier, while the **Lyric,** one of the first theaters on the street, was built in 1888 with profits from a hit musical playing in Leicester Square.

INSIDER TIP:

For discounted theater tickets, join the line at the tkts booth in Leicester Square. You can reserve same-day or advance seats.

—LARRY PORGES
National Geographic Books editor

North of Shaftesbury Avenue

At the west end of the grid of streets north of Shaftesbury Avenue, the stallholders of Berwick Street's lively fruit and vegetable market stand in front of pretty 18th-century houses. On Old Compton Street, once the heart of French London, more recent Italian immigrants run I Camisa & Son deli and grocery and the Sicilian bakery, Patisserie Valerie. Italians left their mark on Dean Street, too, at P. G. Leoni's Quo Vadis restaurant, which opened in 1926. Ronnie Scott's, on Frith Street, continues to host top jazz stars despite the death of its mentor. Across the street, Bar Italia serves up perfect cappuccinos. On Greek Street, the plain facade of the House of St. Barnabas, built in 1746, belies a magnificent interior. Beside it, Charles II's statue in Soho Square testifies to Soho's noble beginnings.

Chinese Soho

Almost all the tall, narrow houses of London's Chinatown have a shop or restaurant at street level. There are Chinese medical shops, news agents selling the British-published *Sing Tao,* and video rental shops with piles of kung fu tapes. But mostly, there are restaurants. In addition to stir-fried or steamed Cantonese food, specialties include dim sum snacks.

In this area, where the Chinese have succeeded in keeping alive their mother tongue, the atmosphere is enhanced by Chinese-style telephone boxes, benches, colorful lanterns, and red-and-gold gateways on either end of Gerrard Street and on Macclesfield Street toward Shaftesbury Avenue.

Tucked down Leicester Place is the distinctly non-Chinese Notre-Dame-de-France—once a theater but converted in 1865 by art nouveau pioneer Auguste Boileau. ■

Courts of law, theaters, shops, markets, and entertainments between the City and Westminster

Covent Garden to Ludgate Hill

Window shopping in Covent Garden

Covent Garden to Ludgate Hill

Hugging the curve of the Thames, this part of London fills the space between the capital's two cities: Westminster and the City. Ancient buildings such as Temple Church and Lincoln's Inn Gateway, Covent Garden's restored market, the Adelphi Theatre, and the Royal Opera House show how it has changed continuously to keep pace with its customers.

When Westminster became the seat of royal and political power, a riverside path linked it to the merchants' City of London. The sweep of the Strand, so called because it ran close to the north bank of the Thames, and Fleet Street, named after the river it crossed, became a favorite address for medieval bishops. Later, after the dissolution of the monasteries, the two parts took on slightly different characters.

Along either side of Fleet Street, toward St. Paul's Cathedral, some bishops' houses evolved into barristers' inns of court, while early printers and booksellers established themselves around the churches of St. Bride and St. Dunstan. Newspaper presses thundered on Fleet Street from 1702 until the 1980s. The printers have gone, but the law remains. Lawyers defend their clients in the great courts, while their pupils hurry through the streets with armfuls of files.

Along the Strand, Tudor and Stuart rulers presented the bishops' former houses and waterside gardens to favored courtiers. George Villiers, a favorite of both James I and Charles I, enlarged the palace of the bishops of Norwich to include a watergate, which survives today in Embankment Gardens, testifying to both the grandeur of these residences and the pre-Embankment width of the river Thames.

The Savoy Theatre reflects the changing roles of the Strand down the centuries. The first building on the site, the sumptuous 14th-century Savoy House, fashionably faced the river. In Covent Garden's 17th-century heyday, the Strand was a smart promenade, but by the late 19th century it had degenerated into a seedy mixture of prostitutes, coffeehouses, and cheap theaters. When Richard D'Oyly Carte built his Savoy Theatre in 1881, he put the entrance on the newly built, clean, and smart Embankment rather than on the Strand. Later, in 1929, the entrance was turned to face a much-improved Strand; the Aldwych crescent had replaced a swath of slums in 1905.

Today, the heart of the area is again Covent Garden. Originally the garden of a convent attached to Westminster Abbey, it was given to the Earl of Bedford after the Dissolution of the Monasteries. Covent Garden Piazza, laid out in 1631, became the blueprint residential

MONMOUTH ST.

London square. Half a dozen others followed nearby, including Lincoln's Inn Fields, to house the gentry who were moving out of the City after the Great Fire. When society moved farther west, the aristocratic tone of the piazza changed to a commercial one with the arrival of the main London fruit and vegetable market, coffeehouses, and gambling dens. When the market moved to south London, the area was cleaned up and became a lively mixture of shops, restaurants, and museums encircled by a dozen theaters. ■

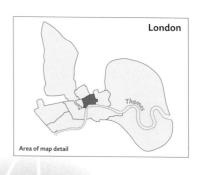

London

Area of map detail

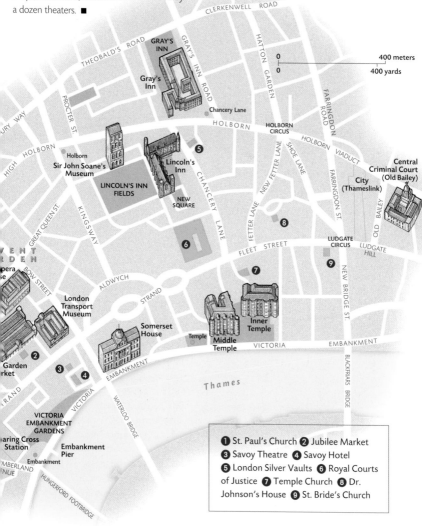

1 St. Paul's Church 2 Jubilee Market
3 Savoy Theatre 4 Savoy Hotel
5 London Silver Vaults 6 Royal Courts
of Justice 7 Temple Church 8 Dr.
Johnson's House 9 St. Bride's Church

Covent Garden

The restored market buildings, chic shops, and entertainers in the piazza typify this much-changed area, bordered by the Strand, Kingsway, High Holborn, and Charing Cross Road.

Jubilee Market in Covent Garden offers a variety of shops.

London Transport Museum

- 🅰 Map p. 123
- ✉ 39 Wellington St., WC2
- ☎ 020 7565 7299
- 💲 $$$
- 🚇 Tube: Covent Garden

www.ltmuseum.co.uk

The 1st Earl of Bedford acquired this land in 1552, after Westminster Abbey was dissolved. But it was the 4th earl who laid out London's first residential square of high-society houses. When the aristocrats moved west, the 5th earl won a license for a fruit and vegetable market in 1671. Traders, prostitutes, and literary types, including Richard Sheridan and James Boswell, met here. Stalls selling everything from lavender to birdcages sprawled over the square.

Order of a sort began in 1831, with the building of the Central Market. Floral Hall (1860), the Flower Market (1870–1872), and the Jubilee Market (1904) followed. This was the Covent Garden of George Bernard Shaw's

Pygmalion: of "low life" in the piazza but high life in the Royal Opera House, first built in 1732.

When the market moved in 1974, protests ensured that the buildings were restored, not demolished, and the area has been revitalized. The **Central Market** is full of shops and restaurants. Street entertainers perform in the traffic-free piazza. **Jubilee Market,** on the south side of the piazza, has stalls selling antiques on Mondays, art and crafts on the weekends, and a general market the rest of the week. The excellent **London Transport Museum** occupies part of the old Flower Market; next door, the refurbished **Royal Opera House** *(tel 020 7304 4000, www .royaloperahouse.org)* has food, bars, and daily quality entertainment. ∎

Somerset House

An extraordinary art collection and a large public piazza that is a fountain in summer and an ice rink in winter have reawakened Sir William Chambers's sumptuous palace, built in 1776–1786 for government bureaucrats.

One of central London's most successful arts complexes is in a refurbished and forgotten building. The 16th-century palace of Edward Seymour, Protector of Somerset was later the domain of various Tudor and Stuart royals, but was demolished on the orders of George III to make way for London's most impressive 18th-century public building. The Navy Board, Inland Revenue, the Register General of Births, Deaths, and Marriages, and a handful of learned societies enjoyed luxurious offices here until 1989. Today, the courtyard draws visitors to enjoy ice skating in winter and water-jet fountains in summer. The River Terrace has a café and excellent views over the Thames.

Inside, the **Courtauld Institute Galleries** (tel 020 7848 2526, www.courtauld.ac.uk) opened first. Samuel Courtauld, industrialist and art patron, founded the Courtauld Institute in 1932, aiming to help art history students experience great paintings in fine settings. His French Impressionist and Postimpressionist canvases were later joined by the Princes Gate Collection's Rubens, Tiepolo, and Van Dyck paintings; by the Lee Collections's Botticellis, Goyas, and Gainsboroughs; and by more than 7,000 old master prints and drawings. Here you can enjoy a roomful of Rubens, Manet's "Bar at the Folies Bergère," magnificent silver, and works by Derain, Turner, van Gogh, Matisse, and Degas. ∎

Somerset House

- 🗺 Map p. 123
- ✉ Strand, WC2
- ☎ 020 7845 4600
- 💲 $$ for each museum
- 🚇 Tube: Temple, Embankment, Covent Garden

www.somerset house.org.uk

Ice rink

- 💲 $$$$ for ice-skating
- 🕐 Closed Feb.– mid.-Nov.

EXPERIENCE: Open-air Ice-skating

Visiting London in the winter? Join the locals for one of the fastest-growing sports in town: outdoor ice-skating at some of the city's most impressive and historic locales.

The summertime fountain at **Somerset House** turns into a skating rink from mid-November until the end of January each year (tickets from Ticketmaster, tel 0844 847 1520 or via www.somersethouse .org.uk/ice_rink, $$$$), the 18th-century mansion a stunning backdrop. Skating lessons, DJ nights, and lunch workout sessions are all in the offing on the spacious 9,700-square-foot (900 sq m) rink.

New for 2011 is **Eyeskate,** the 3,230-square-foot (300 sq m) ice rink at the **London Eye** observation wheel (www .londoneye.com, $$$$) on the south bank.

Other temporary rinks are located amid the wonderfully scenic settings at the **Tower of London** (www.toweroflondonice rink.com, $$$$) and Knightsbridge's **Natural History Museum** (www.nhmskating .com). London's largest open-air rink is found at **Hyde Park's Winter Wonderland** (www.hydeparkwinterwonderland.com/ rink.html, $$$$). One overlooks the Thames at **Canary Wharf** in Docklands (www .canarywharficerink.com, $$$$); another is at Tudor **Hampton Court Palace** (www .hamptoncourtpalaceicerink.com, $$$$).

Inns of Court & Old Bailey

London has four Inns of Court. Each one is an independent society governed by Benchers who call their students, known as pupils, to the Bar—hence the word barristers. Such orders were gradually established after Edward I's Ordinance of 1292 put all men of law under the judges' control, thus ending the clergy's position as lawyers and reducing their power.

The Royal Courts of Justice building was built in the Victorian era.

Royal Courts of Justice (Law Courts)

🏛 Map p. 123

✉ Strand, WC2

☎ 020 7947 6000

🕐 Closed Sat.–Sun. & Aug.–Sept.

🚇 Tube: Temple, Chancery Lane

www.courtservice.gov.uk

NOTE: No cameras, cell phones, jeans, or children under 14 are allowed in the courts.

The Inns have records going back to the 15th and 16th centuries. Each was originally a great mansion, where students and barristers lived. In Tudor times, when litigation was as popular as the arts, lawyers trained at the Inns of Court sat at courts throughout London but enjoyed a high life back at their halls and chambers. Members of Middle Temple treated Elizabeth I to a performance of *Twelfth Night* in their magnificent hall.

Gray's Inn (*High Holborn, WC1, tel 020 7458 7800, www.graysinn.org.uk*), whose students were established in Reginald de Grey's mansion by 1370, has a Tudor screen in its hall. In summer, the garden walks are open to visitors at lunchtime. Early lawyers of **Lincoln's Inn** (*Chancery Lane, WC2, tel 020 7405 1393, www.lincolnsinn.org.uk*), which took over a mansion on the Earl of Lincoln's property, lived in the surviving Old Hall, built in 1490–1492; later lawyers included Oliver Cromwell.

Inner Temple (*Fleet St., EC4, tel 020 7797 8250, www.innertemple.org.uk*) and **Middle Temple** (*Fleet*

INSIDER TIP:

London Walks (*www .londonwalks.com*) is a great way to see London—including Legal London. No bookings, just turn up!

—MARY LAMBERTON
National Geographic contributor

St., EC4, tel 020 7427 4800, www .middletemple.org.uk) derive their names from the Knights Templar, a brotherhood whose members protected pilgrims bound for Jerusalem. At the Dissolution of the Monasteries, their lands became Crown property, which the Benchers leased in perpetuity in 1608. Today, their labyrinth of courts and buildings includes Middle Temple's fine Elizabethan **Hall** (*Middle Temple Lane, call for*

hours), the Inner Temple gateway of 1610–1611, and Wren's King's Bench Walk of 1677–1678. The **Temple Church** (*Inner Temple Lane, EC4, tel 020 7353 3470, www.templechurch.com*), originally a round Norman building with a nave added later, has effigies of 13th-century Templars. When the Embankment's land reclamation provided the barristers with Inner Temple Gardens, they hosted the Royal Horticultural Society's annual flower show, now held at Chelsea (see p. 181).

In the 19th century, a new interest in legal education forced barristers to use their Inns more for work than for pleasure. The courts were centralized in the **Royal Courts of Justice.** Today, the Inns are sandwiched between these courts and the Central Criminal Court, known as the **Old Bailey** after the street beside it. ∎

Central Criminal Court (Old Bailey)
- Map p. 123
- Newgate Street, EC4
- 020 7248 3277
- Closed Sat.–Sun.
- Tube: St. Paul's

www.cityoflondon
.gov.uk

NOTE: A list of the day's programs are noted by the main door. No children under 14. No bags, radios, cameras, cell phones, food, drink, or music players are allowed in the viewing galleries.

Fleet Street Printing

The Law Courts mark the beginning of Fleet Street, which until recently has been synonymous with the printing industry. After the death of William Caxton, who published the first book printed in England in 1477, his commercially acute pupil Wynkyn de Worde moved the presses from Westminster to Fleet Street. De Worde set up England's first press with movable type near St. Bride's Church, close to his clergy customers. Between 1500 and 1535, he published about 800 books and also ran one of the many bookshops in St. Paul's Churchyard. Printers, bookbinders, booksellers, and writers soon filled the lanes off Fleet Street. Dr. Samuel Johnson lived in one (see p. 128) and patronized

the coffeehouses and pubs around it.

On March 11, 1702, Fleet Street added to its ecclesiastical, literary, scientific, and political output by publishing its first newspaper, *The Daily Courant.* But the newspaper industry did not really take off until Alfred Harmsworth, pioneer of popular journalism, bought the *Daily Mail* in 1896 and pushed its circulation up to a million. He later founded the *Daily Mirror* with his brother.

Fleet Street remained the hub of the national newspapers until the 1980s. Then international press baron Rupert Murdoch pushed through the technological revolution that resulted in all newspapers leaving Fleet Street for offices linked to their presses by computer.

A Walk Through Legal London & Covent Garden

This walk is best done on a weekday, when activity in legal London adds atmosphere; but Covent Garden, although busy on a weekday, is at its most bubbly on Saturday, with entertainers and markets. The walk begins at Temple and ends at Covent Garden Tube stations. The first part is a loop, which could be a walk in itself, or which could be omitted.

In & Around the Strand

From the Temple Tube station, walk up to the Strand and turn left past Somerset House containing the Courtauld Institute (see p. 125). Turn left again onto **Waterloo Bridge ❶**, where there are good views east to the City towers and south toward Westminster.

Return to the Strand and turn left. The **Savoy Hotel** (now re-opened after a massive £100 million/$160 million restoration) and **Theatre ❷** are on their own lane to the left. Richard D'Oyly Carte built the theater in 1881, where Gilbert and Sullivan's operas, including the successful *Mikado*, financed the adjoining deluxe hotel as well as Claridges. Both buildings later benefited from work by the art deco architect Basil Ionides.

Along the Strand, opposite Stanley Gibbons (stamp dealers) and the Vaudeville and Adelphi Theaters, turn left by the Coal Hole pub, with its rich Edwardian interior, and go down Carting Lane to Victoria Embankment Gardens. Inside the gardens, turn right at the statue of Robert Raikes. At the end of the paths is **York Watergate** on the right, a survivor from grand riverside York Mansion of 1626.

Backtrack through the garden to the statue of composer Sir Arthur Sullivan (1842–1900) at the far end. Leave the gardens there, cut up Savoy Street, then turn right to return past Aldwych. **St. Mary-le-Strand ❸** stands mid-road, James Gibb's first London church (1714–1717). This was the first of 50 churches Queen Anne planned (she achieved 12) for the capital's growing population. St. Clement Danes, another island church, lies beyond. The Strand ends with the magnificent **Royal Courts of**

NOT TO BE MISSED:

Inner and Middle Temples
• Temple Church • Dr. Johnson's House • Gray's Inn • Lincoln's Inn
• Covent Garden Piazza

Justice ❹ (see p. 127) on the left, and Thomas Twining's tea store and the 1882–1883 Lloyd's Bank banking hall, lined with Doulton tiled panels made at Lambeth, on the right.

The Law Courts & Covent Garden

At the start of Fleet Street, a mid-road memorial topped by a griffin rampant marks the ever tense boundary between the Cities of London and Westminster—between the monarchy and its source of finance. Opposite Chancery Lane, an archway leads into **Inner** and **Middle Temples ❺** (see p. 126). Going straight ahead, then right, find Fountain Court and Middle Temple's Hall (another court); going straight, then left, find **Temple Church** (1160–1185 and 1220–1240) (see p. 127) with splendid effigies of Knights Templar; the Inner Temple Gardens; and Wren's King's Bench Walk, 1677–1678. An opening here leads to Bouverie Street and back to Fleet Street.

Across the road, both Bolt and Hind Courts lead into Gough Square, a patch of 17th-century alleys and houses. Dr. Samuel Johnson lived and compiled his dictionary here from 1749 to 1759. Now it is a simple, atmospheric museum, **Dr. Johnson's House ❻** (*17 Gough Square, EC4, tel 020 7353 3745, closed Sun, www.drjohnsonshouse.org, $$*).

At the back of the square, go to Fetter Lane, then along Norwich and Furnival Streets to High Holborn. Staple Inn's half-timbered houses are to the left. The way into **Gray's Inn** ❼ (see p. 126) is opposite, its narrow entrance next to the Cittie of Yorke Pub; squares lead to the grassy Walks (gardens). Down Chancery Lane, dozens of silver shops make up the **London Silver Vaults** (tel 020 7242 3844, www .thesilvervaults.com, closed Sun.). Farther down, the Gatehouse (1518) leads into **Lincoln's Inn** ❽ (see p. 126). Here New Square leads into Lincoln's Inn Fields and so to **Sir John Soane's Museum** (see p. 130).

From here, Remnant Street and Great Queen Street lead across Kingsway to Bow Street, home of the **Royal Opera House** (see p. 124). Russell Street, on the right, goes into **Covent Garden Piazza** ❾ (see p. 124). The **London Transport Museum** (see p. 124), with fine displays including complete trams and buses, is on the left; the **Central Market** (see p. 124) is straight ahead.

On the far side of the piazza, go along Henrietta Street and turn right on Bedford Street. Inigo Jones's classical **St. Paul's Church** (1631–1633) has memorials to actors. Garrick Street, where the Garrick Club honors actor David Garrick, leads to Long Acre and Covent Garden Tube station. Long Acre and parallel Shelton Street and Shorts Gardens are good for shopping.

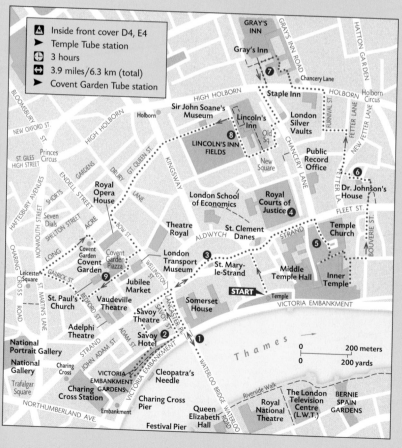

- Inside front cover D4, E4
- Temple Tube station
- 3 hours
- 3.9 miles/6.3 km (total)
- Covent Garden Tube station

Sir John Soane's Museum

One of London's more eccentric and atmospheric house-museums, this was where architect Sir John Soane lived from 1813 until his death in 1837. It is still redolent of his personality. Soane designed No. 12 Lincoln's Inn Fields for himself in 1792; later he bought No. 13 and rebuilt it as a timeless, intensely personal home for his collection. In 1823 Soane expanded to No. 14, which today houses the museum's Picture Room and the Monk's Parlour.

The library of Sir John Soane's Museum

Sir John Soane's Museum

🅐 Map p. 123

✉ 13 Lincoln's Inn Fields, WC2

☎ 020 7405 2107

🕐 Closed Sun.–Mon.

💲 Donation. Tours: $$

Ⓜ Tube: Holborn

www.soane.org

NOTE: Appointment required (tel 020 7440 4263) for groups of six or more.

The best way to arrive is to walk around Lincoln's Inn Fields, a large square laid out in the 1630s, go through the gardens to the north side, and ring the bell at No. 13.

On the ground floor, above the library fireplace, are John Flaxman's reliefs "The Silver Age" and "The Golden Age," two fine pieces of Soane's rich collection of English sculpture. Through the corridor, lined with antique marbles, lies the Picture Room. In this tiny room Hogarth's paintings for "The Rake's Progress" and "The Election" series are stored against the walls in layers that unfold to reveal a view of Soane's model for the Bank of England.

Down in the basement, one of Inigo Jones's original capitals for his Banqueting House was rescued by Soane when it was refaced. Beyond, the Sepulchral Chamber containing the sarcophagus of Seti I, made in 1300 B.C. and found in the Valley of the Kings, reflects Europe's new excitement about Egypt. When the piece arrived in 1824, Soane threw a party.

INSIDER TIP:

Go early to Sir John Soane's Museum to ensure you get the guided tour, or go for a candlelit opening on the first Tuesday evening of each month.

—SIMON HORSFORD
Sunday Telegraph *travel writer*

The museum is currently undergoing a £6 million ($9.6 million) expansion that will provide new exhibition space, an art conservation studio, and improved facilities for visitors. Work is slated to be completed in 2012. ■

Eighteenth-century squares, the British Museum, and a handful of fascinating individual small collections for special interests

Bloomsbury

The exterior of the British Museum's reading room

Bloomsbury

Bloomsbury's air is filled with calm contemplation and wonder, a mood set by the presence of the University of London and the venerable British Museum, plus their satellite institutions. It is hard to believe that Soho's bars, Covent Garden's entertainment, and the bustle of north London's busy railway stations are but a five-minute walk away.

Like much of central London, Bloomsbury has agricultural, monastic, and aristocratic chapters in its book. The Domesday Book, William the Conqueror's 11th-century inventory of his English possessions, records a wood for 100 pigs and vineyards here. Later, Edward III gave the land to the Charterhouse monks. After the Dissolution, Henry VIII gave it to his Lord Chancellor, the Earl of Southampton. The 4th Earl of Southampton laid out the square that is now Bloomsbury Square in 1660. A clever marriage linked the Southampton family with the Bedfords. The 4th Duke of Bedford's widow built Bedford Square in the 1770s, while her son was a minor. After he became the 5th Duke, he recognized the area's potential and, around 1800, began building Bloomsbury.

Land was parceled off to developers, principally James Burton, an ambitious Scot. He was succeeded by his architect son, Decimus Burton, and Thomas Cubitt (see p. 140). The sequence of elegant squares then progressed rapidly: Bloomsbury Square was redeveloped, Russell Square was begun in 1800, Tavistock in 1806, Gordon in 1820, and Woburn in 1825.

Meanwhile, in 1823 work began on replacing Montague House, the British Museum since 1759, with a specially built museum. Soon after, in 1836, England's first nondenominational university, the University of London, was founded in Bloomsbury. East of the patchwork are Brunswick and Mecklenburgh Squares, laid out in the 1790s by the Governors of the Thomas Coram Foundation for Children (now the Foundling Museum, see p. 139), a hospice for abandoned children founded by Captain Coram in 1732 and endowed by Hogarth, Gainsborough, Handel, and others. It overlooked the hospital's land, now Coram's Fields, and set a different tone from the nearby streets—delightful Queen Square, Great James Street, and Lamb's Conduit Street. Handsome Doughty Street was completed in 1812; later Charles Dickens lived here. West, across Tottenham Court Road, Fitzroy Square was laid out by the Adam brothers in the 1790s. ∎

NOT TO BE MISSED:

The Rosetta Stone, Parthenon Marbles, Egyptian mummies, and millions of other priceless artifacts in the British Museum   134–138

The quiet reading rooms of the dignified British Library   139

Exploring the Wellcome Collection's art and science exhibits   139

The stately 18th-century house facades fronting all sides of Bedford Square   140–141

Touring the Dickens Museum, the author's last surviving London residence   142

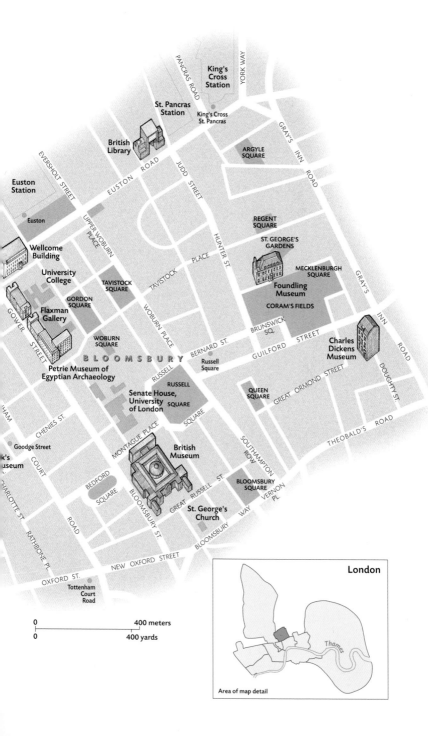

King's
Cross
Station

St. Pancras
Station

King's Cross
St. Pancras

British
Library

PANCRAS ROAD

YORK WAY

ARGYLE
SQUARE

GRAY'S INN ROAD

EVERSHOLT STREET

EUSTON ROAD

JUDD STREET

Euston
Station

Euston

UPPER WOBURN PLACE

REGENT
SQUARE

ST. GEORGE'S
GARDENS

Wellcome
Building

University
College

TAVISTOCK SQUARE

TAVISTOCK PLACE

HUNTER ST.

MECKLENBURGH
SQUARE

Foundling
Museum

GRAY'S

Flaxman
Gallery

GORDON
SQUARE

WOBURN PLACE

CORAM'S FIELDS

GOWER STREET

WOBURN
SQUARE

BRUNSWICK
SQ.

INN ROAD

B L O O M S B U R Y

BERNARD ST.

GUILFORD STREET

Charles
Dickens
Museum

Petrie Museum of
Egyptian Archaeology

RUSSELL

Russell
Square

DOUGHTY ST.

CHENIES ST.

Senate House,
University
of London

RUSSELL
SQUARE

QUEEN
SQUARE

GREAT ORMOND STREET

Goodge Street

k's
useum

COURT

MONTAGUE PLACE

British
Museum

THEOBALD'S ROAD

BEDFORD
SQUARE

BLOOMSBURY
SQUARE

CHARLOTTE ST.

ROAD

BLOOMSBURY ST.

GREAT RUSSELL ST.

SOUTHAMPTON ROW

St. George's
Church

BLOOMSBURY WAY

VERNON PL.

RATHBONE PL.

NEW OXFORD STREET

OXFORD ST.

Tottenham
Court
Road

0   400 meters
0   400 yards

London

Thames

Area of map detail

British Museum

Britain's largest museum is not to be taken on lightly. Its nine departments look after the national collection of archaeology and ethnography. It covers 13.5 acres, employs 1,200 people, has more than six million visitors a year, and cares for more than four million objects ranging from prehistoric bones to chunks of Athens' Parthenon, from whole Assyrian palace rooms to exquisite gold jewels. This is a living museum: It changes daily as different pieces are put on display, special exhibitions are held, and new discoveries change their fields.

The British Museum's famed collection of Egyptian antiquities includes coffins, portraits, sculptures, and masks, as well as mummies.

The Museum

This astounding treasure-house began as the simple idea of one man, Sir Hans Sloane. A physician who lived at nearby Bedford Place, he collected minerals, coins, books, and other objects with rare obsessiveness. On his death in 1753, he suggested the government buy all 80,000 bits and pieces, which they did. The same year, the British Museum Act was passed, creating London's first public museum. Money was raised, Montague House bought, and the museum doors opened in January 1759. Entry was by written application, but the curators were not interested in the public. Groups were escorted through the galleries in just half an hour, and not permitted to linger or gaze at the objects.

The foundation collection also included the library and the finds of antiquarian Sir Robert Cotton and the manuscripts of politician Robert Harley. It expanded alarmingly fast. Even before the museum opened, in 1757 George II donated most of the Royal Library's 12,000 volumes. The Hamilton antique vases, Townley classical sculptures, Elgin marbles, George III's extensive library, Capt. James Cook's collections from his voyages, and the Bank of England's coins all came to Montague House.

The house overflowed. So Robert Smirke's great classical temple to learning was built around the house in 1823–1838. Then the house was demolished to make way for the entrance colonnade and portico, which closed the courtyard, known as the Great Court. The domed Reading Room was built in 1854–1857, and all remaining space was filled with galleries and book stacks. Even then, the museum overflowed. In 1881 the Natural History department went to South Kensington (see p. 174); and in 1973 the Printed Books and Manuscripts department went to the British Library, confusingly situated in a part of the museum.

By the latter part of the 20th century, a radical solution was needed. First, the British Library was given its own building at St. Pancras, just north of Bloomsbury. This released 40 percent of the museum's space, which, crucially, included the Great Court. A program of expansion and renewal was completed in 2003, the museum's 250th birthday. The centerpiece is the Great Court in the middle of the museum. Cleared of all but the Reading Room and roofed in glass, it is another light-filled public Bloomsbury square, this time a covered one. This is the information area for the museum's 100 galleries, a central bureau for its educational events, and a space where visitors can rest, shop, refresh themselves, and cross from one part of the museum to another.

Galleries have been reorganized in response to the reemergence of the Great Court. The suite of ethnography galleries is on the north side, and the Age of Enlightenment gallery fills the former King's Library on the east side.

INSIDER TIP:

Aficionados of Japanese history should not miss the spectacular suit of samurai armor on the upper floors.

—PATRICIA DANIELS
National Geographic contributor

Your Visit

Clearly, this is not a "do-in-a-day" museum. Many visitors will pick up a map and seek out what they know they want to see. For others, the museum is overwhelming. In the Great Court, there is information and lists of the day's events. To help

British Museum

- Map p. 133
- Great Russell Street, WC2; rear entrance on Montague Place
- 020 7323 8299
- For some exhibitions
- Tube: Tottenham Court Road, Holborn, or Russell Square

www.britishmuseum.org

British Museum

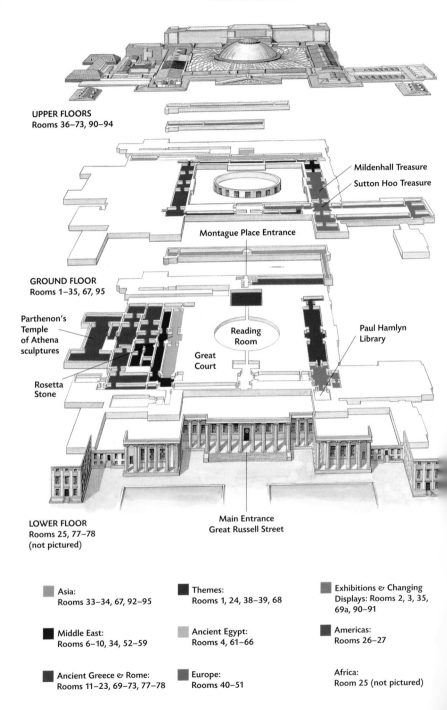

UPPER FLOORS
Rooms 36–73, 90–94

Mildenhall Treasure

Sutton Hoo Treasure

Montague Place Entrance

GROUND FLOOR
Rooms 1–35, 67, 95

Parthenon's Temple of Athena sculptures

Reading Room

Paul Hamlyn Library

Great Court

Rosetta Stone

LOWER FLOOR
Rooms 25, 77–78
(not pictured)

Main Entrance
Great Russell Street

Asia:
Rooms 33–34, 67, 92–95

Themes:
Rooms 1, 24, 38–39, 68

Exhibitions & Changing Displays: Rooms 2, 3, 35, 69a, 90–91

Middle East:
Rooms 6–10, 34, 52–59

Ancient Egypt:
Rooms 4, 61–66

Americas:
Rooms 26–27

Ancient Greece & Rome:
Rooms 11–23, 69–73, 77–78

Europe:
Rooms 40–51

Africa:
Room 25 (not pictured)

transform this into a manage-able, stimulating experience, here is a trail that focuses on just a few objects.

First explore the rooms surrounding the Great Court (see above) ending with the great, long gallery that contains the cream of the finest collection of **Egyptian antiquities** outside Egypt—some 70,000 objects (a few more are displayed upstairs in Rooms 61–66). Sculpture fills this gallery, and among the heads of Rameses II, Amenophis II, and other ancient rulers is the small but significant **Rosetta Stone** (see sidebar at right). The upstairs galleries contain funerary models for the afterlife, painted mum-mies, books of the dead, and Coptic portraits.

Next to the Egyptian sculp-tures is the **Western Asiatic** department in Rooms 6–10. This covers the civilizations that rose and fell in the huge area between Egypt and Pakistan. The **Assyrian friezes** are especially beautiful. Excavated last century, they have come from palaces built in the ninth century in the successive capitals of Nimrud, Khorsabad, and Nineveh. Rooms 7 and 8, the **Nimrud Gallery,** have some colossal, protective winged lions and narrative scenes of the king hunting, the army swimming across a river, and an attack on a town. Room 9, the **Assyrian Saloon,** tells the story of a royal lion hunt and features the animals being released, the people of Nineveh watching from a hill, and a strip cartoon of the kill.

The remaining rooms in this part of the museum, Nos. 11–23, are devoted to **Greek** and **Roman antiquities.** One of the world's finest collections, covering every aspect of life, it ranges from the early simplicity of Cycladic figures to the sophistication of Greek vase paintings. The sculpture is excep-tional and includes pieces from two of the world's best-known buildings. Room 18 contains sculptures from the **Parthenon's Temple of Athena,** built in the

Rosetta Stone

Carved in 196 B.C., when Egypt's pharaohs were dead and the Greek Ptolemy kings ruled the land, the Rosetta Stone—one of the British Museum's prized possessions—would, 2,000 years later, become the key that allowed scholars to unlock the secrets of ancient Egyptian hieroglyphics.

In 1799, Napoleon's soldiers found the stone and its long trilingual inscrip-tions while tearing down an ancient wall. Modern scholars used the more familiar Greek words to decipher the two other sets of writing: the hieroglyphic and demotic scripts of the Egyptians. Less than 4 feet high by 3 feet wide (1.2 m by 0.9 m), the stone heralds a decree from a council of priests.

fifth century B.C. as part of a plan to beautify Athens. Using money intended for the navy, the sculptor Phidias oversaw the decorative work on the most magnificent building from the golden age of ancient Greece. It remained per-fect until gunpowder stored there exploded in 1687. In the early 19th century, Lord Elgin brought many of the surviving sculptures to London: The great frieze of the

Carved female figurines from predynastic Egypt are among the British Museum's millions of objects.

procession to celebrate Athena's birthday, plus sculptures from the pediments and metopes. The other outstanding piece is in Room 17: the **Nereid Monument,** the front of a tomb built like a miniature Greek temple.

Now go up the stairs to the upper levels. In Room 68, the **HSBC Money Gallery** (supported by the Hong Kong Shanghai Banking Corporation) displays 2,000 years of British coinage in commerce, history, and portraiture.

Rooms 49–51 display the **Prehistoric** and **Romano–British Antiquities** spanning early history to the Christian period. There is a gold torque from Norfolk, a bronze mirror, and gaming pieces. At the top of the stairs, a mosaic floor found in Dorset in 1963 contains the earliest known representation of Christ in a mosaic floor in the Roman empire.

Some precious and delicate objects from the **Medieval and Later Antiquities** department fill the corner Rooms 41–47. Several special treasures are worth seeking out here. In Room 41, early pieces include the **Sutton Hoo Treasure,** an Anglo-Saxon royal burial ship that survived intact in Suffolk and was excavated in 1939. Room 41 also includes Byzantine and Early Christian objects, Celtic bowls, Merovingian coins, and high-quality locally made jewelry, all illustrating the diversity and sophistication of Anglo-Saxon high society. Room 40, one of the **Medieval** rooms, contains the **Lewis Chessmen,** possibly carved in Scandinavia in the 12th century and found on the Hebridean island of Lewis in 1831.

Asian & Islamic Pieces

Cut down the east side of the museum through Rooms 49–52 to the North Wing. There are several levels here, connected by stairs and elevators. Rooms 92–94, on Level 5, are devoted to **Japanese art.** Room 95 on Level 2 houses the Sir Percival David collection of exquisite **Chinese porcelain**. On the floor below them, Room 33 is the Joseph E. Hotung Gallery, which begins at the west end with early **Indian Buddhist sculptures** and moves through the cultures of **Southeast Asia.** Beneath this, the ground floor contains the John Addis Gallery of **Islamic arts.**

The British Museum grows almost daily: Most British archaeological discoveries come here; bequests are frequent; and the museum continues to buy new pieces for its collection. ∎

The Museum Trail

The British Museum is the inspiration for a host of other fascinating museums and historical sites scattered throughout Bloomsbury and around Covent Garden. Telephone the smaller ones to confirm opening times before visiting.

Start at the **British Library.** Edouard Paolozzi's sculpture of Newton in the courtyard introduces the headquarters of one of the world's most important library collections, composed of more than 150 million items—George III's 65,000 volumes are housed in a magnificent six-story glass-walled tower. Galleries include the **Sir John Ritblat Gallery,** displaying rare treasures such as the Magna Carta. Other rooms include a philatelic gallery showcasing rare and important stamps.

From here, take in the dependably fascinating science exhibitions at the **Wellcome Collection** *(183 Euston Rd., NW1, tel 020 7611 2222, www.wellcomecollection.org, closed Mon.).* More tricky to find, and visit, are three little museums at the University of London's University College *(www.museum*

.ucl.ac.uk)*: the **Flaxman Gallery** *(Slade School of Fine Art, Gower St., WC1, tel 020 7679 2540, www.ucl. ac.uk/slade)*, in the university library building, has models by neoclassical sculptor John Flaxman; the Slade also displays paintings from its own collection in the **Strang Print Room,** located in the Wilkins building in the quadrangle off Gower Street; and the **Petrie Museum of Egyptian Archaeology.** Finally, the University's School of Oriental and African Studies runs the **Brunei Gallery** *(Russell Sq., WC1, tel 020 7898 4915, www. soas.ac.uk/gallery, closed Sun.–Mon.).* A short detour leads to **Pollock's Toy Museum** *(1 Scala St., W1, tel 020 7636 3452, www.pollockstoy museum.com, closed Sun.),* two houses of childhood treasures.

The route now passes the British Museum (see pp. 134–138). Drop into Nicholas Hawksmoor's lavishly restored Baroque masterpiece, **St. George's Church** *(1716–1731) (www.stgeorgesblooms bury.org.uk)*, on Bloomsbury Way, before crossing onto Drury Lane. East of Drury Lane, the **Hunterian Museum's** astonishing, often ghoulish, collection traces the development of surgery *(Royal College of Surgeons, 35–43 Lincoln's Inn Fields, WC2, tel 020 7869 6560, www.rcseng.ac.uk).* The trail ends at the **Somerset House** (see p. 125) across the Strand. ■

British Library
- Map p. 133
- 96 Euston Rd., NW1
- 0843 208 1144
- Open daily. Reading Room closed Sun. Advance reservations recommended.
- Donation
- Tube/Rail: King's Cross/St. Pancras, Euston

www.bl.uk

The Foundling Museum
- Map p. 133
- 40 Brunswick Sq., WC1
- 020 7841 3600
- Closed Mon.
- $$
- Tube: Russell Square

www.foundling museum.org.uk

Petrie Museum of Egyptian Archaeology
- Map p. 133
- University College, WC1, Malet Place entrance
- 020 7679 2884

www.petrie.ucl.ac.uk

The Foundling Museum

Another route from the British Library to the British Museum takes you via the Foundling Museum (see p. 132), a grand refurbished house that offers a fine picture collection, a Handel room, and galleries recounting the plight of London children in the 18th century.

London Squares

Bloomsbury's squares of flat-fronted, brick houses overlooking gardens of lawns, trees, and the odd statue have a rhythm that sets the tone for much of London. The London square is a very specific piece of urban design, which suited the English social system, love of gardens, and, once the Enlightenment took hold, its sense of order. Introduced in the 17th century, the square reached its peak of popularity in the 19th century. More than 150 of them are spread across central London.

Soho Square features a picturesque gardener's hut.

Inigo Jones, Charles I's favorite architect, laid out Covent Garden Piazza in 1631 for the Earl of Bedford. While the earl was inspired by Paris's Place des Vosges, Jones was remembering Palladio's work in Italy. The result was a handsome residential square whose houses, built behind a uniform facade, overlooked an airy central space. It was quite different from anything the tight-knit City offered, and it was popular. By 1700, a dozen squares had been built for London's wealthy, including Lincoln's Inn Fields, Soho, Leicester, Bloomsbury, St. James's, and several in the Inns of Court.

The squares often proved to be nuclei for 18th-century development, the period when squares were given their most satisfactory sizes and proportions. This is the case in Mayfair, where the concept developed at St. James's Square leaped across Piccadilly to appear as Hanover, Berkeley, and Grosvenor Squares. More isolated gems were built, too, such as the Charterhouse (on the edge of the City) and Smith (in Westminster).

But it is Bedford Square, one of the early Bloomsbury squares, that reached near-perfection, and survives complete. A daring piece of speculative development in the 1770s, Bedford was London's first square to be planned and built as a single architectural unit. Each side follows a simple design, a great palace facade with a pediment in the middle, overlooking a central oval garden.

INSIDER TIP:

Visit Smith Square (Westminster), where the distinctive baroque St. John's Church hosts marvelous concerts.

—MARY LAMBERTON
National Geographic contributor

Originally, the square was gated and guarded, to preserve residents' privacy. Only the residents had keys to the gardens—a practice still in use in many London squares. Tradesmen used the back entrances in the mews lanes behind the buildings, where the stables were. Coal was delivered to the front of the house, however, and poured down coal holes in the pavement, so that it reached the basement kitchens without dirtying the main house. You can still see the metal lids for these coal holes in some sidewalks.

Walking paths wind among plane trees in Portman Square Garden.

During London's rampaging 19th-century expansion, developers constantly utilized the square. Islington's 18th-century terraces were joined first by Canonbury Square in around 1800, then, gradually, by the unpretentious squares of Barnsbury. But a new scale of grandeur was introduced in the creation of Belgravia. Belgrave Square, the centerpiece for Thomas Cubitt's development (see p. 182), begun in 1825, is huge and unashamedly pompous. Mansions mark each corner, each terrace is four stories high, and columns and pilasters are rampant. Working with George Basevi, Cubitt broke the facades up, giving individuality to the houses by varying the entrances, elevations, and decoration.

The break with the austere Georgian square was complete. But individuality kept the square popular. Eaton Square resembles a triumphal way; Chester Square, long and narrow, is surprisingly intimate; Ladbroke Square's Italianate houses overlook what is possibly London's largest private communal garden. Late 20th-century developments at Chelsea Harbour and Broadgate have kept the idea of the square alive.

The Bloomsbury Group

At the beginning of the 20th century, a handful of artists and writers formed a clique devoted to the philosophy of G. E. Moore, which decreed that the most important things in life were the "pleasures of human intercourse and the enjoyment of beautiful objects. It is they that form the rational ultimate end of social progress." Most of the group had Cambridge connections, but they all gathered in Bloomsbury's Gordon Square, where in 1904 the Stephen family—Virginia (later Woolf), her sister Vanessa (later Bell), Toby, and Adrian—moved into No. 46. The economist John Maynard Keynes was part of the group, as were E. M. Forster, Lytton Strachey, Leonard Woolf (Virginia's husband), and Vanessa's husband, Clive Bell. So, too, was Roger Fry, the artist and critic who left his art collection to the Courtauld Institute. Paintings by him and another Bloomsbury artist, Duncan Grant, are in the Courtauld Galleries (see p. 125).

Charles Dickens Museum

Charles Dickens had many London homes, but only this one survives. He, his wife, Catherine, and their young son Charles moved onto Doughty Street in 1837 and lived here for three key years. Dickens wrote the first of his great novels in this house.

Charles Dickens Museum
- 🅰 Map p. 133
- ✉ 48 Doughty Street, WC1
- ☎ 020 7405 2127
- 💲 $$
- 🚇 Tube: Russell Square, Chancery Lane

www.dickens museum.com

The house was well located: in a good residential area, yet close to the City and Thameside streets where he did his research. His daughters Mary and Kate were born here. Not surprisingly, the house holds the world's most comprehensive Dickens library and is a place of pilgrimage for Dickens enthusiasts, many of whom join walks around Dickens's London. Saved from demolition in 1922

INSIDER TIP:

See who you can identify in the "Dickens's Dream" painting, depicting the author amid his characters.

—RACHAEL JACKSON
National Geographic contributor

by the Dickens Fellowship, which now runs it, the house has been skillfully arranged to retain its atmosphere of literary output and early Victorian interior decoration. Seeing the writer's desk and chair, marked-up copies of his readings, and other personal artifacts, it is easy to imagine him polishing off the *Pickwick Papers*, writing *Oliver Twist* and *Nicholas Nickleby*, or beginning *Barnaby Rudge*—feats all achieved here.

The museum is currently in the process of raising several million pounds for what they hope will be a major redevelopment, to include doubling the museum's size and redesigning the interior rooms to a traditional Victorian look. The goal is to have funding raised and work completed in time for Dickens's 200th birthday on February 7, 2012. Either way, the museum is hosting a series of special events and activities in 2012 to mark the occasion. ∎

Charles Dickens's house survives from the 19th century.

Theatrical architecture and two of the city's most glorious parks:
Regent's Park with its gardens and zoo, and Hampstead Heath

Regency London & North

Houseboats in Little Venice

Regency London & North

When the Prince Regent became King George IV he introduced a new order into London with the development of Regent Street and Regent's Park. Not since the great building projects of the Tudors of the sixteenth century had a royal exercised such influence on the shaping of London. The Prince Regent was the energy and inspiration behind the dream. John Nash, his planner and gifted architect, realized this dream with theatrical panache.

When Prince George came of age in 1783, he moved out of St. James's Palace into Carlton House, sited where the bottom of Regent Street is today, and for the next 30 years squandered a fortune having fun. It was during this period that he employed the architect John Nash.

The prince, influenced by the growing English Picturesque movement, which saw architecture as part of the environment, conceived a scheme that would make sweeping changes to the outer reaches of London. In 1811, when he and Nash were already making plans, three key events happened. The lease on 500 acres of Crown parkland, just north of smart Marylebone and Mayfair, expired; George III became so unwell that his son was made Regent; and the tide turned in the Napoleonic Wars, firing London with optimism and jump-starting a building boom.

The idea was to create a garden city for aristocrats, a park dotted with villas, woods, a royal pleasure palace, a lake, and a canal. The plan also included a wide, mile-long street of suitable size for large carriages to link the park to his own home and thus to the Court and Parliament.

Most of the Prince Regent's dream was realized. Regent Street was built at the expense of hundreds of Soho houses, dividing Mayfair and Marylebone from all points east. Today, much rebuilt, it remains a stylish shopping street, and happily links to James Adam's elegant Portland Place of 1776–1780. Carlton House was demolished when the Prince moved to Buckingham Palace and the southern end of Regent Street closed with a staircase leading down to St. James's Park. At the north end, the great circus planned at the crossing with Marylebone Road was only half realized in Park Crescent, but even this is one of London's finest architectural set pieces.

Regent's Park may have fewer villas than planned, and no pleasure palace, but with its meandering lake, northern boundary canal, zoo, immaculate gardens, and gleaming terraces, it is one of London's most breathtaking royal parks.

At the southwest corner, Dorset Square's development in 1811 forced the famous Marylebone Cricket Club to move to Lord's in St. John's Wood (now the country's best known cricket ground). North of the park, as buildings covered the hills, Hampstead and, to a lesser extent, Highgate were brought into the London frame. ∎

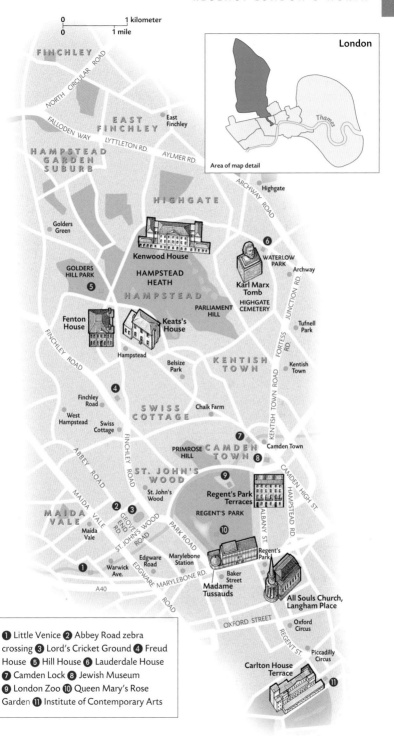

London

Area of map detail

0 ——— 1 kilometer
0 ——— 1 mile

FINCHLEY

NORTH CIRCULAR ROAD

EAST FINCHLEY

East Finchley

FALLODEN WAY

LYTTLETON RD.

AYLMER RD.

HAMPSTEAD GARDEN SUBURB

ARCHWAY ROAD

Highgate

HIGHGATE

Golders Green

Kenwood House

GOLDERS HILL PARK

WATERLOW PARK

Archway

❻

HAMPSTEAD HEATH

Karl Marx Tomb

HIGHGATE CEMETERY

JUNCTION RD.

❺

HAMPSTEAD

Fenton House

Keats's House

PARLIAMENT HILL

Tufnell Park

FINCHLEY ROAD

Hampstead

Belsize Park

KENTISH TOWN

Kentish Town

FORTESS RD.

Finchley Road

SWISS COTTAGE

Chalk Farm

❹

West Hampstead

Swiss Cottage

KENTISH TOWN ROAD

ABBEY ROAD

FINCHLEY ROAD

PRIMROSE HILL

CAMDEN TOWN

❼

Camden Town

❽

ST. JOHN'S WOOD

Regent's Park Terraces

CAMDEN HIGH ST

MAIDA VALE

St. John's Wood

❾

❷ ❸

REGENT'S PARK

ALBANY ST.

HAMPSTEAD RD.

Maida Vale

GROVE END RD.

ST. JOHN'S WOOD ROAD

PARK ROAD

❿

Regent's Park

❶

Warwick Ave.

Edgware Road

Marylebone Station

Baker Street

EDGWARE ROAD

MARYLEBONE RD.

Madame Tussauds

All Souls Church, Langham Place

A40

OXFORD STREET

Oxford Circus

REGENT ST.

Piccadilly Circus

Carlton House Terrace

⓫

❶ Little Venice ❷ Abbey Road zebra crossing ❸ Lord's Cricket Ground ❹ Freud House ❺ Hill House ❻ Lauderdale House ❼ Camden Lock ❽ Jewish Museum ❾ London Zoo ❿ Queen Mary's Rose Garden ⓫ Institute of Contemporary Arts

Regent Street

Oxford Street may have more shops than any other street in Europe, but Regent Street has the edge for its mix of shops, style, and a drop of culture—all wrapped in architectural grandeur.

Regent Street

🅰 Map p. 145

Institute of Contemporary Arts

🅰 Map p. 145

✉ Nash House, The Mall, SW1

☎ 020 7930 3647

🕐 Closed a.m.

💲 $

🚇 Tube/Rail: Charing Cross

www.ica.org.uk

At the south end of Regent Street (and its extension, Waterloo Place), architect John Nash (see p. 148) tidied up the eastern side, creating Pall Mall East and planning for Trafalgar Square. When the prince moved to Buckingham Palace, Nash replaced Carlton House with grand Carlton House Terrace (1827–1832). Today, No. 6 is home to the erudite Royal Society, whose presidents have included Wren, Newton, and Sloane. In the middle of the terrace is Benjamin Wyatt's Duke of York's Column. (The English Tourist Board's center is near this section of Regent Street.) Steps lead down to the **Institute of Contemporary Arts,** which shows state-of-the-art exhibitions and films.

Northward, **Piccadilly Circus** (see p. 118) marks a change of direction and mood. Here is Austin Reed, with its art deco basement barber (see sidebar below), and Burberry. Farther up, Liberty & Co. is known for its quality, exotic goods.

Oxford Circus marks Regent's Street's intersection with bustling Oxford Street, one of the world's great shopping meccas. Stately **Selfridges** and **Marks & Spencer** have their flagship stores here, as do a wide range of 70 clothing retailers. This famously crowded strip has recently been made more user-friendly with wider sidewalks and a pedestrian crossing at Oxford Circus.

North of Oxford Circus, the circular portico of **All Souls Church, Langham Place** has a bust of architect Nash looking down his street. ∎

EXPERIENCE: Have Your Whiskers Trimmed

Combining the best of centuries-old ritual and 21st-century pampering, there are still a few spots in town where you can go for a traditional straight-edge wet shave, complete with scented hot towels, a hearty bristled brush, and thick lather.

Austin Reed (103 Regent St., W1, tel 020 7534 7719, www.austinreed.co.uk, $$$$$) has been offering wet shaves and other face and body treatments in its lower ground floor salon since the 1930s.

Geo F. Trumper (www.trumpers.com, $$$$$) has two locations in London—in Mayfair (9 Curzon St., W1, tel 020 7499

1850) and St. James's (temporarily, 1 Duke of York St., SW1, tel 020 7734 1370). You can further your education with a private shaving lesson at the Mayfair location.

Pall Mall Barbers (27 Whitcomb St., WC2, tel 020 7930 7787, www.pallmallbarber .com, $$$$$) is an independent barber near Leicester Square with more than 25 years experience providing straight-edge shaves.

The Refinery at Harrods (Harrods basement level, tel 020 7893 8332, www .the-refinery.com, $$$$$) offers massages, waxing, and manicures in addition to their wet-shave service.

Regent's Park

This is where John Nash left the French formality of Regent Street behind and returned to English Picturesque. Almost 500 acres of farmland had been appropriated by Henry VIII from the Abbey of Barking. These were sold by Cromwell, then reclaimed by Charles II and leased out (see p. 148). It was these leases that reverted to the Crown in 1811. Of Nash's 56 planned villas, only 8 were built, but the terraces at the sides were completed.

Regent's Park offers boating on its lake and relaxing on its shores.

Regent's Park

- Map p. 145
- 020 7486 7905
- Closed at night
- Tube: Regent's Park, Baker Street, Great Portland Street, or Camden Town (especially for zoo)

www.royalparks .gov.uk

Regent's Park Open-Air Theatre

- Inner Circle, Regent's Park, NW1
- Tickets: 0844 826 4242
- June–Sept.
- $$$
- Tube: Baker Street

www.openairtheatre .org

London Zoo

- Map p. 145
- Regent's Park, NW1
- 020 7722 3333
- $$$$
- Tube: Camden Town, Regent's Park

www.zsl.org

Regent's Park has great variety. In the southeast corner, the Victorian complexity and density of planting in Avenue Gardens, laid out in 1864, has been restored to full glory. Beside them the Broad Walk runs the length of the park, bordered by mature horse chestnuts. About 6,000 forest trees grow in the park.

Halfway up the Broad Walk, Inner Circle protects the park's most private and magical area, Queen Mary's Rose Garden. Laid out to celebrate the Jubilee of George V and Queen Mary in 1935, it includes formal and alpine gardens and a glorious rose garden. More than 30,000 plants and 400 varieties, both old and new, perfume the air with blooms throughout the summer. Rambling and climbing roses encircle beds of flowers, creating peaceful corners in the park.

The **Regent's Park Open-Air Theatre,** which offers Shakespeare and classic musical productions during the summer months, is in Inner Circle, too, near the modest Rose Garden Restaurant. Regent's Park Lake, a sanctuary for waterbirds, meanders around Inner Circle; the bandstand's music floats over it, and boaters enjoy views of the Holme, a villa designed by Decimus Burton.

North across the lawns, the roaring of lions announces the **ZSL London Zoo,** opened in 1828. A bridge over Regent's Canal leads to Primrose Hill, with views across London. ∎

Regency Architecture

Architect John Nash's vision for London became the capital's chief expression of Regency architecture and town planning. Inspired by the Picturesque movement, it was a style of architecture that reacted against the Enlightenment's classical severity.

The emphasis turned from quality of building and detail to overall effect; from a preoccupation with interior space to a desire for impressive facades; from a serious, formal approach to a more capricious, eclectic one that took inspiration from any period or culture.

Born in 1752, Nash produced his best work in his sixties and seventies when, as the Prince Regent's town planner, he brought freedom and imagination to the city's "metropolitan improvements," as the prince dubbed his project. Nash's gleaming stuccoed streets, terraces, and villas introduced a new theatricality and dignity to a city transforming itself from a port into the capital of a worldwide empire.

This Regency style is best displayed in Nash's imposing Regent's Park terraces, which surround the park: York, Cornwall, Clarence,

John Nash's architecture at Regent's Park

Sussex, and Hanover, built in 1821–1823, were followed by Ulster, Cambridge, Chester, and Cumberland, and finally Gloucester in 1827.

York Terrace is strung along the south side of the park in two sections. In the middle, the stage-set design of York Gate cleverly frames Marylebone Church, built in 1813 with gilded caryatids supporting the tower's dome. The other early terraces are strung along the west side. York, Cornwall, and Clarence, ambitious conceptions by Nash, were built under his direction by James Burton and his son, Decimus. In Sussex Place, Nash drew on his Brighton Pavilion: The curved end wings, octagonal domes, and polygonal bay windows seem better suited to the seaside. Finally, Hanover Terrace returns to a classical simplicity.

Where the architecture lapses, however, the lighthearted theatrical effect does not. This is even more true of the terraces on the east side, which follow the south side's Ulster Terrace with its simple lines and bay windows at each end. Between the relatively modest Cambridge Terrace and the asymmetrical Gloucester Gate, Chester Terrace's 940-foot-long (287 m) facade is broken up by giant Corinthian columns; at either end, projecting wings are joined with thin triumphal arches. This is fun, but for architectural frolic Cumberland Terrace tops it. With its seven porticoes, courtyards, and arches, it makes one of the most impressive panoramas in London, a perfect backdrop to aristocratic partying.

Of the eight villas once sprinkled through the park, just three remain. Seen from across the lake, the Holme, designed by Decimus Burton for his father, looks just as it should: part of a suburban idyll of country houses surrounded by spacious grounds.

Madame Tussauds

Drawing some of the largest crowds in London, this waxwork temple to the famous, infamous, and sometimes unremarkable opened in 1835. Today it is especially popular with children and can make for a fun outing, even though it is of relatively minor importance in a city blessed with so many truly amazing museums for history, art, and science.

Madame Tussaud, whose real name was Marie Grosholtz, fled revolutionary Paris in 1802, toured England with her uncle's waxworks, then settled near here. Fans kept returning because she was always adding people in the news. Her sons moved the collection to this site, and today's owners keep the show up-to-date. Bring your camera; the photo ops come fast and furious.

The best comes first: the section called "Blush" where the visitor is a star amid waxworks stars and paparazzi flashing cameras.

A motley collection of personalities includes Hollywood favorites such as John Travolta, Robin Williams, and Shrek; David Beckham, Tiger Woods, and other sports figures; the Beatles, Freddie Mercury, and Michael Jackson from the world of music; and a selection of U.S. presidents, British prime ministers, and members of the British royal family.

The "Scream" attraction pits you against live actors jumping out from the shadows to startle you. The old planetarium building continues the celebrity show, plus screens a changing selection of "4-D" features. ■

Soccer star David Beckham in wax at Madame Tussauds

Madame Tussauds

🗺 Map p. 145
✉ Marylebone Road, NW1
☎ 0870 400 3000
🕐 Best to book tickets online in advance
💲 $$$$$
🚇 Tube: Baker Street

www.madame tussauds.com

Lord's Cricket Ground

England's most famous cricket club, the Marylebone Cricket Club (MCC), lies behind high walls. Thomas Lord moved the MCC northwest of Regent's Park when he sold the club's Dorset Square ground for development. The ground hosts club and Middlesex County matches and international test matches. Visitors may tour the buildings (one designed by Michael Hopkins) and museum (tel 020 7616 8500, www.lords.org, closed on major match days). Cricket memorabilia include Donald Bradman's boots, the sparrow killed by Jehangir Khan's ball in 1936, and the tiny urn containing the Ashes. The Ashes—of the stumps burned after Australia's first victory over England in 1882—is a mock trophy awarded to the winner in test matches between the two countries.

Regent's Canal, Camden & Little Venice

In the 18th century, England was crisscrossed by canals—water highways that transported much of the industrial revolution's new trading wealth. Regent's Canal, built as the park's north border, provided a vital link in the system. It ran from Paddington Basin, where the Grand Union Canal from the Midlands then ended, to the Port of London 8.5 miles away, and quickly became England's busiest stretch of canal. Even after the railways were built, it was used for delivering expanding London's building materials.

Regent's Canal in Camden is a favored spot for relaxing on a summer day.

Regent's Canal Pleasure Boats

 Tube: Camden Town, Warwick Avenue

www.canal museum.org.uk

Today, Regent's Canal is quiet. The towpath is a favorite spot to fish or take a stroll, and pleasure boats ferry passengers 45 minutes between Camden Lock and Little Venice, stopping at London Zoo.

The two destinations are quite different. Camden's modest, small-scale houses are now gentrified. Weekend life with its banter and noise focuses in and around Camden Lock, whose ethnic market began in the 1970s and is now spruced up. Thousands of bargain hunters flock to the markets that have spread up Camden High Street and Chalk Farm Road (see p. 164). The **Camden Arts Centre** (Arkwright

EXPERIENCE: Crossing Abbey Road

For visitors of a certain age, there's an almost inexorable draw to the famous crosswalk (generically called "zebra crossings" in the U.K. for their distinctive black-and-white stripes) that appears on the cover of the Beatles' 1969 album, *Abbey Road*.

To get there from Little Venice's pretty Blomfield Road (a 15- to 20-minute walk), follow Randolph Avenue and turn right onto Sutherland Avenue (which becomes Hall Road), then turn left onto Grove End Road. The crosswalk will be about 200 yards (182 m) in front of you. (Or take a short walk down Grove End Road from the St. John's Wood Tube stop.) You should be able to spot the crosswalk by the clusters of tourists loitering on either side of the street, waiting their turn to parade back and forth. Luckily, British law requires that drivers give pedestrians the right of way at zebra crossings (which, by and large, they do), but Abbey Road is a busy street, so don't dally too long trying to perfectly recapture the pose of the four Liverpudlians.

A few yards up Abbey Road, on the southwest side of the street, is **Abbey Road Studios**, where the Beatles recorded 90 percent of their music. You aren't able to visit, as it's still a working studio, so you'll have to make do with photos shot through their iron gates.

In 2010, both the zebra crossing and the Abbey Road Studios were approved for listing by the Department for Culture, Media and Sport, affording them protected status.

INSIDER TIP:

In Little Venice, drop into Clifton Nurseries at Clifton Villas. It's London's oldest garden center and has a lovely café for breakfast, lunch, or tea.

—SIMON HORSFORD
Sunday Telegraph *travel writer*

Rd., NW3, tel 020 7472 5500, *www.camdenartscentre.org, closed Mon.*), a free exhibition space for contemporary art, perfectly embodies Camden's alternative and artsy feel. Meanwhile, the recently expanded and relocated **Jewish Museum** (*129–131 Albert St., NW1, tel 020 7284 7384, www.jewishmuseum.org.uk*), off the northeast corner of Regent's Park,

displays particularly good collections of Jewish art and objects.

Little Venice, a couple of miles southwest, is, by contrast, a leafy and stylish haven. Painted barges are moored at the canal's end, including one that is a **puppet theater** (*opposite 40 Blomfield Rd., W9, tel 020 7249 6876, www.puppet barge.com, moored in Richmond Aug.–Sept.*).

A walk here passes by the grand houses of the neighborhood of Maida Vale—the elegant ones on Blomfield Road border the canal—and a couple of notable pubs: the **Bridge House,** where upstairs the renowned Canal Café Theatre (*www.canalcafetheatre.com*) performs frequent comedy shows; and the perfectly preserved **Prince Alfred,** an old Victorian gin palace on Formosa Street behind the Warwick Avenue Tube stop. ■

Clifton Nurseries
- 5A Clifton Villas, W9
- 020 7289 6851
- www.clifton.co.uk

London Waterbus Company
- 020 7482 2550
- Closed Mon.–Fri. Nov.–March
- $$$
- www.londonwaterbus.com

Jenny Wren
- 250 Camden High St., NW1
- 020 7485 4433
- Closed Oct.–Easter
- $$$
- www.walkersquay.com

Hampstead

Distanced from the central London developers, Hampstead watched the builders climb up the hill toward its doors but retained its distinct, hilltop village character. Healthy air and panoramic views across London to the Surrey hills attracted Tudor merchants to Hampstead. By the 18th century, its popularity ran parallel with Islington's, but its position farther from town made it a more select pleasure resort, and it has never lost its fashionable image.

Fenton House

- Map p. 145
- Hampstead Grove, NW3
- 014 9475 5563
- Closed Mon.–Tues. mid-March–Oct. & Nov.–mid-March
- $$
- Tube: Hampstead

www.nationaltrust
.org.uk

Burgh House & Hampstead Museum

- New End Square, NW3
- 020 7431 0144
- Closed Mon.–Tues.
- Tube: Hampstead

www.burghhouse.org.uk

The wealthy, artistic, and intellectual came to take the health-giving mineral waters at Hampstead's spa, and some stayed—statesman William Pitt and writers Lord Byron, Robert Louis Stevenson, and John Galsworthy all lived here. Despite the restaurants and shops that line High Street today, houses in Hampstead Square, Church Row, Flask Walk, Well Walk, and their surrounding streets still echo with Georgian holiday mood.

Hampstead's contemporary intellectuals have saved several fine houses and gardens and made them museums. **Fenton House,** at the top of the hill, is perhaps the grandest. It is a William-and-Mary house of 1693, filled with fine ceramics and musical instruments, and set in a delightful garden.

Burgh House & Hampstead Museum, located in the village center, a perfect Queen Anne house of 1703, was once owned by Hampstead physician Dr. William Gibbons.

Among the writers attracted to Hampstead was the poet John Keats, who lived between 1818 and 1820 in Keats Grove, a modest Regency house *(Keats Grove, tel 020 7332 3868, www.keatshouse .org.uk, closed Mon.–Thurs. Nov.–Apr.)* now furnished with his belongings. The psychoanalyst Sigmund Freud lived at 20 Maresfield Gardens *(tel 020 7435 2002, www.freud.org .uk, closed Mon.–Tues.),* today the **Freud Museum London,** where his analyst's chair is displayed. Finally, the National Trust has bought and opened **2 Willow Road** *(tel 020 7435 6166, www. nationaltrust.org.uk),* designed by Erno Goldfinger in 1939.

Another way to take in the area is to walk around **Hampstead Garden Suburb,** an "ideal" garden city of vernacular houses north of Hampstead Golf Club, conceived by Raymond Unwin and Barry Parker in 1907. It was laid out with houses of three sizes for different income groups. ■

Hampstead's handsome brick houses have long attracted writers and other intellectuals.

Kenwood House & Hampstead Heath

Fine art in a spectacular setting is matched by panoramic views, rolling hills, and woodland, making this house and its surroundings one of the great joys of London.

In 1754 the brilliant lawyer the Earl of Mansfield bought the early 17th-century, hilltop Kenwood House with its fashionable "prospects" as a summer retreat from his city home in Lincoln's Inn Fields. Robert Adam, a fellow Scot, remodeled it in 1764–1769. Exhibiting his mastery of both exterior and interior design, Adam added another story to the long, classical garden front and balanced the older orangery with a sumptuous library, one of his best rooms anywhere. The ceiling is decorated with plasterwork by Joseph Rose and paintings by Antonio Zucchi.

After Mansfield, the house languished until 1925, when Edward Guinness, Earl of Iveagh, bought it along with 80 acres (32 ha) of park and hung his pictures in Adam's suite of rooms. Guinness left the house and gardens to the nation, along with the paintings, which include Vermeer's "Guitar Player," Rembrandt's late "Portrait of the Artist," and a Constable oil sketch, "Hampstead Heath."

From the front terrace, the lawns sweep down to an ornamental lake, now the setting for summer concerts; to the left (east), a path leads to the summit for breathtaking views of London. Walkers will itch to step out across Hampstead Heath, a tract of

Parliament Hill in Hampstead Heath offers fine kite flying and sweeping views of London.

789 acres fought for in the face of developers and accumulated piecemeal since 1829. Plunge down to **Highgate Ponds,** then climb **Parliament Hill** where Sunday kite flyers make their fragile, colorful paper shapes perform acrobatics in the skies; continue to **Hampstead Ponds** and perhaps take a walk in **Hill House's** *(Sandy Lane, by Jack Straw's Castle apartments)* secret garden of heavily scented azaleas. ∎

Kenwood House, Iveagh Bequest

- Map p. 145
- Hampstead Lane, NW3
- 020 8348 1286
- Charge for special exhibitions
- Tube: Hampstead, then walk 1 mile (1.6 km)

www.english -heritage.org.uk

Highgate

Living slightly in the shadow of fashionable Hampstead, Highgate's story has been a similar but quieter one. A hamlet grew up on land belonging to the bishops of London. By the end of the 16th century its waters and air were worth the journey from London, as were its open spaces for exercise and fun; wealthy merchants built their country mansions here. Today, Highgate is best known for its beautiful cemetery, where many famous Londoners lie.

Lauderdale House

- Map p. 145
- Highgate Hill, N6
- 020 8348 8716
- Tube: Highgate, Archway

www.lauderdale house.co.uk

Highgate Cemetery

- Map p. 145
- Swain's Lane, N6
- 020 8340 1834
- East side: $ West side, guided tours: $
- Tube: Archway

www.highgate -cemetery.org

One of the earliest mansions to be built here, **Lauderdale House** (1580) survives in part, with later additions. The large sloping garden, confusingly called Waterlow Park, has great beech, catalpa, and yew trees shading the heavily scented summer azalea blossoms.

INSIDER TIP:

Highgate's West Cemetery has more imposing monuments than the East Cemetery, but you must take a guided tour to see it.

—LARRY PORGES
National Geographic Books editor

The nucleus of Highgate, however, is farther up the hill, where the eccentric philanthropist William Blake built houses at Nos. 1–6 of The Grove in the 17th century. Nearby, delightful houses fill Pond Square, and more survive in South Grove: Old Hall at No. 17 (1690s), Moreton and Church Houses at Nos. 10 and 14, and the stuccoed Literary Institute (1839). Cromwell House, at 104 Highgate Hill, is a rare survivor: a large

London house of the 1630s. The High Street has more 18th-century houses at Nos. 17–21, 23, and 42, and several attractive Georgian shopfronts.

Highgate Cemetery, next to Waterlow Park, is the burial place of numerous interesting people, and well worth a visit. Opened in 1839, it was so popular for its ornate catacombs and fine views that an extension was opened in 1857, with an under-road tunnel to take the biers to the graves. In the eastern part today, obelisks and other elaborate monuments are shaded by mature trees.

Memorials in the cemetery include those to writer George Eliot (under the name Mary Anne Cross), who died in 1880, philosopher Herbert Spencer (1903), and Karl Marx, who died in 1883. Tours to the western side may pass memorials for the Rossetti family, Dickens family (he himself is in Westminster Abbey), Charles Chubb, who invented Chubb locks, and Charles Cruft, founder of Cruft's Dog Show. The most ostentatious mausoleums, though, are the Terrace Catacombs, supposedly the inspiration for Bram Stoker's *Dracula*. This sacred ground is closed during funerals; children are not welcome. ■

A family-friendly area with everything: a palace, gardens, parks, markets, and museums galore

Kensington & South Kensington

A marker for the Princess of Wales memorial walk, which wends though Hyde Park and Kensington Gardens

Kensington & South Kensington

In 1689 the asthmatic and bronchitic William III left dank Whitehall Palace with his wife, Mary II, for the fresh air of Kensington village, then well outside London. Thus began a royal association with the area that continues, for members of the royal family still live in Kensington Palace. The State Apartments are open to the public.

William and Mary invited Sir Christopher Wren and Nicholas Hawksmoor to remodel their house as Kensington Palace. They also fenced off some of Hyde Park to create the nucleus of Kensington Gardens. The palace still lies at the heart of Kensington. This was a favorite official palace of the 18th-century Hanoverian rulers until George III moved to Buckingham Palace in 1762. The proximity of royalty attracted the rich and wellborn: Even today, Kensington contains many of London's most fashionable residential streets.

London's grandest and most ostentatious street, Kensington Palace Gardens, was laid out in 1843 as a gated, tree-lined avenue. Edged with palatial mansions, it was soon nicknamed "millionaires' row." Today it is mostly devoted to foreign missions. Less ostentatious Kensington survives beyond, in the area bordered by

NOT TO BE MISSED:

The new landscaping and layout of Kensington Palace 158–159

Visiting the inspiring Albert Memorial 160

A Saturday shopping spree among the stalls of Portobello Road market 166–167

The amazing decorative arts collection at the sprawling Victoria & Albert Museum 169–171

The Natural History Museum's fossils and galleries 174–176

two great shopping streets: Kensington Church Street, which curls up the hill to Notting Hill Gate and so to Portobello Road as a continuous parade of antiques shops; and Kensington High Street, which rose to prominence for more practical shopping after the Underground was built in 1868. The large estate of Holland Park was parceled off to become grand Holland Park houses at one end and a leafy idyll for artists such as the 19th-century painter Lord Leighton at the other.

A monument to Prince Albert stands across the road from the Royal Albert Hall, completed in 1871. Royal colleges for art, organists, and music are nearby, together with the Royal Geographical Society, the Imperial College of Science and Technology, and the Goethe Institute. The area is also the home to three of London's great museums: the Victoria & Albert, Science, and Natural History. ■

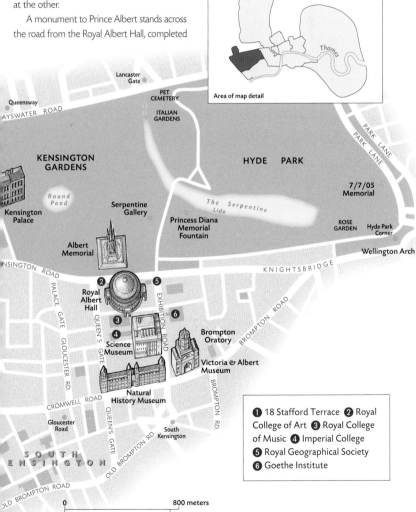

London

Thames

Area of map detail

Lancaster Gate

Queensway

BAYSWATER ROAD

PET CEMETERY

ITALIAN GARDENS

KENSINGTON GARDENS

HYDE PARK

PARK LANE
PARK LANE

Round Pond

Serpentine Gallery

The Serpentine
Lido

7/7/05 Memorial

Kensington Palace

Princess Diana Memorial Fountain

ROSE GARDEN

Hyde Park Corner

Albert Memorial

KENSINGTON ROAD

KNIGHTSBRIDGE

Wellington Arch

❷
Royal Albert Hall

❺

PALACE GATE

QUEEN'S GATE

GLOUCESTER RD

❸
❹
Science Museum

❻

EXHIBITION ROAD

Brompton Oratory

BROMPTON ROAD

Victoria & Albert Museum

Natural History Museum

CROMWELL ROAD

Gloucester Road

QUEEN'S GATE

South Kensington

BROMPTON RD

OLD BROMPTON RD

SOUTH KENSINGTON

OLD BROMPTON ROAD

❶ 18 Stafford Terrace ❷ Royal College of Art ❸ Royal College of Music ❹ Imperial College ❺ Royal Geographical Society ❻ Goethe Institute

0 ——————— 800 meters
0 ——————— 800 yards

Kensington Palace

With its warm redbrick exterior and small, comfortable rooms, Kensington Palace instantly gives a feeling of informality that contrasts with the formal splendors of Hampton Court or Buckingham Palace. This family mood was created by William and Mary. In 1689 they bought their country mansion from Sir Heneage Finch, Duke of Nottingham. Sir Christopher Wren and Nicholas Hawksmoor made changes so the royal family could move in for Christmas.

Fronted by its gardens, Kensington Palace displays its characteristic red brickwork.

The south and east facades, with their fine brickwork, are Wren's signature. The grounds feature statues of William III and Queen Victoria (by her daughter Louise) and a sunken garden enclosed by pleached lime trees (their branches entwined to form a solid mass). On the right of the palace stands Hawksmoor's Orangery, built in 1704–1705 and now a café where customers can admire Grinling Gibbons's elaborate carved pine and pearwood festoons at either end. The building adjoining the back of the palace is home to some members of the royal family. After her separation from Prince Charles, Princess Diana lived here; and it was from Kensington Palace that her funeral procession left for Westminster Abbey.

Kensington Palace is undergoing a major £12 million ($19 million) redesign and redevelopment that will transform both the exterior of the palace as well as the visitor experience inside. By the anticipated completion date (summer 2012), the fences and trees that currently cordon off the view of the palace from Kensington Gardens will be removed, opening up the gardens and landscape, restoring the traditional east-west axis, and making the palace more accessible in look and feel.

Upon entering the building, the visitor will find a new central, glass-ceilinged **Hub,** with several rooms that can be visited for free. From here, it's decision time: You'll be able to tour the **State Apartments,** visit temporary exhibits, or enter the new permanent **Queen Victoria** narrative, which tells the story of Victoria's life in the very rooms in which she grew up. After 2012, similar visitor routes will be created to feature the lives of William & Mary, Queen Anne, King George II, and 20th-century princesses Diana and Margaret.

The State Apartments

Selected art from the Queen's Royal Collection fills the State Apartments. The plain oak Queen's Staircase rises to an

INSIDER TIP:

Have an ale at the cozy Windsor Castle (a few hundred yards west of the palace), an old-style pub that hasn't changed since the 1830s.

—NATASHA SCRIPTURE
National Geographic contributor

intimate suite of Queen Mary's rooms. Her gallery has more Gibbons carvings on the overmantle mirror frames while the Dining Room retains its original paneling. Mary's Drawing Room has the Thomas Tompion barometer made for the palace around 1695, while her Bedchamber has original elm floorboards and a bed, complete with hangings, used by James II.

The Privy Chamber marks the beginning of the high-ceilinged rooms designed by Colen Campbell for George I in 1718–1720. The rooms' gentle Palladian style is complemented by William Kent's ceiling decorations. The Privy Chamber decor shows Mars and Minerva, symbolizing the king's military prowess and the queen's patronage of the arts and sciences. Seventeenth-century Mortlake tapestries hang on the walls of this private audience chamber. The public audience room, or Presence Chamber, is next. Here, Kent decorated the ceiling in cheerful Pompeiian colors.

The King's Grand Staircase was designed by Wren, with ironwork by Jean Tijou. Kent's painting of the walls and ceiling is his most important decorative work: a Venetian-style view of a crowded gallery, inspired by Versailles and Blenheim (see p. 225). Courtiers and visitors to Kensington Palace would have climbed this appropriately grand staircase to the King's Gallery, built by Hawksmoor in 1695–1696 and painted by Kent in 1725–1726 with scenes from *The Odyssey*. The walls of the gallery are now rehung with George II's paintings as he had them.

The State Room tour also includes Victoria's old bedroom, where the teenage princess was awakened during the night of June 20, 1837, and informed that she was now queen. Memorabilia include her own children's cot and David Roberts's views of the Great Exhibition. But keep looking upward in these State Rooms. The King's Drawing Room has yet another splendid Kent ceiling. Wren and Kent together created the Cupola Room, next, where Victoria was baptized in 1819. ■

Kensington Palace

- 🅰 Map p. 157
- ✉ Kensington Gardens, W8
- ☎ 020 7937 9561 Booking: 0870 751 5180
- 💲 $$$
- 🚇 Tube: High Street Kensington

www.hrp.org.uk

Windsor Castle Pub

- ✉ 114 Campden Hill Rd., W8
- ☎ 020 7243 8797
- 🚇 Tube: High Street Kensington, Notting Hill Gate

www.thewindsor castlekensington .co.uk

Kensington Gardens

William and Mary's creation of a Dutch garden on the 26 acres (11 ha) they bought with Kensington Palace was the humble origin of the 275-acre (111 ha) Kensington Gardens. Queen Anne anglicized and enlarged those gardens and built the Orangery; she also laid out the promenade, Rotten Row. In 1728, George II's wife, Queen Caroline, and her gardener, Charles Bridgeman, fenced in more Hyde Park acres, dug the Round Pond, laid out the radiating avenues, and diverted a stream to make the Long Water. The gardens fully opened to the public in 1851.

Walk: Kensington Gardens

A meander through Kensington Gardens is the prelude to a cornucopia of cultural feasts set in remarkable buildings.

Kensington Gardens (see sidebar p. 159), begun by William and Mary in the 17th century, were expanded by a succession of later rulers. From the Lancaster Gate Tube station, you enter the gardens at the **Italian Gardens,** added by Victoria and Albert in 1861. Follow the path beside the Long Water—perhaps spotting grebes and other waterfowl—to find George Frampton's 1912 statue of J. M. Barrie's fictional hero, **Peter Pan.** Through the trees to the right is George Frederick Watts's powerful 1904 bronze, "Physical Energy," and Queen Caroline's Round Pond. Back toward the Long Water, look for her Temple and the **Serpentine Gallery ❶** (tel 020 7402 6075, www .serpentinegallery.org), displaying contemporary art. Nearby, the **Princess Diana Memorial Fountain** was designed by American architect Kathryn Gustafson.

The **Flower Walk** leads to Sir George Gilbert Scott's flamboyant **Albert Memorial ❷** (tel 020 7495 0916, guided tours), created between 1864 and 1876. John Foley's statue has the seated prince holding the catalog of his Great Exhibition and looking down on his lasting legacy, the South Kensington cultural compound that dominates the hillside.

Kensington Cultural Institutions

This honeypot of institutions begins with the **Royal Albert Hall ❸** (Kensington Gore, SW7, tel 020 7589 8212, www.royalalberthall .com) in front of the memorial. Inspired by Roman amphitheaters, the great oval Hall is encircled with a frieze made by the Ladies' Mosaic Class of the Victoria & Albert Museum. The frieze depicts the Triumph of Arts and Letters. Inside, the iron-and-glass-dome is an engineering triumph. The Henry Wood Promenade Concerts (www.bbc.co.uk/

NOT TO BE MISSED:

Albert Memorial • Royal Albert Hall • Royal Geographical Society • Brompton Oratory

---

proms), an annual seven-week-long summer festival of nightly concerts known as the Proms, were transferred here in 1941, after being bombed out of Queen's Hall.

A cluster of small institutions surrounds the hall. Upon leaving it, turn left (west) to find the **Royal College of Art** (Kensington Gore, SW7, tel 020 7590 4444, www.rca.ac.uk), founded in 1837, in H. T. Cadbury-Brown and Sir Hugh Casson's building (1962–1973). Farther along, F. W. Moody's multicolored graffito facade now fronts one of London's largest houses. Go behind the Royal Albert Hall to Prince Consort Road. To the left is the **Royal College of Music ❹** (tel 020 7589 3643, www.rcm.ac.uk), founded in 1882, whose instrument collection includes Haydn's clavichord. Students perform in Sir Hugh Casson's Britten Opera Theatre.

Keep on to the end of Prince Consort Road to find Exhibition Road. The energetic can divert uphill to the **Royal Geographical Society ❺** (Kensington Gore, SW7, tel 020 7591 3000, www.rgs.org, closed Sat.–Sun.), founded in 1830 in Norman Shaw's Lowther Lodge (1873–1875), and the **Polish Institute** (20 Princes Gate, SW7, tel 020 7589 9249, www .pism.co.uk) and its Sikorski Museum. This is the major Polish museum outside Poland because, after the German invasion in 1939, the government-in-exile came to London.

The route downhill passes the **Goethe Institute ❻** (50 Prince's Gate, Exhibition Rd., SW7, tel 020 7596 4000, www.goethe.de/ins/gb/

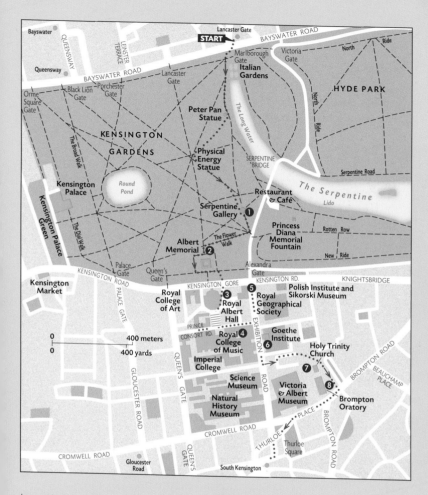

Map labels:
- Bayswater
- QUEENSWAY
- Queensway
- LENSTER TERRACE
- Lancaster Gate
- START
- BAYSWATER ROAD
- Marlborough Gate
- Italian Gardens
- Victoria Gate
- North
- Ride
- HYDE PARK
- Black Lion Gate
- Porchester Gate
- Lancaster Gate
- BAYSWATER ROAD
- Orme Square Gate
- North
- Ride
- Peter Pan Statue
- The Long Water
- KENSINGTON GARDENS
- Physical Energy Statue
- SERPENTINE BRIDGE
- Serpentine Road
- The Broad Walk
- The Serpentine
- Kensington Palace
- Round Pond
- Restaurant & Café
- Lido
- Serpentine Gallery ❶
- Kensington Palace Green
- The Dial Walk
- Albert Memorial ❷
- The Flower Walk
- Serpentine Gallery
- Princess Diana Memorial Fountain
- Rotten Row
- Palace Gate
- Queen's Gate
- Alexandra Gate
- New Ride
- KENSINGTON ROAD
- KENSINGTON GORE
- KENSINGTON RD.
- KNIGHTSBRIDGE
- Kensington Market
- Royal College of Art
- ❸ Royal Albert Hall
- ❺ Royal Geographical Society
- Polish Institute and Sikorski Museum
- PALACE GATE
- PRINCE CONSORT RD.
- ❹ Royal College of Music
- Goethe Institute ❻
- Holy Trinity Church
- BROMPTON ROAD
- BEAUCHAMP PLACE
- 0   400 meters
- 0   400 yards
- Imperial College
- EXHIBITION ROAD
- ❼
- ❽
- Brompton Oratory
- QUEEN'S GATE
- GLOUCESTER ROAD
- Science Museum
- Natural History Museum
- Victoria & Albert Museum
- BROMPTON ROAD
- CROMWELL ROAD
- THURLOE PLACE
- Thurloe Square
- CROMWELL ROAD
- Gloucester Road
- QUEEN'S GATE
- South Kensington

ion, opening times vary) on the left and **Imperial College** on the right. The **Science Museum** (see pp. 172–173) and the back entrance of the **Victoria & Albert Museum** (see pp. 169–171) are beyond. Turn left into Prince's Gate Mews, then walk right, down past the mews cottages and through **Holy Trinity's garden ❼**. Go around the church and up the drive, then turn right to find the Oratory of St. Philip Neri. Known as the **Brompton Oratory ❽** (*Brompton Rd., SW7, tel 020 7808 0900, www .bromptonoratory.com*), this branch of the oratory founded in Rome in 1575 was established by Father Faber in 1849. Inside the baroque

⚑	Inside front cover A3
►	Lancaster Gate Tube station
⊕	2 hours
↔	2.5 miles (4 km)
►	South Kensington Tube station

church, Giuseppe Mazzuoli's exceptional "Twelve Apostles" from Siena Cathedral surround the huge nave.

Turn right out of the church along Brompton Road, past the V&A, then cross the road into Thurloe Place and Thurloe Square, built in the 1840s. The South Kensington Tube station is a couple of minutes away.

Hyde Park

Stretching east of Kensington Gardens, Hyde Park is 350 acres (140 ha) of green and mostly open space, making it the perfect venue for lazy walks, jogs, pick-up soccer games, concerts, and the occasional mass demonstration. Originally a hunting ground for Henry VIII, the park was first opened to the public in the early 17th century and contains a number of interesting sites.

Hyde Park contains a popular cycling route.

Just off Bayswater Road, an old **Pet Cemetery** lies behind Victoria Gate Lodge. The cemetery began in the 1880s when a local dog met his end and was buried in the garden of the kindly gatekeeper. Eventually, more than 300 pets were buried here. The cemetery is closed to the public, so you'll have to content yourself with pictures taken through the bars.

Speakers' Corner is located at the northeast corner of Hyde Park. Busiest on Sunday mornings, this famous platform of free speech is a meeting point for anyone who wants to stand on a soapbox and speak his or her piece (usually about politics or religion). The free speech goes both ways; sometimes the speakers end up in hearty debates with disagreeing crowd members.

Just outside the park, across Cumberland Gate from Speakers' Corner, is **Marble Arch,** an 1827 ceremonial arch designed by John Nash to honor British victories in the Napoleonic Wars. Originally situated on the Mall as an entrance to Buckingham Palace, it was moved to its present location in 1851. Continue down the east side of the park to the simple and moving **7/7/05 Memorial** (*www.royalparks.org.uk),* commemorating the 52 lives lost in the London terrorist attacks of July 7, 2005.

Farther south stands the impressive 18-foot-high (5.5 m) **statue of Achilles** on the Wellington Monument that memorializes the great duke's campaigns against Napoleon. The metal statue was created from the molten munitions of some of the duke's defeated enemies.

Head west from Hyde Park Corner to reach a lovely **rose garden.** From here, continue west to the **Serpentine,** the large lake that bisects the park. Both row- and paddleboats are available for rent *(Easter–Nov., $$$),* while sunbathers and swimmers should head to the small **lido** (waterfront) on the southern edge of the lake. Nearby is the popular **Princess Diana Memorial Fountain** (see p. 160), opened in 2004 to honor the late Princess of Wales. ■

Holland Park & Leighton House

Holland Park is, confusingly, the name for both the park surrounding Holland House and the two roads at the park's northwest corner, as well as for the whole area stretching from Kensington High Street to Holland Park Avenue.

First, the house: Holland House, now ruined, was built in 1606–1607 by Sir Walter Cope, minister to James I. It is the only Jacobean manor built to an E-shaped plan in London, and enough remains to enable us to imagine the grand life enjoyed by its owners. One was Henry Fox, created Baron Holland, who, using public funds for private speculation while paymaster-general in the government, bought it in 1768. The house became a center of Whig politics and literature, where Palmerston, Macaulay, Wordsworth, and Dickens made it a more significant court than the royal one. The picturesque ruins are now a backdrop for summer opera. The **Orangery Gallery** holds periodic art exhibitions and has lovely terraced gardens.

The 54 acres (22 ha) of Holland Park, opened to the public in 1950, begin with these terraces, shaded by magnificent horse chestnut trees. Newer additions include the Japanese **Kyoto Garden,** created in 1991, where resident peacocks strut their stuff. Cricket lawns to the south contrast with the wooded walks to the north. The rich woodland, with mature rhododendrons and azaleas, rose walks, and spring daffodils gives an idea of what first lured the nobility to Kensington.

18 Stafford Terrace

Behind its stuccoed, classical, Italianate facade in Kensington's Stafford Terrace, a perfect cameo of Edwardian London is lovingly preserved by the Victorian Society. The political cartoonist Linley Sambourne, born in 1844, moved into his newly built house in 1874, and by his death in 1910 he had filled it to capacity. Rooms are hung with Sambourne's own cartoons for *Punch* magazine. Decorative china lines the shelves and early photographs fill the bathroom walls. Do not miss Sambourne's illustrations to Charles Kingsley's famed novel, *The Water-Babies,* in the bedroom upstairs.

All this is part of today's district of Holland Park. At the south end, a leafy residential enclave became home to wealthy artists and architects at the end of the 19th century, producing a crop of exotic houses. The most remarkable home in Holland Park is Frederick Lord Leighton's, designed by his friend George Aitchison in 1864–1866. It is London's first full expression of the aesthetic movement. The interior of **Leighton House** is a bachelor's indulgence typified by the lack of guest rooms. Red walls, ebonized wood, and gilt decorate the main rooms downstairs. Richly glazed tiles line the beautiful Arab Hall and staircase. ∎

Leighton House
🅰 Map p. 156
✉ 12 Holland Park Rd., W14
☎ 020 7602 3316
🕐 Closed Tues.
💲 $$
🚇 Tube: High Street Kensington or Holland Park
www.rbkc.gov.uk

18 Stafford Terrace
🅰 Map p. 156
☎ 020 7602 3316
🕐 Open Wed. & Sat.–Sun. by guided tour only
💲 $$$
🚇 Tube: High Street Kensington
www.rbkc.gov.uk

London's Markets

London has more than 340 markets of all sizes and themes, from Sunday's huge Petticoat Lane to Berwick Street's weekday produce market in Soho.

Portobello Road market offers clothing, antiques, food, and more.

Food

All the big wholesale markets need to be visited early. Smithfield Meat Market (see p. 66), the last wholesale fresh market remaining in central London, sells its bloody carcasses in the early weekday hours. Billingsgate fish market left the City and is now at West India Dock on the Isle of Dogs, and New Covent Garden Market still trades in fruit, flowers, and vegetables but has moved over the river to Nine Elms Lane in Vauxhall.

A destination recommended by many Londoners is the amazing array of food stalls at Borough Market, *(www.boroughmarket.org.uk),* south of the Thames in the shadow of Southwark Cathedral. Hundreds of vendors sell (and offer free samples of) fruit, cheese, spices, vegetables, fish, olives, sausages, fresh meat (including some exotic varieties such as boar, venison, and grouse), as well as prepared international foods for the noshing

such as Middle Eastern falafel, German wurst, Indian chutneys, and Greek fried halloumi cheese. The market is open Thursdays 11:00 a.m.–5:00 p.m., Fridays noon–6:00 p.m., and Saturdays 8:00 a.m.–5:00 p.m. It is busiest on Saturdays and can get packed; smart money arrives before 11:00 a.m. to beat some of the crowds.

Clothes, Antiques & Crafts

Other big markets specialize in clothing and antiques, such as Portobello Road on Saturdays (see page 166). Camden Lock Market, by the canal, thrives on the weekends (be prepared to mingle with 150,000 other shoppers), but its hundreds of stalls selling gifts, jewelry, books, food, and crafts are open all week. Several other markets branch out on Camden's side streets; Camden Stables Market, for one, has more than 700 stalls selling alternative fashions. The souvenir, clothes, and antique markets that now fill Covent Garden's buildings daily make up one of London's newest markets, established in the 1970s. The weekend market at Greenwich, which has echoes of the great market that was closed down last century, is down by the Thames on King William Walk and has an almost seaside feel to it. The whole atmosphere is fresh and lively, and stalls stocking clothes, antiques, books, and prints are complemented by the craft market in Bosun's Yard.

The best known large Sunday market is Petticoat Lane, where hundreds of stalls fill Middlesex and Wentworth Streets and the surrounding lanes to sell clothing of all kinds. Here, London's best East End street salesmen-entertainers run through their patter to gullible crowds. Vendors from nearby Brick Lane sell excellent Bengali and Indian food. A short walk away, Spitalfields Market survives in its old building.

Local Markets

Dotted across London, little local markets vary their stock to suit their customers' tastes and traditions. Berwick Street's weekday market just north of Shaftesbury Avenue in Soho dates back to the 1840s when the area was an Italian and French quarter, and its quality vegetables, herbs, and flowers balance the supplies sold in nearby Italian food shops. Chapel Market in

Islington has been lively for a century, serving the local population with no-nonsense food and basic household goods. Ridley Road market at Dalston is quite different: It has been thriving since the 1880s, but its injection of postwar Afro-Caribbean, Asian, and Turkish immigrants means such delicacies as live catfish are now on sale. Brixton Market is best for pure West Indian goods. Here, in the lanes around Brixton Underground station, you can find reggae and soul music shops, fish such as goat fish, smoked angera, and blue runner, Nasseri African fabrics, and calves' hooves.

Specialist Markets

For antiques, Camden Passage has a fine set of shops and stalls, with plenty of good restaurants nearby. Portobello has a similar mix. Bermondsey Market, held in Bermondsey Square on Fridays, has the largest and best value stalls, but means a 5:00 to 6:00 a.m. start for bargains, which are inspected by flashlight. Prices vary, and only the most knowledgeable will be able to compete with the dealers and the clients, who would be as at home bidding in Sotheby's auction rooms. Safer to pick up a painting along Bayswater Road on Sunday, or a coin at the Collector's Fair on Villiers Street on Saturday. And there are markets in the courtyards of St. James's Piccadilly on Friday and Saturday, or St. Martin-in-the-Fields any day except Sunday.

EXPERIENCE: Learn to Cook Seafood

Poach, grill, and pan-fry your way to culinary excellence under the guidance of expert fishmongers and chefs at the **Billingsgate Seafood Training School** at Billingsgate Fish Market (*Trafalgar Way, E14, tel 020 7517 3548, www.seafood training.org, $$$$$*). The school, located amid the largest selection of seafood in the United Kingdom, teaches students to select and prepare everything from trout to cuttlefish. Courses range from full-day affairs to two-hour evening classes and may include a market tour, preparation of several types of seafood, and at least one meal. Students often leave with extra food, so if your accommodations don't include a kitchen, opt for the shorter classes.

Notting Hill & Portobello Road

While Holland Park lured high society, the area to its north was developed with slightly lower aspirations to attract London's affluent Victorians. Farms, potteries, and piggeries were soon mere memory as pretty villas and terraces spread north. Today, Notting Hill is best known for its Portobello Road antiques market and the annual Caribbean carnival.

The Travel Bookshop in Notting Hill was featured in the 1999 movie *Notting Hill*.

Notting Hill &
Portobello Road
 Map p. 156

At the bottom of Notting Hill, Norlands Farm was transformed into the pretty, small-scale Norland Estate during the 1840s and '50s. Farther up, developer James Weller Ladbroke bought Notting Hill Farm, planning to create a utopian garden city of large villas with their own private gardens, which in turn opened onto communal gardens. When the estate was finished in 1870 it was London's most spacious, and its architecture was of unusually high quality. Handsome Lansdowne Road and Crescent, Stanley Crescent, and Ladbroke Square illustrate the achievement.

Portobello Road

Portobello Road slips northward down the side of, and in contrast to, the grandeur of Ladbroke Grove. It was once the farm track leading down to Porto Bello Farm. By the 1870s Gypsies were trading horses and herbs here and in the 1890s Saturday-night markets were established. The antique

Notting Hill Carnival

Every August Bank Holiday weekend, the streets of Notting Hill are one continuous Caribbean party. The Caribbean community grew here after World War II, when citizens of newly independent British Empire countries were given British citizenship. The immigrants replaced Londoners who had left for a suburban life. They held the first African-Caribbean street festival in the 1960s, evoking the Trinidad Carnival that envelops the island for two days before Ash Wednesday. Today, it is Europe's largest street festival, drawing a million people and filling the areas between Chepstow Road and Ladbroke Grove.

The action consists of music and parades and builds up over Saturday and Sunday. On Monday, dozens of bands play reggae, soul, hip-hop, Latin jazz, funk, and calypso in Powis Square, or tour the streets playing in open-back trucks. Trinidadian influence is in the steel bands—whose use of steel oil pans evolved in response to the colonial ban on playing drums—and the costume parades. These parades are spectacular, up to 200 people in each, all in fantastical costumes following themes such as African warriors, butterflies, and flowers; central characters may have costume extensions held up by wire frames. The best music and costumes win cash prizes. (See *www.thenottinghillcarnival.com* for details.)

INSIDER TIP:

If you must visit Portobello Road on a busy Saturday and want to find genuine bargains, go at 6 a.m., when the dealers are buying from each other.

—TIM JEPSON
National Geographic author

dealers that now make the street famous began to arrive in 1948, when Caledonian Market near King's Cross closed.

Today, the **Portobello Road market** *(www.portobelloroad.co.uk)* is one of Britain's longest and, when augmented by its Saturday stallholders, provides a daylong party of guaranteed fascination, noise, and color—and possibly a bargain or two.

At the end of Notting Hill, the established antique shops and stalls between Chepstow Villas and Lonsdale Road have quality, often rare, collectors items, with few bargains. The sharp-eyed and informed may have a better chance down the hill. Good food shops between Lonsdale and Lancaster Roads can restore strength.

Beyond the Westway flyover, the imaginative hunter may find secondhand clothes and bric-a-brac to give individual character to an outfit or a room. Golborne Road has a fruit and vegetable market, and the shops between Aklam Road and Oxford Gardens sell the latest street fashion, worn by stylish Londoners sitting in the neighborhood bars. Beyond that, find vendors with secondhand bicycles, new clothes, and household goods. ■

Prince Albert's Dream

South Kensington is the living legacy of one man, Prince Albert of Saxe-Coburg-Gotha. From the day of his marriage to Queen Victoria in 1840, he was her closest adviser and worked ceaselessly for his adopted country.

Prince Albert, Queen Victoria's consort, has a gilded memorial in Kensington Gardens.

provide free learning for all people. The plan was to have an avenue of colleges for the arts and sciences leading to a huge national gallery, with museums and learned societies, concert halls, and a garden beyond.

Albert's devotion to his project, soon known as "Albertopolis," was unstinting. Tragically, he died of typhoid in 1861. While the queen withdrew into seclusion, Prime Minister Benjamin Disraeli told a stunned public: "This German Prince has governed England for twenty-one years with a wisdom and energy such as none of our Kings have ever shown."

Nothing stopped Albert's dream, the biggest development for public use that London had yet seen. When the National Gallery refused to move, the Royal Albert Hall took its place in the scheme, and music and art colleges surrounded it. The Victoria & Albert Museum,

INSIDER TIP:

The Albert Memorial is stunning at night, when its bronze statue and marble figures seem to glow against the sky.

—LARRY PORGES
National Geographic Books editor

Albert's crowning achievement was the Great Exhibition of the World of Industry of All Nations, held in Hyde Park in 1851. It was a celebration of Victorian dynamism. Sir Joseph Paxton, once gardener to the Duke of Devonshire, designed a great cast-iron-and-glass building, nicknamed the Crystal Palace. In it, 100,000 exhibits were shown by 13,937 exhibitors, half of whom were from Britain and its empire. Conceived as a platform for and celebration of industrial enterprise worldwide, the exhibition ran from May to October and was visited by six million people, a third of Britain's population.

The exhibition's success, and its substantial profits, inspired Albert to an even more ambitious dream: a cultural campus that would

which Albert hoped would be of practical help to students, grew so fast that its art college became the separate Royal College of Art, and its science collections became the Science Museum. Meanwhile, the British Museum's natural history departments overflowed and were given space here; the Geological Museum arrived from St. James's in 1935, and was later absorbed by the Natural History Museum.

Victoria & Albert Museum (V&A)

The world's largest museum of decorative arts and design is encyclopedic. In fact, it is several museums in one. Primarily the national museum of art and design, it also includes the national collections of sculpture, watercolors, portrait miniatures, art photography, wallpaper, and posters, as well as the National Art Library. It has the best set of Italian sculpture outside Italy and the finest Indian decorative arts collection in the world.

The V&A began as a collection of plaster casts, engravings, and a few objects from the Great Exhibition. It was Prince Albert who, with art patron Henry Cole, conceived the idea of a museum of objects "representing the application of Fine Art to manufacture," to inspire British people. Cole, the first director, wanted a museum about design and craft in a commercial context, not craft for craft's sake. This is still the museum's philosophy today.

The humble museum with big ideas was first housed in wooden sheds, then in an engineer's iron-and-glass building known as the Brompton Boilers. It grew fast. While the keeper amassed quality objects for his students, gifts began to arrive: Sheepshanks's British paintings, the Bandinel Collection of pottery and porcelain, the Gherardini Collection of models for sculpture, and many more. Various rooms were built piecemeal to form the central quadrangle and the eastern courts, and Sir Aston Webb's slab of galleries was added to the front in 1899–1909. Whole departments later left to find space as V&A outposts or as independent museums, such as the Science Museum and the V&A Museum of Childhood.

The best of past and contemporary design was bought by, or given to, the museum. Some pieces were tiny, such as the Canning Jewel; others were vast—the Raphael Cartoons, for instance, and whole rooms, including the Duke of Norfolk's Music Room. Today, most of the 2,000 or so

EXPERIENCE:
V&A Programs

If the holdings in the V&A's extensive collection leave you wanting to know more, you can immerse yourself in the world of British design through the museum's wide variety of special programs, classes, and lectures. The eclectic series includes designers, writers, and other artists discussing their work; live presentations of music and poetry; practical workshops on everything from weaving tapestries to creating hand-printed silk scarves; and seminars and classes on important people and movements in the history of design, style, and art that range in length from an afternoon to a full year.

Some programs are free, but many have a fee ($$–$$$$$). Check out www.vam.ac.uk for complete information. Reservations can be made on the website or by phone at 020 7942 2211.

The Future at the V&A

The Victoria & Albert Museum is in the midst of an extensive, ten-year (and counting) renovation program to provide new exhibition spaces and facilities for visitors as well as to restore original architectural elements to historic galleries. Funded almost completely by private donors, FuturePlan work has so far refurbished dozens of galleries, at a cost to date of more than £120 million ($192 million).

So far, projects completed include the lovely John Madejski Garden at the rear of Level One, as well as a new museum café behind it. Recently reopened galleries include the renovated Cast Courts (containing plaster copies of monumental sculptures) in Rooms 46 and 46b; the V&A's collection of more than 3,000 gems in the jewelry collection (Rooms 91–93); and the new exhibition space for 14th- to 16th-century European stained glass and sculpture in Rooms 16a and 25–27, which opened in 2010.

And it doesn't stop there. Projects still under construction include a furniture gallery, featuring British and international pieces from the 15th century onward, slated to open in early 2013, and a new courtyard and entrance onto Exhibition Road, which should be finished by 2014.

Victoria & Albert Museum

- 🅰 Map p. 157
- ✉ Cromwell Road, SW7
- ☎ 020 7942 2211
- 🕐 Check website for schedule during construction
- 💲 Charge for some exhibitions
- Ⓜ Tube: South Kensington

www.vam.ac.uk

annual acquisitions for the design, prints, and drawings departments are contemporary, and the museum regularly commissions silver, furniture, and other pieces. In addition, galleries are constantly being added; recent ones include ceramics, glass, and photography.

Just some of the museum's 4.5 million objects are exhibited in more than 170 galleries arranged on seven levels around four courts and organized by five main themes: Europe, Asia, Materials and Techniques, Modern, and Exhibition.

Basically, there are two types of rooms: art and design galleries, such as Europe 1600–1700, where objects of a type are exhibited in their cultural context; and materials and techniques galleries, such as silver, where objects of one material or type are displayed to show their form, function, and technique.

For those who know what they want to see, a combination of the map, the list of galleries, and a keen sense of direction will be enough. For those who feel overwhelmed before they start, here are some interesting stops on an easy route (with room numbers indicated, as marked on the free museum maps available at the information desk).

The Trail

Note: The museum is undergoing a ten-year refurbishment (see sidebar above). Achievements so far include the John Madejski Garden, the Sacred Silver and Stained Glass gallery in Rooms 83–84, and the Islamic Middle East gallery in Room 42. Temporary closures may affect this trail.

From the entrance hall, turn right and go through Rooms 50a and 50b, part of the museum's impressive **Medieval and Renaissance** collection. Then turn left from Room 50b (through the Korean gallery), into Rooms 46 and 46B, crowded with Victorian casts, where Trajan's Column and Michelangelo's "David" have inspired countless students; here, too, is the museum's collection of splendid fakes.

Backtrack through the Korean and Chinese art in Rooms 47g and 47f and turn right into the **T. T. Tsui Gallery of Chinese Art** in Room 44. Next door is the **Toshiba Gallery of Japanese Art** (Room 45); one of the museum's best buys was 12,000 woodcuts in 1886. Down the steps, turn left for the Hintze sculpture collection in Rooms 24–21a before turning left again to Room 41, the **Nehru Gallery of Indian Art,** where a tiny fraction of the Indian collection is on show, usually including some exquisite miniature paintings and some fine textiles. Southeast Asian objects fill the corridor Rooms 47a and 47b, which lead to the **hall of fashion,** Room 40, a feast of European costumes from the permanent collection and temporary exhibits from the 16th century to today.

Across the corridor, stroll through the older rooms that surround the **John Madejski Garden,** pausing in Rooms 17–20 to enjoy the collection of Buddhist sculpture. Now visit the **Canon Photography Gallery** (Room 38) on the east side of the garden. The display has some of the museum's 300,000 photographs that date back to an 1839 daguerreotype of Trafalgar Square by M. De Ste. Croix.

Three more stops complete this introduction. The first is a wander through the stunning, renovated **British Galleries**

upstairs, feasting your eyes on a jewel Francis Drake gave Elizabeth I, Huguenot silver, and whole rooms saved from Jacobean and Georgian London houses. The second is to go up the **Ceramic Staircase,** decorated with Minton tiles, to find the dazzling national collection of English silver. And the third is the **Gilbert Collection** of gold, silver, portrait miniatures, and mosaics that moved to the V&A from Somerset House in 2008. ∎

Two Victorian rooms in the V&A display plaster casts of famous sculptures, such as Michelangelo's "David."

Science Museum

The most unscientific person will be excited by Britain's National Museum of Science and Industry, where learning often demands more active participation than merely reading labels. In 1909 it became fully independent of the V&A, and in 1928 completed its move into Richard Allison's new building. His department-store format, with big windows and large, simple spaces, has been ideal. As the collection has grown, there is flexibility to display the full thrill of scientific discoveries through the ages, and it is easy to find one's way around.

The National Museum of Science and Industry has plenty of hands-on activities for kids.

Science Museum

- 🗺 Map p. 157
- ✉ Exhibition Rd., SW7
- ☎ 0870 870 4868 or 020 7942 4000
- 💲 Charge for special sections
- 🚇 Tube: South Kensington

www.science museum.org.uk

Today, some of the 200,000 items are displayed in 70 galleries on 7 floors covering 8 acres (3.2 ha) of floor space, telling stories of inventions and discoveries that have affected our lives, from the plastic bag and the telephone to the offshore oil rig and the airplane. And yet the arrangement is straightforward: Lower galleries are geared to young people and are often more crowded; upper ones are dedicated to a more sophisticated level of interest. This trail explores every floor, seeking out one or two highlights on each.

The Trail

At the main entrance, there is information on the day's events and demonstrations, with a useful introduction to science on the mezzanine. Here, too, is the Dana Centre schedule for debate on scientific issues.

The ground floor's **Energy Hall** includes James Watt's steam engines and models of early locomotives. **Exploring Space** provides a history of rockets from 10th-century China until today. **Making the Modern World**—a family favorite—explains landmark modern inventions from the Ford Model T to the brain scanner. **The Garden** exhibition in the basement satisfies young children's natural curiosity.

Now go to the **Wellcome Wing,** where state-of-the-art galleries include the **IMAX 3-D cinema**, **Antenna,** which presents the latest science news on interactive screens, and **Pattern Pod,** an educational play area for children under 8 years of age.

On the first floor, gas, agriculture, meteorology, surveying, and time measurement are tackled at the back. With plenty of hands-on equipment, **Telecommunications** presents the history of electronic communications, from the first electric telegraphs and telephones to wireless technologies. **Challenge of Materials** explores the world of materials using installations, audiovisual displays, and interactive computers. In the Wellcome Wing at the other end of the floor, the **Who Am I?** exhibition challenges young visitors to think about their own personalities, use of language, and the other workings of their brains through artwork, quizzes, and interactive displays.

Up on the second floor, you can see how the paper that fills our lives is made and how it was imprinted before computer typesetting confined metal type to museums. Other subjects, which need more scientific interest and application to appreciate, include chemistry, measuring, lighting, and nuclear physics and power. Sections on petroleum and computing lead to a large space devoted to navigation, marine engineering, docks, and diving—with lots of superb model ships.

From here, steps lead up to the third floor. This is all about flight: **Flight** has hands-on exhibits for testing the principles of flight, while a hangar full of aircraft includes Amy Johnson's *Jason,* in which she flew to Australia in 1930. A walk down the hallway leads to the museum's elaborate flight simulators, basically motion rides, for which a fee is charged.

INSIDER TIP:

The museum's "Who Am I?" exhibit makes science personal: You can see your face age and hear your voice as from the opposite sex.

—RACHAEL JACKSON
National Geographic contributor

The other end of this floor includes the **Health Matters** area, where vaccinations are explained, and the popular **Launchpad,** an interactive gallery that demonstrates the science of lights, sound, and energy. Roaming the exhibit are live "Explainers" to answer visitors' questions.

The smaller fourth and fifth floors cover medical history with **Glimpses of Medical History.** Upstairs, the undervisited Wellcome Museum's gallery is a magpie hoard: a mummified head, African fetish objects, George Washington's false teeth, Napoleon's toothbrush, and more. ■

Natural History Museum

Both the collection—consisting of more than 68 million specimens and one million books and manuscripts—and the magnificent building could be daunting. But this museum has made its exhibits and knowledge highly accessible and exciting for the general public without sacrificing the prime job of informing and educating. The famous dinosaur exhibition explains what we can learn from these ancient bones about the evolution of modern animals.

Visitors to the Natural History Museum's Central Hall swirl around the reproduction of a Diplodocus skeleton.

The Building

The building is as remarkable as its contents. When in 1882 the natural history collection of the British Museum (see pp. 134–138), including pieces from Sir Hans Sloane's collection, came to the burgeoning South Kensington cultural campus, it needed a suitable home. This was realized in the cathedral-like proportions of Alfred Waterhouse's Romanesque building, whose towers, spires, arches, and columns look to the churches of the Rhineland. The iron-and-steel framework is covered with cream, blue, and honey-colored terra-cotta, which introduced color into dirty Victorian London.

The Layout

The museum has recently been reorganized into four distinct color-coded zones.

The **Green Zone** includes the impressive main Central Hall, accessed from the Cromwell Road entrance, dominated by the 85-foot-long (26 m) replica skeleton of a Diplodocus. Spreading east from the Central Hall, the rest of the Green Zone highlights fossils, minerals, primates, ecology, insects, and birds, including a model of the extinct Dodo, and the place of humans in evolution.

At the end of the 20th century,

the Natural History Museum formally amalgamated with the Geological Museum next door. The geological collection, now called the **Red Zone,** tells the story of the Earth itself and the natural forces that shape it, from a delicate 330-million-year-old fern fossil to the reenactment of an earthquake in Japan in 1995. The Red Zone connects to the eastern end of the Green Zone and can also be entered directly from Exhibition Road.

West of the Central Hall lies the **Blue Zone,** which gets a lot of foot traffic from its galleries featuring dinosaurs; fishes, amphibians, and reptiles; marine invertebrates; and mammals, including a 75-year-old model of a massive blue whale, which at the time was one on the mystery creatures of the deep.

Head west from the Blue Zone to reach the **Orange Zone** and its **Darwin Centre,** which opened in 2002 and houses the museum's research facilities and specimen collection. The best way to see the Darwin Centre's zoological specimens (in the delightfully Victorian-named Zoology Spirit Building, after the industrial alcohol used to preserve the creatures) is to sign up for a guided tour. Lasting about 30 minutes, visitors get a closer look at some of the museum's vast store of animal specimens, including some kept in tanks, see the laboratories, and talk to scientists.

In 2009, the center expanded and the **"Cocoon"** opened; here you can take a self-guided tour of some of the 30 million insect and plant specimens in the museum's extensive collection.

The Trail

Plans are afoot to shift galleries around over the next few years, so be sure to pick up the free museum map when you arrive.

Start in the vast **Central Hall,** where Waterhouse's painted ceiling and zoo of terra-cotta animals, birds, flowers, and reptiles running up the columns and hiding in the arches is the setting for the famous Diplodocus skeleton.

INSIDER TIP:

Explore the atmospheric balconies around the Central Hall. Specimens there range from diamonds to a slice of a Sequoia.

—ESZTER DOBOS
*Natural History Museum
visit planner*

Turn left, westward, and follow **Dinosaur Way** to the dinosaurs in the Blue Zone. Here are bones from creatures that roamed the Earth for 160 million years until their extinction 65 million years ago. They come in all varieties, and from these skeletons we can understand their lives—whether they lived alone, fought by charging like a ram, or hunted in packs.

Across Dinosaur Way, the **"Human Biology"** gallery takes a closer look at a recent development, human beings. Models show how the memory works and the development of a baby from a single cell; optical illusions explain the relation between sight and knowledge.

Now cross the Central Hall to **"Fossil Way,"** which is lined on either side with fossils of marine reptiles, from tiny ammonites found in Jurassic rocks in Dorset to sea dragons. To the left is a kid-popular gallery devoted to **"Creepy Crawlies":** insects, spiders, crustaceans, and centipedes, whose highly adaptable nature, sophisticated social systems, and defense mechanisms have helped them survive the eons. The last gallery at the end of Fossil Way explains our **"Ecology":** How we are linked to one another

INSIDER TIP:

Join a free Nature Live talk in the Attenborough Studio. It's an amazing opportunity to meet the scientists in person.

—ESZTER DOBOS
*Natural History Museum
visit planner*

and how crucial air, soil, sunlight, energy, and water are to survival. Across from Ecology, the **"Birds"** gallery seems untouched by time, with several specimens (and specimen cases) dating to the 1880s.

Return to the Central Hall. From here, stairs lead up to the first floor and the story of Charles Darwin's theory of human evolution. Look for the plaster cast of the **fossil of Ida,** a creature that emerged just after a critical split

in the human evolutionary tree about 47 million years ago. One branch led to lemurs and bushbabies, while the other headed off to evolve into primates. Nearby, the **"Tree"** gallery features a super-thin cross-section of the entire length of a 200-year-old tree, installed in 2009 to celebrate the 200th anniversary of Darwin's birth and representing the ever-branching tree of life he theorized. This area also contains galleries devoted to plants around the world, minerals, and meteorites, and offers great views down onto Central Hall and its decoration.

"Earth Hall," in the Red Zone, is the big introduction to the Earth galleries, focusing on the planet itself. Displays of specimens line the gallery, including a piece of the moon and another of soft graphite, which is chemically identical to hard diamonds.

Then take the escalator on a journey through a vast iron, zinc, and copper globe. Upstairs, **"The Power Within"** chronicles the restless surface of the Earth. Here, the forces that propel change in the Earth are considered, resulting in such disasters as Mount Pinatubo's 1991 volcanic eruption and Kobe's 1995 earthquake. A free earthquake simulator brings these awesome experiences to life. To end, the visitor is reassuringly given the power to polish rocks, change the direction of rivers, and alter the Earth's climate, but a poignant exhibit on the ground floor (**"Earth Today and Tomorrow"**) shows how humans are wasting the planet's non-renewable natural resources. ■

Four London neighborhoods and two favorite institutions: Harrods in Knightsbridge and Tate Britain in Pimlico

Chelsea, Belgravia & Knightsbridge

A statue of a Chelsea Pensioner in his red uniform sits outside the Royal Hospital Chelsea.

Chelsea, Belgravia & Knightsbridge

It was when the trendsetting Prince Regent became George IV in 1820 and began to remodel Buckingham Palace that developers recognized the promise of this area. Open fields and marshy but drainable land lay right next to the palace. Soon bargeloads of building materials were being unloaded along this stretch of the Thames. So began Belgravia. This, together with the Great Exhibition of 1851 and the development of South Kensington's museums and upmarket housing, stimulated the creation of Knightsbridge.

Chelsea

The most interesting area is Chelsea, which had been a favorite aristocratic country retreat from London since Tudor times, when manor houses set in spacious orchards grew up around a fishing village. King William and Queen Mary chose Chelsea for their Royal Hospital in the next decade, and Sir Hans Sloane bought Chelsea Manor in 1712 and made it the repository for his collection (see p. 134).

Later, 19th-century Chelsea attracted writers and artists, from Thomas Carlyle to Oscar Wilde. Architects returned to a more vernacular Queen Anne style using red brick. First adopted for houses along the Embankment, this style was chosen by the Cadogan family when, in the 1870s, they laid out Cadogan Square and its surroundings. More recently, the King's Road, running through the hearts of Chelsea and Fulham, was reborn in the 1960s as a catwalk for the avant garde, while the terraces off it, built as mass-produced housing for artisans, became the immaculate, if cramped, homes of successful City businesspeople.

Belgravia

Belgravia's story is shorter, but spectacular. With Mayfair and St. James's overflowing, this was the last London project to be developed by the rich (the Grosvenors) for the rich. Begun in 1824, the scheme centered on Belgrave Square, where the Regency style was taken to new heights. It was here that architect Thomas Cubitt brought success and quality to a wobbling project; such success that the Grosvenors

Carlyle's House

NOT TO BE MISSED:

Christopher Wren's magnificent
Royal Hospital Chelsea **180**

Taking a meditative stroll among
the herbs and rare plants at the
Chelsea Physic Garden **181**

Pimlico and Belgravia's Regency
squares and majestic curving
building facades **182–183**

Browsing Harrods' 540,000 square
feet (50,000 sq m) of retail
space **184–185**

Exploring 500 years of British art at
Tate Britain **186–188**

themselves have left Mayfair for Belgravia,
and Belgrave Square accommodates a clutch
of foreign missions.

Knightsbridge

Knightsbridge, meanwhile, was boosted
not only by the Great Exhibition but by the
building of Belgravia. The first village on
the road that led west out of London from
Mayfair was transformed from fields into a
densely packed area whose heartbeat was,
and is, retail commerce. Today, the heart of
Knightsbridge is Harrods, whose international
shoppers are content to feel they have visited London if they have shopped there. ■

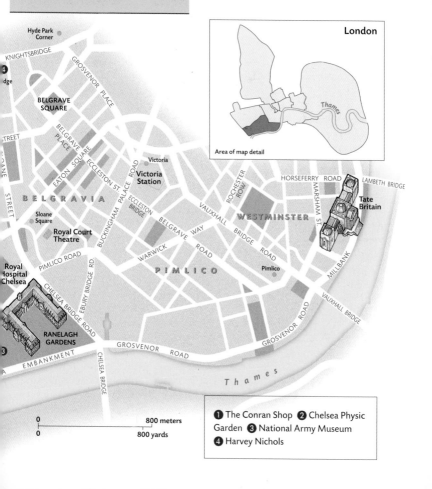

London

Area of map detail

0   800 meters
0   800 yards

❶ The Conran Shop ❷ Chelsea Physic
Garden ❸ National Army Museum
❹ Harvey Nichols

Chelsea

When the Scottish historian and philosopher Thomas Carlyle (1795–1881) chose to live in Chelsea in 1834, the lanes that are now so sought after were unfashionable.

A statue of King Charles II stands proud in front of the Royal Hospital Chelsea.

Royal Hospital Chelsea

- 🅐 Map p. 179
- ✉ Royal Hospital Road, SW3
- ☎ 020 7881 5200
- 🕐 Open 10–12 a.m. & 2–4 p.m. Mon.–Sat.
- 💲 Donation
- 🚇 Tube: Sloane Square

www.chelsea pensioners.org.uk

Chelsea Flower Show

- ☎ 0845 260 5000
- 💲 $$$–$$$$$, reservations required

www.rhs.org.uk

Royal Hospital Chelsea

First views of London buildings can be stunning. For the Royal Hospital, designed by Sir Christopher Wren for Charles II to house almost 500 army veterans, and still home to red-coated Chelsea Pensioners (residents) today, there are two such views: from a leafless, wintertime Royal Avenue off King's Road, or from a boat on the river, looking up the lawns to the main river-facing facade.

Wren broke new ground with this, his first large-scale secular work. Inspired by Louis XIV's Les Invalides in Paris, it became a blueprint for institutional buildings in Europe and America: a central hall and chapel flanked by two side courts for the dormitories. The stables were added in 1814 by Sir John Soane, while he was Clerk of Works to the hospital.

On the garden facade, benches in Figure Court overlook Grinling Gibbons's bronze of Charles II and the formal gardens that once ended at the water. The more informal gardens to the left were, from 1742 to 1803, the infamous Ranelagh pleasure gardens.

Inside the hospital are three magnificent rooms. In the paneled Great Hall, today's pensioners dine beneath Verrio's painting of Charles II. In the chapel, they pray in box pews amid decoration that includes Sebastiano Ricci's "Resurrection" altarpiece.

National Army Museum

Next to the western flank of the Royal Hospital Chelsea stands the upbeat National Army Museum *(Royal Hospital Rd., SW3, tel 020 7730 0717, www.national-army-museum .ac.uk)* The permanent galleries explore the army's role in British history from 1066 on and also display works from the museum's impressive art collection. A rich array of temporary exhibits highlights the museum's extensive holdings of artifacts from the reaches of the old British Empire.

The army museum also hosts special events, celebrity speakers on a wide range of topics, and features Kids' Zones for family-friendly activities.

INSIDER TIP:

Just a short walk from the Royal Hospital, Elizabeth Street is a focus for a wide range of excellent specialty stores.

—TIM JEPSON
National Geographic author

Carlyle's House

Despite its then unfashionable location, Carlyle relished his "old-fashioned" street and his "most massive, roomy, sufficient old house" at 24 Cheyne Row.

Today, like so many house-museums, the personality of its owner still pervades it. Carlyle would wander the house and quiet back garden in his dressing gown, smoking hat, and pipe. Here the intellectual, famous after his account of the French Revolution was published, and his witty wife would receive John Stuart Mill in the drawing room, Dickens and Browning in the parlor, and Darwin or Thackeray in the back dining room. Carlyle lived here for 47 years, and his ghost seems to haunt the garden and its vines.

EXPERIENCE:
Chelsea Flower Show

Immerse yourself in all things botanical at the Royal Horticultural Society's (RHS) annual spectacle, held in and around huge marquees erected in the Royal Hospital's gardens. For a week in late May, Chelsea's streets are crowded with plant-minded people. Nurseries and plantsmen, garden designers, and manufacturers of gardening equipment exhibit their triumphs, from a new rose to a repellent for slugs. Visitors can glean ideas or just enjoy the show's profusion of perfect blooms. Check the RHS website *(www.rhs.org.uk/Shows-Events)* for the public access days.

Chelsea Physic Garden

Carlyle undoubtedly visited this walled garden located a mere two minutes' walk from his house. Founded in 1673 by the Society of Apothecaries to grow plants for medical study, the 4-acre (1.6 ha) garden was stocked with specimens cultivated for the first time in England. Today, with its herbs and exotic trees, the garden remains a place of serious study as well as a peaceful haunt for visitors. ∎

Carlyle's House

◭ Map p. 178

✉ 24 Cheyne Row, SW3

☎ 020 7352 7087

🕐 Open Wed.–Sun. 11 a.m.–5 p.m. March–Oct.

$ $$

🚇 Tube: Sloane Square

www.nationaltrust .org.uk

Chelsea Physic Garden

◭ Map p. 178

✉ 66 Royal Hospital Road, SW3; entrance on Swan Walk

☎ 020 7352 5646

🕐 Closed Sat., Mon.–Tues., & Nov.–March

$ $$$

🚇 Tube: Sloane Square

www.chelseaphysic garden.co.uk

Belgravia & Pimlico

With Britain enjoying an economic boom and George IV rebuilding Buckingham Palace, the 2nd Earl of Grosvenor focused on his 400 undeveloped acres south of Hyde Park. Over this marshy scrubland, notorious for its highwaymen and duels, he created a 200-acre (81 ha) estate that stole the limelight from his 100-acre (41 ha) Mayfair estate. Georgian brick, simplicity, and modest scale gave way to high Regency stucco. Thus Belgravia was born, a suburb for the very grand. Soon society moved west to take up residence there, Knightsbridge and South Kensington moved upscale to meet it, and Chelsea was linked to the continuous London sprawl.

The elegant stucco facades of Belgravia are exemplified in the buildings of Cadogan Place.

Belgravia

The master plan had a traditional square (Belgrave) surrounded by a network of streets, Georgian in concept but Regency in scale. Three big developers took on the site. Two went bankrupt; the third, Thomas Cubitt (see sidebar opposite), made a fortune. Work began in 1824 and continued for 30 years. Cubitt, backed by three Swiss bankers, took the lease on Belgrave Square and employed George Basevi as architect. The square was an instant social success: Dukes and duchesses moved into the palatial mansions and held glittering parties in their first-floor ballrooms. Work continued. Soon Cubitt had added Upper Belgrave Street, Chester Square, and Eaton Place (where he had his offices).

To appreciate Belgravia's magnificence, take a walk around these awe-inspiring streets and squares. From Sloane Street, walk east on Pont Street and Chesham Street, past Cadogan Place's stucco. Turn left into Belgrave Mews, once the stables for the grand houses in the square in front and now converted into

Thomas Cubitt

London's most successful developer in the early 19th century was Thomas Cubitt. Born in 1788 near Norwich, he revolutionized the building industry and, with a mixture of commercial acuteness and bold imagination, oversaw a series of large construction projects across the breadth of London.

As a young man, he worked as a ship's joiner on a voyage to India, making enough money to start his own business on his return. By 1815, the 25-year-old Cubitt had recognized that contracting each building trade as needed was not the most efficient way to work. So at his Gray's Inn Road workshops he employed a full set of laborers and craftsmen on a permanent wage, creating London's first modern building firm. The need to keep these workers busy encouraged his hugely successful career as a speculative builder.

Cubitt's London work took off in Bloomsbury, where he laid out Gordon Square, Endsleigh Place, and Tavistock Square. When the Grosvenor family developed Belgravia, he moved into the big time. He crowned his career with Pimlico, a daring piece of speculation. In Belgravia, Pimlico, and the government project that created Battersea Park, Cubitt raised the low-lying land and firmed up the clay by using the earth that was being excavated from the great docks in the East End, in which he was heavily involved. Meanwhile, he baked his bricks on site. This rags-to-riches builder also fought for the improvement of London's drainage system and the creation of open spaces for public use.

---

attractive (and pricey) little houses, to find Halkin Place leading into the grandeur of Belgrave Square.

Turn left and walk the sweep of Wilton Crescent, which will bring you back to Belgrave Square. On the opposite side, Upper Belgrave Street leads to magnificent Eaton Square.

Today, foreign embassies and high-flying international entrepreneurs fill Belgravia houses and streets, along with a sprinkling of old British aristocrats.

Pimlico

The dry, formal atmosphere of Belgravia is quite different from Pimlico's, where Londoners step out of less opulent houses to join their lively community in Tachbrook Street's market and Warwick Way's restaurants.

INSIDER TIP:

Check out the retail enclave, Pimlico Green, best known for the food emporium and café Daylesford Organic (44b Pimlico Road).

—TIM JEPSON
National Geographic author

Pimlico was Thomas Cubitt's own project. After years of negotiation, Cubitt finally persuaded the Grosvenors to lease him the land south of the canal, today cut off by Victoria Station. On this land, he laid out two squares, Eccleston and Warwick, set on terraced streets of houses. ■

Harrods & the Knightsbridge Shops

The most devoted shopper can no more "do" Harrods than the most curious art lover can "do" the British Museum. The world's most famous store is enormous. Its 300 departments on seven floors spread over 20 acres. Every day, 4,000 staff serve 35,000 customers and take in around £1.5 ($2.4) million.

The vast, landmark department store Harrods is lit by thousands of bulbs at night.

Harrods

- 🅰 Map p. 178
- ✉ 87–135 Brompton Rd., SW1
- ☎ 020 7730 1234
- 🚇 Tube: Knightsbridge

www.harrods.com

It all started when Charles Henry Harrod, a tea merchant, opened a grocery shop in the hamlet of Knightsbridge in 1849, bringing in about £20 (equivalent to around $38) a week. Two years later, the Great Exhibition brought plenty of trade and, as Knightsbridge began to expand and move up the social scale, business boomed. Charles's son, another Charles, took over in 1861, rebuilt, and soon quintupled his takings. After a devastating fire in 1883, he simply informed his customers that their deliveries would be delayed "a day or two." Harrods' service was established. When Richard Burbidge took over the shop in 1894, he created the slogan "Harrods serves the world." In addition, he installed London's first escalator in 1898.

Burbidge also rebuilt. The pink, domed Edwardian building we know today was designed by Stephens and Munt and built between 1901 and 1905. Louis de Blanc added the back extension in the 1920s. The Food Halls were decorated with W. J. Neatby's mosaic friezes and tiles. Burbidge's store has always been a royal favorite: George V made him a baron for his service.

Many visitors to London feel their trip is incomplete without a Harrods' session, and most are not content merely to window-shop at the 80 displays or gaze at the thousands of light bulbs illuminating the building; 40 percent of all sales go abroad, packed in the now famous moss-green bags. Londoners may say they can do without Harrods, but many go there for something—perhaps the patient children's hairdresser, or the health juice bar, or the massive greeting card department, and almost always their route will go via the Food Halls to pick up some perfectly ripened cheeses, fine patisserie, or delicious terrines.

To go inside Harrods is truly to enter the ultimate self-contained retail city. It has everything a dedicated shopper needs to survive the day, or several days. Most entrances have an information desk, which supplies events information and the essential free map of the store. Bars and restaurants are scattered throughout the store. Departments range from beauty parlor, pet shop, and bridal gowns to London's best toy department, Harrods own brand shop, a sweet-smelling Perfume Hall, a ticket agency that can get tickets for almost anything officially sold out, a choice of more than 150 whiskeys, and the irresistible Food Halls.

Naturally, other retailers hoping to benefit from Harrods' shoppers set up nearby. Using profits from the Great Exhibition's visitors, Benjamin Harvey's daughter brought an experienced silk buyer, Colonel Nichols, to the family drapery business. The long-term result, **Harvey Nichols,** is a paradise for women: floors of designer clothes and accessories topped by the Fifth Floor, a stylish food hall, bar, and restaurants.

The Harvey Nichols store stands a few hundred yards east of Harrods at the corner of Sloane Street, the site of a solid string of international designer clothing stores that rivals New and Old Bond Streets. Other recent designer shop arrivals fill Brompton Road. A honeypot of home furnishing and fashion shops surround the **Conran Shop** in the decorated Michelin building at Brompton Cross, where Brompton Road meets Walton Street and Fulham Road.

None of the competition has a building to compare with Harrods, but several entice customers with inspired modern structures. Eva Jiricna's signature staircase, cable balustrades, and polished white plaster walls are in the remodeled **Joseph** chain of shops, including 16 Sloane Street. ∎

Harrods Trivia

Harrods has an unparalleled shopping legacy, with a storied retail history going back more than 160 years. As a savvy customer, you might indeed know that the store contains a wine shop, a men's grooming center, and more than two dozen restaurants. But did you also know...?:

• Harrods sells airplanes through its Harrods Aviation subsidiary. The store first began selling airplanes (and accompanying flying lessons) in 1919.
• More than 11,000 lights illuminate the store each night. This practice began in 1959 when Harrods started dressing itself up for Christmas.

• In the early 1900s, Harrods had its own Ladies Club where female customers could write letters, leave messages for each other, or simply relax in luxury.
• Harrods once had its own embalming and funeral service. Established in 1900, some of its "clients" included psychologist Sigmund Freud (d. 1939) and British prime minister Clement Attlee (d. 1967).
• The store offers safety deposit boxes on the lower ground floor for customers to stash their cash and jewelry. The service started in 1896 and is still available today.
• A memorial to the staff members who were killed in World War I stands near Door 3 (leading to Basil Street).

Tate Britain

A century after it opened in 1897, the Tate split in two. Its superb national collection of British art from 1500 to the present day—the foremost collection of its kind—fills the renovated and expanded buildings here on the north bank of the Thames. Its modern international collection is now housed in the separate Tate Modern at Bankside in Southwark on the south bank (see p. 104). Tate Boat water taxis ply between the two. The Tate has two outposts: one in Liverpool and the other in St. Ives, Cornwall.

Art in Tate Britain ranges from the 16th through the 21st centuries.

The Site & the Building

The story of the Tate begins with controversy. Henry Tate, an 18th-century sugar millionaire, led a public movement demanding a showcase for British art. Tate himself offered the nation his collection of Victorian paintings and some money to pay for housing it. The government dithered before grudgingly accepting Tate's offer. There was then a wide debate on its location: South Kensington, Blackfriars, or Millbank, whose land became available first. Tate's money paid for Sidney Smith's building. The new gallery replaced the octagonal Millbank Prison, built between 1812 and 1821.

Smith's neoclassical facade, entrance hall, and rotunda were completed for the opening. Many additions followed. The most significant were nine galleries added in 1899 and the central cupola and sculpture galleries given by the art dealer Joseph Duveen and his son in 1937. One small but delightful addition in 1983 was the Whistler Restaurant, where Rex Whistler's landscape mural called "Expedition in Pursuit of Rare Meats" (1926–1927) keeps art and food in harmony.

Stirling and Wilford's Clore Gallery opened in 1987 to house the Turner Bequest. The artist left some 300 paintings, 20,000 drawings, and nearly 300 sketchbooks to the nation. Eight top-lit galleries admit natural light without damaging Turner's fragile watercolors.

The Centenary Development increased gallery space by a third and renewed Henry Tate's vision of a showcase for British art. The foundation collection had grown quickly since 1916, when the Tate was given the additional responsibility of forming the national collection of international modern art (which is now at Bankside).

The Collection

Tate Britain holds nearly 3,500 paintings, plus prints—including those belonging to the Turner Bequest—and sculptures. Visitors can walk though a new chronological display of 20th-century art along the western side of the building, view more than 120 significant works from the 16th to the 19th centuries in the central gallery space, and explore other galleries and temporary exhibitions. Following are some stars that may be on view.

The earliest work on display is John Bettes's "A Man in a Black Cap" (1545). The artist is said to have spent several years doing decorative work for Henry VIII's court in the 1530s.

Later, the 18th century saw British painters responding to the Enlightenment. Look for George Stubbs's "Reapers" (1785) and "Haymakers" (1785), Sir Joshua Reynolds's "Three Ladies Adorning a Term of Hymen" (1773), and several Thomas Gainsborough works, including the delightful "Rev. John Chafy Playing the Violoncello in a Landscape" (1750–1752). Also check out William Hogarth's "The Painter and his Pug" (1745). The artist, England's first great native-born painter, is said to have included his pug dog, Trump, in the self-portrait to represent his own pugnacious personality.

INSIDER TIP:

Explore art after hours on the first Friday of every month, when Tate Britain keeps its doors open to 10 p.m. to host Late at Tate.

—AIMÉE TAYLOR
Tate information assistant

Nineteenth-century British painting developed in several directions, and the Tate has examples of each. The great visionary poet and painter William Blake is represented by his illustrations for Dante's *Divine Comedy* and others. Several paintings by John Constable include the well-loved "Flatford Mill" (1816–1817). Pre-Raphaelite paintings include many of the best-known: John Millais's "Ophelia" (1851–1852), William Frith's "The Derby Day" (1856–1858), and William

Tate Britain

▲ Map p. 179

✉ Millbank, SW1; secondary entrance on Atterbury Street. The Clore Gallery has its own entrance.

☎ 020 7887 8888 Information: 020 7887 8008

$ Charge for temporary exhibitions

🚇 Tube: Pimlico

www.tate.org.uk

Holman Hunt's "The Awakening Conscience" (1853). Look for John William Waterhouse's "The Lady of Shalott" (1888), inspired by the Alfred Tennyson poem of the same name.

This diversity and originality continued into the 20th century. Stanley Spencer's mystical paintings include "The Woolshop" (1939). Works by Francis Bacon are equally powerful.

More recently, the Tate's remit to buy contemporary British art has, inevitably, generated controversy given the nature of some such work (bricks, sliced-up animals, and so on). Much of the gallery's art was questioned when the gallery acquired it. Looking at works by Anthony Caro, Richard Hamilton, and David Hockney, now classics, it is hard to understand the fuss. The same is true of Edouardo Paolozzi, Frank Auerbach, Lucian Freud, and Richard

Long, as well as Bridget Riley's black-and-white geometry. Future visitors must judge purchases of the still-controversial Damien Hirst.

In addition to modern art, the Tate's collection of works on paper ranges from 18th-century watercolors to postwar prints. There are also good examples of Britain's preeminent achievement in sculpture in the 20th century, notably by Henry Moore and Barbara Hepworth.

Tate Britain has two important spaces devoted to temporary exhibitions. The museum runs and exhibits the annual Turner Prize (see p. 41) and the Tate Triennial, showcasing art made in Britain today. The Tate also recently dedicated some of its gallery space to "in-focus" displays, which highlight pieces not usually displayed to the public and showcase new acquisitions and work conducted by specialists. ■

Gillian Ayres's "Phaethon" (1990) is among Tate Britain's many modern works.

Elegant houses and their parks, Kew botanical gardens, and Hampton Court Palace, as seductive now as they were centuries ago

West London

Fuschias at Kew Gardens

West London

From Tudor times until the 20th century, the Thames was the principal highway for escaping the city. Kings, queens, aristocrats, and merchants wound their way up the river to reach their country estates. More modest Londoners boarded pleasure boats for day trips upstream to the taverns strung along the waterside at Chiswick, Kew, and Richmond. Most of the splendid buildings were built alongside the Thames, or within easy reach of it. Even today, by far the most pleasant way to reach them is by boat (see p. 52).

Though now surrounded by urban sprawl, these one-time rural estates have preserved pockets of green space for Londoners.

As the Thames begins to turn southward (see map p. 48), large patches of parkland, some wild, some tamed, lie on either bank. Inside the curve, there are the wide open spaces of Barnes Common and the adjoining Putney Lower Common. Together, Wimbledon Common and Putney Heath make up London's largest common, 1,060 protected acres (429 ha) of rough grassland, with heather and gorse bushes, oak and birch woodland, wildflowers, and many bird species. Farther upstream, the 2,358 acres (954 ha) of Richmond Park make it the largest of London's royal parks and one of southern England's important nature reserves. Its mixture of grass, woods, lakes, marsh, and managed forest includes more than 200,000 trees, many of them descendants of the ancient oak, elm, and lime forest once surrounding London. Highlights here include the herds of dappled fallow and red deer, Isabella Plantation's azaleas and rhododendrons, and magical views through the trees over the Thames.

Beside the river lie the intricately planted Royal Botanic Gardens at Kew, with their remarkable glasshouses and renovated royal palace, and the evocative 17th-century Ham House at Twickenham, whose garden has been partially reconstructed. Enjoy the square lawns, hornbeam hedges, and cherry garden.

Outside the Thames's curve, the grounds surrounding Chiswick House, Osterley Park, Syon House, and Marble Hill House were all tamed in the 18th century. Richmond's royal connections made this a favorite spot, as did the fashionable prospects from Richmond Hill.

Royal gardener Charles Bridgeman and poet Alexander Pope designed Marble Hill's garden, and both they and William Kent worked with Lord Burlington at Chiswick. For Syon House, the Northumberland family brought in Capability Brown, who created lakes and a formal rose garden, and planted specimen trees such as swamp cypresses and sessile oaks. At Osterley, banker Francis Child improved his flat, viewless estate with garden follies and trees. The lake now attracts great crested grebes, corn buntings, kestrels, kingfishers, and other birds.

The river twists back northwest again at Kingston. The whole bowl contained within is filled with Hampton Court Palace, whose gardens include the restored Dutch garden, the deer park, and the deliciously wild Bushy Park. ■

NOT TO BE MISSED:

0 ———— 2 kilometers
0 ———— 1 mile

M4

OSTERLEY PARK
Osterley Park

Osterley

GREAT WEST ROAD

BRENTFORD

M4

KEW BRIDGE
Kew Bridge

KEW BRIDGE

KEW

Chiswick House ❷

GREAT CHERTSEY ROAD

Thames

Hounslow East

SYON PARK
Syon House

Royal Botanic Gardens

KEW RD.

MORTLAKE RD.

Kew Gardens

CHISWICK BRIDGE

Chiswick

BARNES

DUKE'S MEADOWS

ISLEWORTH

OLD DEER PARK

TWICKENHAM RD.

Richmond

MORTLAKE

TWICKENHAM BRIDGE

RICHMOND

RICHMOND ROAD WEST

EAST SHEEN

GREAT CHERTSEY ROAD

RICHMOND BRIDGE

MARBLE HILL PARK

Twickenham

Marble Hill House

ROEHAMPTON

ROEHAMPTON LANE

❶

TWICKENHAM

Ham House

PETERSHAM

RICHMOND PARK

HAM COMMON

ROEHAMPTON VALE

HAM

TEDDINGTON

WIMBLEDON COMMON

ROBIN HOOD WAY

HAMPTON HILL

BUSHY PARK

HAMPTON WICK

KINGSTON BRIDGE

HAMPTON COURT RD

HOME PARK

KINGSTON UPON THAMES

HAMPTON COURT BRIDGE

Hampton Court

Hampton Court Palace

Thames

❶ Orleans House Gallery
❷ Hogarth's House

London

Thames

Area of map detail

Royal Botanic Gardens, Kew

This is London's living museum of plants, landscapes, buildings, and statuary. The 300-acre (121 ha) garden of perfect specimen trees and plants is part of an institute of botanical research. Visitors gasp at some of the 50,000 species of plants and explore glasshouses (greenhouses) full of lilies and orchids. Meanwhile, behind the scenes, for more than a century this has been a major center for the identification and distribution of plants from around the world.

Kew's giant South American waterlilies can support weights up to 100 pounds (45 kg).

However, you need no botanical knowledge to revel in the sheer beauty of the gardens. They began as two very different estates. The part on the west, bordering the river, belonged to George II and Queen Caroline's country house, White Lodge on the Richmond Estate. Capability Brown created the original lake and the dell, now planted with rhododendrons. The eastern part was the 9-acre (3.6 ha) Kew estate, where Prince Frederick's widow, Princess Augusta, lived in Kew Palace. Now exquisitely refurbished, it was built in 1631 by a London merchant of Dutch descent (hence the Dutch gables).

In 1759 the princess took up gardening. In 1761 her builder Sir William Chambers designed the Orangery, now the Tea House, and the Pagoda, Kew's ten-story landmark. George III, who came t the throne in 1760, inherited bot estates from his mother, Princess

INSIDER TIP:

On select Sunday nights, Kew Palace offers behind-the-scenes tours that include access to the Tudor undercroft.

—RACHAEL JACKSON
National Geographic contributor

Augusta, and his grandfather, George II. George III stayed in tiny Kew Palace and soon employed Sir Joseph Banks to enlarge and replant both gardens, now joined. Banks had collected specimens on his travels with Captain Cook, and he sent gardeners off to find additional plants.

More acres were added, and in 1841 the gardens were given to the state, with Sir William Hooker as director. It was Hooker who founded the Department of Economic Botany, the museums, the herbarium, and the library. And in 1844 the first of Kew's custom-designed glasshouses was built (see sidebar below). Later, W. A. Nesfield, who also worked

at Regent's Park, laid out the four great vistas—Pagoda Vista, Broad Walk, Holly Walk, and Cedar Vista. He also designed the lake and pond. His son, W. E. Nesfield, designed the delightful Temperate House Lodge in 1866–1867, one of London's first Queen Anne Revival buildings. Note the fine detailing of the central chimneys.

Whatever the season, Kew has something glorious for you to see. Kew Palace or the Orangery are good places to start. Then, the magic of a perfect garden is yours to explore. In spring, there are the daffodils, crocuses, tulips, and bluebells, especially surrounding Queen Charlotte's Cottage. Early summer shrubs and trees include azaleas, magnolias, rhododendrons, and flowering cherries—there is a fine view across to Syon House from the end of the azalea walk. After the autumn color, there are winter-flowering prunus, the Heath Garden by the pagoda, and the glasshouses. At all times, Nesfield's great vistas are impressive, as are the groves of tree collections including willow, beech, and birch. Each tree is identified by its country of origin. ■

Royal Botanic Gardens

- 🅰 Map p. 191
- ✉ Kew, Richmond, Surrey, TW9
- ☎ 020 8332 5655 Information: 020 8940 1171
- 🕐 Check occasional area closures. Queen Charlotte's Cottage: closed Mon.–Fri. & Oct.–March
- 💲 $$$$
- 🚇 Tube/rail: Kew Gardens, then walk; riverboat (see p. 52)

www.kew.org

Kew Glasshouses

Kew's seven glasshouses possibly look for inspiration to Syon's huge Great Conservatory (see p. 195), built in the 1820s by Charles Fowler. The gardens' first glasshouse was the Aroid House, designed by Nash in 1836 as a garden pavilion for Buckingham Palace. The Palm House, though, was specially designed in 1844–1848 by Decimus Burton and Richard Turner. Its slender cast-ironwork makes it the finest glass-and-iron structure in England. The Palm House predates Paxton's Crystal Palace by three years. The Water Lily House (1852) was followed by Burton's Temperate House, built between 1860 and 1898 as the world's largest glasshouse. More recently, the Princess of Wales Conservatory, completed in 1987, contains ten climatic zones and replaces 26 old glasshouses.

Eighteenth-Century Country Retreats

With a new appreciation for the picturesque sweeping the country, and in particular for fine prospects, the pretty stretch of the riverside that included Chiswick, Richmond, and Twickenham villages became the favorite choice for aristocratic country houses. It also had royal associations and was accessible by the river, the preferred method of travel.

Marble Hill House

- 🏛 Map p. 191
- ✉ Richmond Road, Twickenham, TW1
- ☎ 020 8892 5115
- 🕐 Closed Mon.–Fri. & Nov.–March
- 💲 $$
- 🚇 Tube: Richmond, then walk over the bridge

www.english-heritage .org.uk

Twickenham

Several 18th-century country idylls survive, with settings that evoke the elegance of their period. **Marble Hill House** is an early one, built between 1723 and 1729 for George II's mistress, Henrietta Howard, Countess of Suffolk. This restored, white Palladian villa overlooks the Thames between Twickenham and Richmond. Both

house and park were inspired by the classical idea of an earthly Elysium, as revived in the 16th-century villas of the Italian Veneto. Nature was tamed to produce good views down to the river and, just as important, up from the river for arriving guests. Just off the northwest corner of the park, Montpelier Row, dating from about 1720, is one of Twickenham's gracious early terraces. Follow the riverside path through the woods to James Gibbs's octagonal 1720 **Orleans House** (*Riverside, tel 020 8892 0221, www.richmond.gov.uk/ orleanshouse, closed Mon.*); just enough survives to hint at its former grandeur. Bell, Water, and Church Lanes have more old houses, and the ferry to **Ham House** runs from here.

Chiswick

Downriver from Twickenham, Richard Boyle, 3rd Earl of Burlington and a connoisseur of great refinement, built his perfect Palladian temple to the arts, **Chiswick House**, in 1725–1729. Burlington's town house, the inner part of what is today the Royal Academy, had already broken with Wren's English baroque for Palladio's light, Italian style. Here, at Chiswick, the earl went further. Inspired by Palladio's Villa Capra near Vicenza, he built an exquisite Palladian villa and garden in which to display his

Elegant details abound in Syon House's anteroom.

EXPERIENCE: See a Polo Match

Players on horseback still gallop between goalposts at the **Ham Polo Club** *(Petersham Road, Richmond, Surrey, TW10, tel 020 8334 0000, www.hampoloclub.com, $$)*, the only surviving polo club in London's metropolitan area. Pack a picnic and catch Sunday games in the summer, but dress sharp—no shorts allowed at this establishment, which was founded in 1926 beside Ham House (see p. 196) and across the Thames from Marble Hill House. To reach it, take the train or Tube to Richmond, then bus no. 65 or 371, or enjoy the pretty 20-minute Thameside walk. The more adventurous can saddle up and learn *($$$$$)* how players whack a 3-inch (8 cm) ball while riding a horse.

The game is divided into "chukkas," or seven-minute segments, and you may notice something different about the horses—their manes are shaved so loose hair doesn't affect the game. But don't call them horses. In polo parlance, regular-sized horses are "ponies," a term dating from a 19th-century rule that the animals be less than five feet (1.5 m) tall.

art and entertain his friends, rather than a house to live in. William Kent added ideas on decoration and greatly influenced the design of the garden, one of London's most interesting.

Like the house, the garden breaks away from the geometric designs of English baroque. Its design moves toward the freer, curves of Capability Brown, which evolved into later English landscape garden concepts. The layout is given informality through the use of statuary, garden buildings, and unevenly planted trees.

The property reopened in 2010 after a two-year, £12 million ($19 million) restoration project that returned the gardens to their 18th-century look: 1,600 new trees were planted, and others removed, to restore historic sightlines and views.

Syon & Osterley

The mansions of Syon and Osterley are grand indeed. Sumptuous and magnificent **Syon House** is a 16th-century stone building, totally remodeled in 1761 by Robert Adam for Sir Hugh Smithson, 1st Duke of Northumberland. Adam controlled the whole project, from the building and fine plasterwork to the gilding, carpets, and even the doorknobs. Most of it survives in perfection: the Matthew Boulton fireplaces, the Wedgwood pottery, the Spitalfields silks. Later, in 1827, Charles Fowler's magnificent **Great Conservatory** was added, linking the house to its gardens, landscaped by Capability Brown in 1767–1773. Do not miss the 6-acre (2.5 ha) **Rose Garden,** which blooms from June to September.

Adam created another masterpiece nearby, **Osterley Park** *(tel 020 8232 5050, www.nationaltrust .org.uk, closed Mon.–Tues.).* Again, he took a 16th-century house— this one of red brick—and transformed it into a Palladian mansion suitable for City bankers Francis and Robert Child. Today, Adam's great portico leads to a string of state rooms furnished with Gobelin tapestries. ∎

Chiswick House
- 🅰 Map p. 191
- ✉ Burlington Lane, Chiswick, W4
- ☎ 020 8995 0508
- 🕐 House closed Nov.–March
- 💲 House: $$
- 🚇 Tube: Turnham Green, then walk south. Rail: Chiswick, then walk along Burlington Lane.

www.chgt.org.uk

Syon House
- 🅰 Map p. 191
- ✉ Brentford, Middlesex, TW8
- ☎ 020 8560 0882
- 🕐 Closed Mon., Tues., Fri., & Sat.; and Nov.–mid-March
- 💲 $$$ Gardens only: $$
- 🚇 Tube: Gunnersbury, or rail or Tube to Kew Bridge station, then bus 237 or 267

www.syonpark.co.uk

Ham House

This is one of London's earliest and loveliest grand houses. Scrupulously run by the National Trust since 1949, it is furnished with pieces lent by the V&A. Built in 1610 for Sir Thomas Vavasour, Knight Marshal to James I, it was dramatically remodeled in 1673–1675 by William Samwell for Elizabeth, Countess of Dysart, and her second husband, John Maitland, Duke of Lauderdale, who was the virtual ruler of Scotland for some time after the Restoration. Together they created a flamboyantly palatial baroque home.

Ham House

- 🏔 Map p. 191
- ✉ Richmond, Surrey, TW10
- ☎ 020 8940 1950
- 🕐 House open April–Oct. Sat.– Wed. p.m. Gardens open all year.
- 💲 $$$
- 🚇 Tube/rail to Richmond, then bus 65 or 371

www.nationaltrust .org.uk

Using house records and plans, the Trust has fully restored both house and gardens, so that it gives a more accurate and extensive idea of grand domestic 17th-century life than any other house in England.

Start by looking at the facade of the house: three simple stories of brick with stone dressings. The busts in the oval niches, however, give a taste of what is to come once you enter the house.

INSIDER TIP:

A short walk through the meadows that front Ham House brings you to the quiet banks of the Thames. The pathway here leads you a very pleasant 1.5 miles (2.4 km) to Richmond.

—LARRY PORGES
National Geographic Books editor

Inside, the two-story, galleried Great Hall has a pre-refurbishment ceiling by Joseph Kinsman dating from 1637–1638. Here, too, are 18th- and 19th-century paintings

of the Dysart family by artists such as Sir Joshua Reynolds and John Constable. Up the great staircase, the North Drawing Room is hung with English tapestries depicting the months of the year, probably woven in Soho around 1700. The Long Gallery, decorated in 1639, has a remarkable set of 17th-century portraits in contemporary gilded frames. The Cabinet of Miniatures, also known as the Green Closet, has exquisite works by Hilliard and Cooper.

The rooms of the Queen's Apartment, added in the 1670s, are at the other end of the Long Gallery. The Queen's Closet, the richest room of all, has a Verrio ceiling, marbled flat surfaces, early examples of scagliola decoration around the fireplace, and full baroque carving on the wainscoting.

Return through the State Rooms and head back downstairs: Several ground-floor rooms have ceilings painted by Neapolitan artist Antonio Verrio; the Dining Room has leather wall hangings; and the Duchess's Private Closet has its original japanned furniture. Outside, the 18 acres (7 ha) of formal gardens should not be missed. ∎

Hampton Court Palace

Of all London's royal palaces, Hampton Court has the most to offer the visitor, including two sets of regal rooms (intimate Tudor and grand Wren), numerous gardens (Tudor, Dutch, the Maze, and more), and two great parks (Home and Bushy). In all, more than 500 years of tip-top royal patronage is now conserved by a huge team of specialists.

Henry VIII appropriated the magnificent Hampton Court Palace from disgraced Cardinal Wolsey.

Choices will have to be made, and the first is whether to whisk out there by train to enjoy the rooms relatively empty in the morning, possibly returning to London by riverboat; or to glide up by riverboat, find busier rooms, and spend a summer's afternoon and early evening in the gardens and parks.

History

The palace began as a 12th-century moated estate office. By 1514, it was a courtyard house. That year, Thomas, Cardinal Wolsey, Henry VIII's chief minister, leased it as his country house. Wolsey built grandly and copiously. He added most of the Tudor buildings that stand today: 44 lodgings for his guests in Base Court; three stories of rooms expressly to honor Henry VIII's visit in 1525; a long gallery; and a magnificent chapel.

When Wolsey fell from favor in 1528, Henry VIII took over this ready-made palace. He immediately extended the kitchens, and in 1532–1535 added the Great Hall. His daughter Elizabeth laid out formal gardens. Of the Tudor sovereigns' 60 residences, Hampton Court was one of the few capable of housing the entire 1,000-strong court. Yet it was not the service rooms that impressed visitors so much as the royal apartments; most are gone now, and only the Great Watching Chamber, the chapel, and Wolsey Closet remain.

William and Mary, after

Hampton Court Palace

- Map p. 191
- East Molesey, Surrey, KT8
- 0870 751 5175 or 0870 752 7777
- Palace & gardens: $$$$. Gardens only: $$. Parks: free
- Rail: Hampton Court, then walk over bridge. Riverboats from Westminster pier in summer (see p. 52).

www.hrp.org.uk

NOTE: The palace offers an extensive program of tours, talks, & special events.

Rooms at the palace range from grand to intimate.

1694, building stopped for four years. The work was completed in 1700 and William moved in, but died two years later.

Queen Anne redecorated the chapel and the Queen's Drawing Room, employing the Neapolitan artist Antonio Verrio. Georges I and II resided in Hampton Court. After Queen Caroline's death, the Court ceased to stay here. Gradually, the rooms became "grace and favor" apartments for retired servants of the Crown. The royals continued to care for Hampton Court. Queen Victoria added the Great Hall's stained glass, "improved" the Palace's Tudor style by adding most of the tall, brick chimneys, and, in 1838, opened it to the public. The railway station opened in 1849, making the palace easily accessible.

their accession in 1689, made dramatic changes. They brought in Sir Christopher Wren to create a new baroque palace. Wren began by replacing Henry's royal apartments. The queen's room overlooked Charles II's garden and his Long Water. The king's overlooked his Privy Garden and the Thames. After Mary died in

Hampton Court Palace

Great Gatehouse

Hampton Court Routes

Because the palace is so vast, its curators have devised several routes, each exploring a theme. Guides can be booked for routes and plans are available for self-guidance. Here are two approaches, one Tudor, the other William and Mary.

Trail 1—The Tudors: The Tudor visit begins with the **"King's Beasts"** at the palace entrance, although these are 20th-century replacements.

Henry VIII's **State Apartments** are found through Wolsey's Great Gatehouse in Base Court. The **Great Hall** (1532–1535), with its painted hammerbeam roof, is hung with Henry's 1520s Flemish tapestries. Through the **Great Watching Chamber,** a gallery leads to the **Chapel Royal** and its sumptuous Tudor ceiling.

From here, visit Henry VIII's kitchens, entered between the Clock and Base Courts. They occupied 50 rooms, and 200 staff fed Henry's 1,000-strong court. Ten rooms are open, including the Beer Cellar, Boiling House,

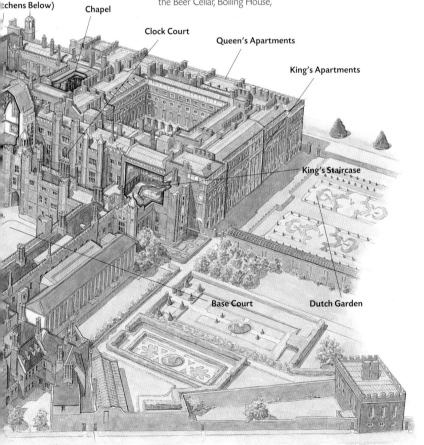

eat Hall
:chens Below)

Chapel

Clock Court

Queen's Apartments

King's Apartments

King's Staircase

Base Court

Dutch Garden

INSIDER TIP:

Hampton Court Palace has what may be the most famous maze in the world. Try not to get lost as you take each twist and turn!

—KATIE BLAKE
Historic Royal Palaces press assistant

and Wine Cellar—where some of the 600,000 gallons of ale drunk annually were stored.

Go across Clock Court and upstairs to find the **"Young Henry VIII"** exhibit. Here are Tudor paintings and exhibits that tell the story of the famous king's formative years. The art collection includes the great panorama of the "Field of the Cloth of Gold," recording Henry VIII's meeting with Francis I of France in 1520.

Trail 2—William & Mary:
To see the two grand suites of Mary II's apartments, begin in Fountain Court and go up a grand staircase painted by William Kent in 1735. The Queen's Presence Chamber leads to the grandest rooms: the **Public Dining Room** and then the **Queen's Audience Chamber.** Next, the Drawing Room, the Bedchamber (prepared for Queen Caroline in 1715), the Gallery, and the Closet.

Go down the back staircase and return to Clock Court to visit **William III's Apartments.** Up the monumental King's Staircase, decorated with Verrio's allegory of William's good government, find the Guard Chamber, which stored 3,000 weapons. The Presence Chamber has its original throne to which courtiers would bow, even if empty; Sir Godfrey Kneller's equestrian portrait of the king; and tapestries made for Whitehall Palace. Ahead you'll come to the grand King's Eating Room, Privy Chamber, Withdrawing Room, Great Bedchamber, and Closet. The King's private apartments continue downstairs. ∎

Hampton Court Gardens

The Tudor, baroque, and Victorian gardens are minutely tended by a bevy of 41 gardeners. Of Henry VIII's grand layout, little survives. The secluded Knot and Pond Gardens give a flavor—Henry's Pond Garden (1536) was stocked with edible fish for the kitchens. The Great Vine is grown from a cutting taken in 1768 from the original. In the nearby Mantegna Gallery, the painter's stage designs "Triumphs of Caesar" (circa 1486–1494) are on display.

William's 3-acre (1.2 ha) Privy Garden is now restored to its 1702 state, complete with authentic flowers, shrubs, and 33,000 box plants. Wren designed the riverside Banqueting House and Jean Tijou the ironwork gates. Other parts to enjoy include the Maze, first planted in 1690, and the Wilderness, with a million bulbs. Beyond Charles's Long Water, Home Park's 300 fallow deer are descended from Henry VIII's herd. This is where the annual Royal Horticultural Society Hampton Court Palace Flower Show, the largest of its kind in Europe, is held in July.

The Tower of London, jolly East End markets, the reborn Docklands, and maritime Greenwich

East London

Tower Bridge is a gateway to
East London.

East London

Here is the flipside to stuccoed Belgravia and the art dealers of St. James's. The medieval Tower of London still slams its doors shut against the London mob each night. Downstream, the palatial splendors of Royal Greenwich Palace and Park are matched by its maritime museum and ships. In between, the East End throbs once more with a vitality that first exploded into life when the enclosed docks were built following the 18th-century industrial revolution.

The romance of the overcrowded, poor, but spirited East End—of Cockney rhyming slang, pearly kings, and music halls—was born in the 19th century. Older areas, such as Spitalfields and Whitechapel, and the East End villages of Hackney and Limehouse, were swallowed into the giant Victorian sprawl of housing for British workers from rural areas and migrants from other countries. Men and women worked on the docks and in their related trades—shipbuilding, engineering, furniture-making, and, at the Whitechapel Bell Foundry, making bells for London's many Victorian churches. They brewed beer, ran the street markets, and entertained great crowds in the music halls. Here Charlie Chaplin made his stage debut at the Royal Cambridge music hall. Meanwhile, the government created a "green lung," Victoria Park, and well-wishers and missionaries started such charitable institutions as the Ragged School.

Today, having slumped after the docks were closed, the heart of the East End beats again. The map is once again dotted with interesting places to visit.

Spitalfields, focused on Christ Church, mixes new gentility with the rag trade, restaurants, and the mosques of the Bangladeshis. Whitechapel Art Gallery is the heart of a large community of artists, who live in the surrounding cheap and disused warehouses. Jazz has replaced the music hall, and one set of almshouses in Bethnal Green is home to the Geffrye Museum. Farther north, the Hackney Empire variety theater entertains full houses, while just around the corner the National Trust tends Sutton House, a rare surviving 16th-century merchant's home. Most surprising of all, a few streets southwest of Victoria Park the V&A has its easternmost outpost: the Bethnal Green Museum of Childhood.

Down by the Thames, the revival of the 11-mile strip of once-disused docks began in 1981 with massive government help. It is now established and self-reliant, as evident in the success of London City Airport and the soaring beauty of Canary Wharf towers.

Docklands building continues on this massive chunk of London. The Isle of Dogs now has the Museum in Docklands and a host of restaurants at West India Docks. Farther east, Royal Victoria Docks has Excel, the London International Exhibition Centre. Still farther east, Royal Albert Dock has the Royal Albert Dock Regatta Centre. At Greenwich, the *Cutty Sark* is restored, and refurbished Ranger's House has reopened, while the Millennium Dome, where the new millennium officially began, is the world's largest dome.

But the biggest boost to the whole East End is yet to come: The 2012 Olympic Games will be staged at Lower Lea Valley, now being revitalized. ■

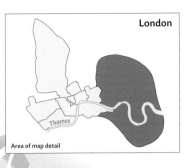

London

Area of map detail

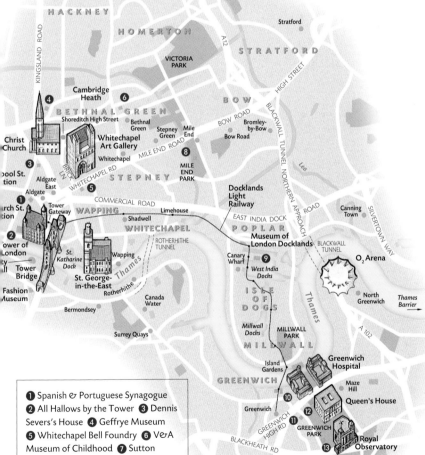

HACKNEY

HOMERTON

KINGSLAND ROAD

Stratford

STRATFORD

A12

VICTORIA PARK

Cambridge Heath ⑥

HIGH STREET

BOW

BETHNAL GREEN

Shoreditch High Street

Bethnal Green

Stepney Green

Mile End

BOW ROAD

Bromley-by-Bow

Bow Road

Christ Church

④

Whitechapel Art Gallery

Whitechapel

MILE END ROAD

Lea

BLACKWALL TUNNEL NORTHERN APPROACH

③

ool St. tion

Aldgate East

BRICK LANE

WHITECHAPEL RD

⑧

MILE END PARK

STEPNEY

Aldgate

⑤

Docklands Light Railway

ROAD

Canning Town

SILVERTOWN WAY

①

rch St. tion

Tower Gateway

COMMERCIAL ROAD

Limehouse

WAPPING

Shadwell

WHITECHAPEL

EAST INDIA DOCK

POPLAR

ower of London

St. Katharine Dock

ROTHERHITHE TUNNEL

Wapping

Museum of London Docklands

BLACKWALL TUNNEL

O₂ Arena

ty

Tower Bridge

Canary Wharf

⑨

West India Docks

Thames

North Greenwich

Thames Barrier

Fashion Museum

St. George-in-the-East

Rotherhithe

Thames

ISLE

Bermondsey

Canada Water

OF

DOGS

A 102

Surrey Quays

Millwall Docks

MILLWALL PARK

MILLWALL

Island Gardens

Greenwich Hospital

GREENWICH

Maze Hill

① Spanish & Portuguese Synagogue
② All Hallows by the Tower ③ Dennis Severs's House ④ Geffrye Museum
⑤ Whitechapel Bell Foundry ⑥ V&A Museum of Childhood ⑦ Sutton House ⑧ Ragged School Museum
⑨ Canary Wharf Tower ⑩ Cutty Sark
⑪ Fan Museum ⑫ National Maritime Museum ⑬ Ranger's House

⑩

Greenwich

⑪

⑫

Queen's House

GREENWICH HIGH RD

GREENWICH PARK

BLACKHEATH RD

⑬

Royal Observatory

0   2 kilometers
0   1 mile

Tower of London

Britain's most perfect surviving medieval fort is tucked behind the sleek City towers, forgotten by most Londoners but ever popular with visitors. In fact, the Tower is not just a fort; it contains a palace, prisons, an execution site, chapels, and museums. Since William the Conqueror began building it soon after his 1066 conquest, it has served the sovereign. Today, covering 18 acres (7.3 ha), it is London's smallest village, with a population of 36 families.

The story of the Tower is as much about people as about buildings. Following its story is a good way of familiarizing yourself with the kings of England.

The Tower of London began

The medieval Tower of London was a fort, a prison, a palace, and a jewel house.

as a temporary fort, constructed by William to keep watch on untrustworthy City merchants. He built it between their Saxon walls and the high surviving Roman ones. Later, he built what is now the central White Tower, completed by William II and Henry I. Constructed of stone from Caen in France, this keep had walls 90 feet (27 m) high and 15 feet (4.6 m) thick, with room inside for three wells, a banqueting hall, a council chamber, and even the tiny St. John's Chapel, plus a prison and dungeon. Henry I also built the Tower's second church, St. Peter ad Vincula. The last Norman king, Stephen, was the first to live in the Tower.

The Plantagenet kings used the Tower well. Henry II added kitchens, a bakery, and a jail. William of Longchamp, loyal servant of Richard II, added more wall, the Bell Tower, Wardrobe Towers, and the ditch while the king was at the Crusades—to no avail, however. Prince John besieged it, became king, and further strengthened the walls. Henry III began the inner wall, the moat, his own watergate, and the royal palace. He whitewashed the White Tower and began a zoo—the King of Norway gave him a polar bear that went fishing in the Thames on a leash. Edward I completed the western

Inner Wall and the Outer Wall including Byward Tower and Traitors' Gate. He moved the mint and Crown Jewels here from Westminster.

Since then, the Tower has changed little. Such extras as the Tower's 14th-century cupolas, Henry VIII's half-timbered houses and two circular bastions on Tower Green, and the barracks of 1840 are minor additions.

INSIDER TIP:

Check out the exhibition of Henry VIII's armor in the White Tower: It ranges from slim (young Henry) to XXL (old Henry).

—PATRICIA DANIELS
National Geographic contributor

The Tower witnessed both great joys and great horrors. Henry IV initiated the Ceremony of the Bath here in 1399. Under Henry VI, the Duke of Exeter introduced the rack for torture and Edmund Campion, the English Jesuit martyr (1540–1581), was stretched on it three times. The Yorkist Edward IV picnicked and played on the Tower lawns. But when Richard III went off to be crowned in 1483, his two prince nephews were murdered in the Bloody Tower. Then came the Tudors: Henry VIII may have built houses on Tower Green, but he also had two of his wives executed there: Anne Boleyn and Catherine Howard. In fact, they were comparatively lucky; Thomas

Cromwell, Archbishop Laud, and others ending with Lord Lovat in 1747, provided public spectacle when they were beheaded up on Tower Hill. Princess Elizabeth first arrived through Traitors' Gate, but later began her coronation procession in a golden chariot from here. Then the Stuarts: James I, the last king to live in the Tower, watched his lions and bears fighting from the Lion Tower. Charles I sent six Members of Parliament to the Tower for insulting his favorite, the Duke of Buckingham. Charles II held the Tower's last pageant in 1661, extravagant spring festivities that included an entire new set of Crown Jewels, as Cromwell's men had stolen the previous ones.

Visiting the Tower

The Tower is very popular. Early arrivals can rush to the Crown Jewels and see them in relative peace. However, the most exciting way to arrive is by riverboat (see p. 52), which means arriving too late for this. There is much to see; reentry tickets allow for a lunch break on Tower Wharf or at nearby St. Katharine Dock. If the lines are horrendous, consider visiting the nearby fascinating church of All Hallows by the Tower, Tower Bridge (see p. 210), and St. Katharine Dock, or taking the ferry from Tower pier to H.M.S. *Belfast* (see p. 106); then return to the Tower later.

The Trail

Arrival by river means going under London Bridge, where prisoners such as Princess Elizabeth would have gazed up at the severed

Tower of London

- Map p. 203
- 0844 482 7777
- $$$$$
- Tube: Tower Hill; or Monument, then walk to it through the City

www.hrp.org.uk

NOTE: Worth booking online in advance

All Hallows by the Tower

- Map. p. 203
- Byward Street, EC3
- 020 7481 2928
- Donation
- Tube: Tower Hill

www.ahbit.org.uk

heads of previous inmates, exhibited on spikes. Arrival on foot from the City allows a visit to All Hallows and a first view of the Tower, with the Victorian Tower Bridge beyond.

You enter the Tower of London through the Byward Tower, at the southwest corner, not far from Tower pier. You can walk around on your own or join a free tour led every half hour by one of the Yeoman Warders, or Beefeaters, who have guarded the Tower since 1485.

It is best to visit the Crown Jewels, housed in the Waterloo Barracks, first. To get there, go straight ahead and find Traitors' Gate on the right; turn left, go up the stairs past Tower Green and straight on. There are plenty of sparkling, egg-size diamonds to note: the First Star of Africa (530 carats), in Charles II's scepter; the 2,800 diamonds in the Imperial State Crown worn for the State Opening of Parliament; and the Koh-I-Noor diamond from India, in the Queen Consort's crown. Also exhibited are the ampulla and

spoon for anointing the sovereign, made in 1399, and the beautifully ornate baroque plate made for Charles II. The Crown Jewels display will be refurbished in time for 2012 (the year of the Queen's Diamond Jubilee, celebrating 60 years on the throne), and will provide improved visitor access and labeling of the jewels.

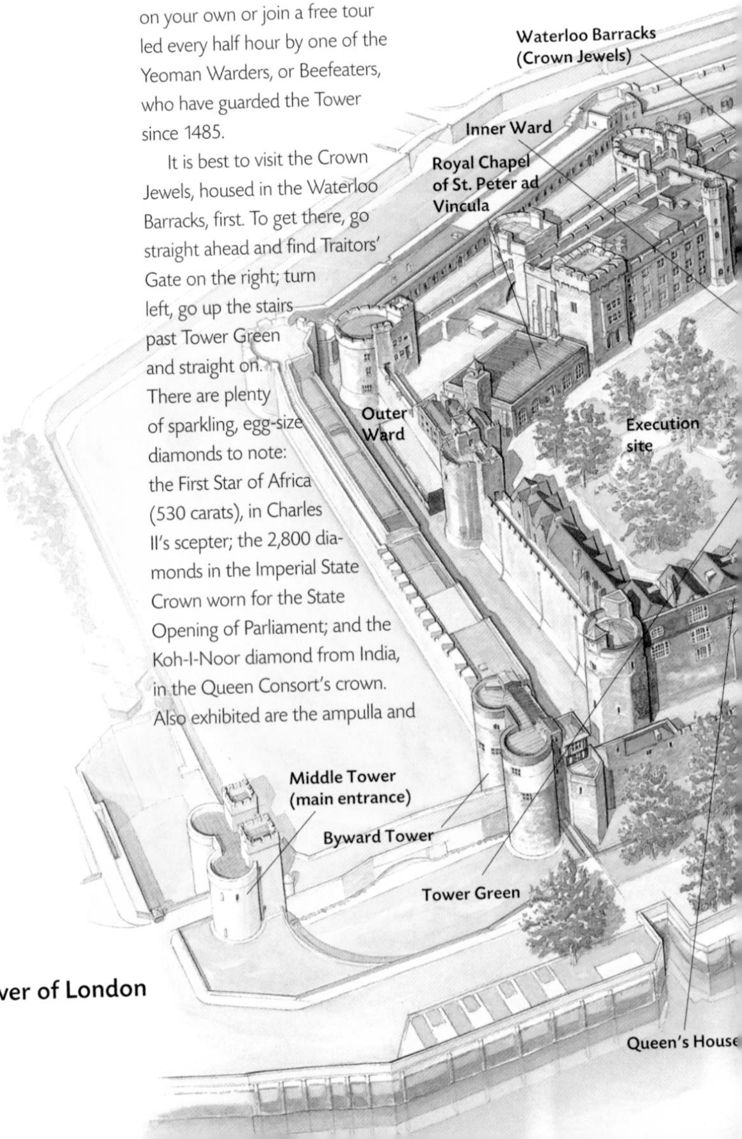

Waterloo Barracks
(Crown Jewels)

Inner Ward

Royal Chapel
of St. Peter ad
Vincula

Outer
Ward

Execution
site

Middle Tower
(main entrance)

Byward Tower

Tower Green

Tower of London

Queen's House

The Brick Tower, just behind Waterloo Barracks, reopens in 2011 with an exhibit on the historic menagerie that the Tower housed for many centuries. Sculptures and wire art of animals will also dot the complex grounds.

From here return to Tower original keep, the White Tower, whose most magical room is the tiny St. John's Chapel on the second floor. Beside this, a chunk of Roman wall leads down to the home of the six Tower ravens, who have their own Raven Master.

Alternatively, Martin Tower in the northeast marks the start of the Wall Walk through Henry III's towers and walls, down to Salt Tower. To finish, see some of the

Martin Tower

St. John's Chapel

Salt Tower

Moat

White Tower

Wakefield Tower

Traitors' Gate

St. Thomas's Tower

THAMES RIVER

Bloody Tower

Tower's best rooms, in the medieval palace. Strung along the south side, overlooking the river, they include St. Thomas's and Wakefield Towers, sensitively restored to give an idea of their structure, possible decoration, and probable use during Edward I's reign. ■

Green to see the Chapel Royal of St. Peter ad Vincula, the execution site, and, in Bloody Tower, the rooms where Elizabeth I's favorite, explorer Sir Walter Raleigh, spent 13 years. Then proceed to the

London's 2012 Olympics

From July 27 to August 12, 2012, London will host the Olympic Games (followed directly, from August 29 to September 9, by the Paralympic Games). The organizers have committed themselves to ensuring that these Olympics are the greenest ever and that they provide a lasting, positive legacy for the city.

The new Aquatics Centre will have a dolphinesque look (shown here in an artist's rendering).

The Rejuvenation of Stratford

The epicenter of the London Olympics is Stratford, in East London. Stratford and the surrounding Lower Lea Valley—once an area of scenic wetlands—became an industrial suburb in the mid-19th century, containing factories for engineering, spinning, printing, and other uses. Well connected to the city and docks thanks to the arrival of workers' train lines and the navigable River Lea, the area's population further increased when the Great Eastern Railway sited its locomotive works at Stratford. By the turn of the 20th century, the Lower Lea's waterways were heavily polluted and silted up, and Stratford had a deteriorating economy and poor health and hygiene.

The Docklands revival of the 1980s kickstarted its rebirth; the Olympics will fast-track this. The waterways will be dredged and widened, with the aim of restoring the ecosystem—and the community around it—back to health.

The Olympic Park & Athletes Village

The cornerstone of the effort to revitalize Stratford is the creation of the Olympic Park, a 650-acre (250 ha) swath of green space. Nearly 4,000 hardy trees and 300,000 wetland plants representing 250 species will be planted in the new park and the adjoining Athletes Village. The northern part of the park will be reserved as an undeveloped haven for wildlife, while the southern half will host a weeks-long riverside festival in its cafés, bars, gardens, and markets.

The Olympic Park will also be home to a majority of the venues for the Games themselves. The 80,000-seat Olympic Stadium will host the opening and closing ceremonies as well as the main athletic events. Other purpose-built Olympic venues include an aquatics center for diving and swimming, a basketball arena, a velodome for track cycling, a handball arena, and a hockey center. Some of these facilities will be dismantled after the games, while others will be maintained for future competitions or converted for community use.

The Athletes Village, which nearly 17,000 athletes and officials will call home during the course of the Olympics and Paralympics, will be located directly next to the Olympic Park. Keeping with the mandate that the Olympics provide a positive future impact, at the end of the Games the residences will be converted into a new community of 2,800 homes (including nearly 1,400 affordable houses), a health center, parklands, and a new educational campus for 1,800 children and teenagers.

Elsewhere in London

The festivities won't be confined to Stratford alone. The whole of London, including several of its best known monuments, will become the backdrop for Olympic events. Sand is being imported to turn the normally staid Horse Guards Parade, at the other end of the Mall from Buckingham Palace, into the beach volleyball venue; Lord's Cricket Ground will host the archery competition; Greenwich Park will hold equestrian events and the modern pentathlon; and Hyde Park will feature the triathlon and marathon swimming. Hyde Park is also going to host a series of music, film, and cultural events that will take place throughout the summer of 2012.

In addition, giant outdoor screens will be set up at several "Live Sites" venues throughout the city (and around Britain), allowing Londoners the chance to watch the events in a festive, community-based atmosphere. The Live Sites will operate at Hyde Park and Victoria Park during the Olympic Games; at Trafalgar Square during the Paralympic Games; and at Potter's Fields Park (next to City Hall in Southwark) over the course of both the Olympic and Paralympic Games. Venues may still be added, so check www.london2012.com for the latest information.

Getting to the Games

Olympic organizers have invested heavily in public transportation upgrades that will benefit Stratford for decades to come. Several hundred million pounds are being spent to upgrade the Stratford Tube stop (serving the Central and Jubilee lines), the local National Rail and London Overground station, and the Dockland Light Railways (DLR) system. In addition, during the Games a high-speed rail service will whisk guests, in just seven minutes, from St. Pancras station in central London to the new Stratford International station. From here, it will only be a short walk to most of the events.

EXPERIENCE:
Attending the Games

Overseas visitors wishing to purchase any of the 8 million tickets for the 671 events at the London 2012 Olympics will need to plan ahead. While in 2011 residents of the U.K. can join a lottery for tickets through the **London 2012** website (www.london2012.com), others will need to apply for tickets via their country's National Olympic Committee. For the U.S., check the **U.S. Olympic Committee** website (www.teamusa.org) for information.

Tickets will be available at a variety of price points, ranging from £20 ($32) for football (soccer) matches to as much as £725 ($1,160) for the men's 100-meter sprint final. On the upside, tickets include the free use of London's public transportation on the day of the event.

You can enjoy some of the flavor of the Olympics for free by standing along the route of some of the endurance events, namely the 26.2-mile (42 km) marathons and the 156-mile (250 km) road cycling races (both of which start and end on the Mall), or the triathlon, which will take place in Hyde Park.

Tower Bridge

This is the capital's only bridge downriver of London Bridge and, begun in 1886, it is also one of its newest. It was designed to relieve congestion on the other City bridges, while still enabling large vessels to enter the Upper Pool of London's port.

The lower span of Tower Bridge opens to allow tall ships to pass through.

Tower Bridge

- Map p. 203
- 020 7403 3761
- $$
- Tube: Tower Hill
  Tube/rail:
  London Bridge

**www.towerbridge
.org.uk**

A special Act of Parliament in 1885 authorized the construction of a double drawbridge. It stipulated a Gothic-style bridge to sympathize with the neighboring Tower of London and an opening span width of 200 feet (61 m) and 135 feet (41 m) of headroom.

The Prince of Wales opened the bridge in 1894. It was 800 feet long and cost the huge sum, for the time, of £800,000 ($1.3 million). The elevators now take visitors to the **Tower Bridge Experience.** Here are changing exhibitions on the history and mechanisms of the bridge, whose coal-fired boilers drove the hydraulic system until electrification in 1976. ∎

Tower Bridge Mechanics

Despite its Gothic design, Tower Bridge was extremely modern for its day. The bridge's two towers have a steel frame covered in stone to house the hydraulic machinery and to support the 1,000-ton (1,016 tonne) weight of each bascule; they also contain the elevators to the footbridge. The two side-spans are on the suspension principle, the decks being hung from curved girders.

It takes just 90 seconds to raise the bridge. In its heyday, it was opened up to 50 times a day. Today, with the wharves closed, the bridge opens about 500 times a year (up to 15 times a day in summer). Sometimes the openings are for ceremonial occasions, such as the arrival of the royal yacht *Britannia* for the 50th anniversary celebrations of the end of World War II.

East End & Spitalfields

A day spent in this up-and-coming area, though still slightly rough around the edges, is rewarding for its local flavor and relative lack of tourists. Plan your schedule carefully to be sure the places that interest you are open.

Whitechapel Art Gallery, a ten-minute walk north from the Tower, was founded as a permanent showcase for the visual arts in the East End. C. H. Townsend's art nouveau building of 1897–1899 is still that, and local artists can be found through the gallery. The museum reopened in 2009 after an expansion that doubled the size of its exhibition space.

Wending its way north from Whitechapel Road (via Osborn Street) is **Brick Lane,** center of the East End's Bangladeshi community (and subject of Monica Ali's 2003 novel of the same name). The area has a long history of attracting immigrants: Huguenots settled the area in the 17th century and Jews migrated en masse in the late 19th century, as did Bengalis a century later. As a result of the latter, the street is famous for its many curry houses serving tasty South Asian cuisine and for its distinct Bengali Muslim atmosphere. Meanwhile, Jack the Ripper buffs will be interested to know that several of the notorious 19th-century murders centered around events on or near the street.

Back on Whitechapel Road is an unusual stop—the **Whitechapel Bell Foundry** *(32–34 Whitechapel Road, E1, tel 020 7247 2599, www.whitechapelbellfoundry .co.uk),* where descendants of the men who made Big Ben still

practice their skills. Farther west, Aldgate has the sumptuous **Bevis Marks Spanish and Portuguese Synagogue** *(entrance on Bevis Marks, EC1, tel 020 7626 1274, www.bevismarks.org.uk, $$),* built in 1701 by a Quaker, Joseph Avis, for Jewish refugees.

Spitalfields, east of Liverpool Street station, has several

Spitalfields Market has operated since the 19th century.

interesting sites. On Commercial Street, the covered **Spitalfields Market,** dating from 1893, is liveliest on Sundays. Across from the market's eastern exits, Nicholas Hawksmoor's painstakingly restored **Christ Church** (1720) should not be missed. A few blocks south, the market on **Petticoat Lane** (actually named Middlesex Street) offers clothes, shoes, handbags, jewelry,

Whitechapel Art Gallery

- Map p. 203
- ✉ Whitechapel High Street, E1
- ☎ 020 7522 7888
- 🕐 Closed Mon.
- 🚇 Tube: Aldgate East

www.whitechapel.org

Christ Church

- Map p. 203
- ✉ Commercial Street, E1
- ☎ 020 7247 7202
- 🚇 Tube: Aldgate East
  Tube/rail: Liverpool Street

www.christchurch spitalfields.org

Dennis Severs's House—A House Tour Like No Other

A glimpse of the unassuming three-story house just off Bishopsgate (18 Folgate St., E1, tel 020 7247 4013, www.dennissevers house.co.uk) reveals few clues about the unusual experience that awaits inside. The Georgian home has been turned into a living work of art, a three-dimensional canvas that was the brainchild of artist Dennis Severs, who ran the house from the 1970s until his death in 1999.

Each of the ten period rooms is packed with dozens of subtle details to evoke the daily lives of the elusive (and fictitious) Jervis family who theoretically lived in the house from the 18th to the 20th centuries.

As you stroll from room to room and absorb the atmosphere, a sense of place and time slowly emerges. It's all in the details: a toppled glass; crumbs from a half-eaten muffin; a live pet cat meandering about; the haunting sound of distant footsteps on creaking wooden steps; ticket stubs and other personal keepsakes tucked into a mirror edge; the warmth of a glowing fire; the muffled voices of what purports to be our just-out-of-sight family. The tours are conducted in total silence and soft light to help evoke the mood.

The house's motto is, "You either see it or you don't."

Geffrye Museum

🅰 Map p. 203

✉ Kingsland Road, E2

☎ 020 7739 8543/9893

🕐 Closed Mon.

💲 Donation

🚇 Tube/rail: Liverpool Street, Old Street, then bus or taxi

www.geffrye -museum.org.uk

and bric-a-brac of non-designer quality. The market teems with life on Sundays, when more than 1,000 vendors hawk their wares on Middlesex and neighboring streets; the action is confined to perpendicular Wentworth Street from Monday to Fridays.

Spitalfields also is home to a rare concentration of fine houses. By the end of the 18th century, 12,000 silk looms built by immigrant French Huguenots thundered in the Georgian lanes. Many houses have been restored, including **Dennis Severs's House** (see sidebar above).

Just north of Spitalfields lies **Hoxton,** one of London's hippest neighborhoods. The scene is constantly in flux, but the streets around Hoxton Square and Old Street host a variety of trendy bars, clubs, restaurants, and art galleries.

The East End is also home to three excellent small museums. The **Geffrye Museum** has

furniture, textiles, and woodwork arranged chronologically in 11 period rooms, built in 1715, plus four period gardens, a walled herb garden, contemporary pieces, and a restored 18th-century historic almshouse (open the first Saturday of each month). About a mile (1.6 km) east, the Victoria & Albert Museum's dollhouses, teddy bears, model circus, and much more fill the **V&A Museum of Childhood** (Cambridge Heath Rd., E2, tel 020 8983 5200, www .museumofchildhood.org.uk). A couple of miles farther northeast, **Sutton House** (2–4 Homerton High St., E9, tel 020 8986 2264, www.nationaltrust.org.uk, $) is a redbrick Tudor merchant's home. You can tour the historic rooms and bask in the quiet courtyard; there's also a café and art gallery.

Farther east still lies Stratford and the Lee Valley, which are being transformed into the epicenter of London's 2012 Olympics (see pp. 208–209). ■

Docklands

The saving grace of this forthright example of free-market inner-city redevelopment is its setting. For this was a renovation scheme that both flew in the face of the great conservation movement and passed up the opportunity to create something that would be a British 20th-century city of architectural significance. Use the Docklands Light Railway (DLR) to enjoy a spectacular overview of one section, from the Tower down to Island Gardens.

Canary Wharf contains some of London's tallest buildings.

The DLR has numerous lines—the route described below terminates at Lewisham and its trains are so marked.

Board your DLR train at either the Bank or Tower Gateway DLR station. (Tower Gateway is a short walk to **St. Katharine Dock,** just east of the Tower of London, an oasis of dockside pubs and restaurants.) The first stop east from both Bank and Tower Gateway is Shadwell, the station to alight for Hawksmoor's handsome church of **St. George-in-the-East** (1714–1729). Next comes Limehouse station, near another magnificent Hawksmoor church, **St. Anne's** (1714–1730),

and **Narrow Street's** pretty houses and pub.

The dock views begin just before the line turns southward after Westferry station. Look left to see Greenwich Peninsula's **O₂ Arena,** formerly called the Millennium Dome. West India Quay is the station for the excellent new **Museum of London Docklands** (see p. 214), Canary Wharf for the three soaring **Canary Wharf** towers and its associated shopping malls. Heron Quays hovers between two strips of dock, while Island Gardens has the best views of Greenwich—reach it by a long, narrow pedestrian tunnel under the Thames. ∎

Docklands

Map p. 203

see p. 214

Museum of London Docklands

Housed in a Georgian warehouse across the waters from Canary Wharf's gleaming high-rises, this is the ideal spot to explore the turbulent story of the Thames and London's great port. You can come to grips with 2,000 action-packed years, from Roman times to the river's heyday as the entrepot for a world-encircling empire, from wartime years to its revival as a modern landscape for living and working.

**Museum
of London
Docklands**

Map p. 203

No. 1
Warehouse,
West India
Quay, E14

020 7001 9844

Tube: West India
Quay (DLR),
Canary Wharf

**www.museumin
docklands.org.uk**

The museum shares many of its objects with the Museum of London. And more are found almost daily by archaeologists working on the city's many building sites such as the Jubilee Tube line or No. 1 Poultry. Here, though, the museum itself is an object: a handsome, three-story brick building that once stored exotic spices, rum, and cotton.

Starting on the top floor, the chronological arrangement of galleries makes London's story about as clear as possible. But it is never dull.

After the intriguing sections on the early Londons—Londinium, Lundenwic, and Lundenburh, each

in a slightly different location— the medieval highlights include two large models of Old London Bridge covered in houses, each of a different historical period. Later, to highlight the times when Tudor explorers left London in search of riches overseas, there is a splendid interactive story of a voyage on an East Indiaman.

As London's wealth grew, so did its quays, and by 1794 some 3,663 laden ships arrived and departed annually. Hence the enclosed docks that surround the museum. Their complexity and atmosphere are captured in the full-scale models of ship's chandlers, alleys, taverns, and shops. Goods of all kinds arrived, from tobacco and sugar to rum and timber; some 14 million tons of tea alone were being unloaded annually in the 1930s.

The museum also holds a gallery of boats, an extensive exhibit on the slave trade, the full story of the 1889 Great Dock Strike, and a "Black Saturday" film about the 1940s Blitz, featuring rare British and German archival footage. The final chapter, "New Port, New City," looks at the Docklands today, after which you long to go out and explore them. ∎

A family works on model buildings at the Museum of London Docklands.

Greenwich

The elegant buildings and excellent museums in and around the expansive Greenwich Park and the delightful town of Greenwich are a peaceful refuge from the resurging Docklands and Greenwich Peninsula, its neighbors.

Greenwich's National Maritime Museum stands out against the skyscrapers of Canary Wharf.

The view of Greenwich from the riverside is one of London's finest. It is best to arrive by river, or by Docklands Light Railway at Cutty Sark. Otherwise, go along King William Walk, and then along a path beside the college railings, called Five Foot Walk. It was here that George I landed on September 18, 1714, to succeed to the throne.

The fabulous setting was created piecemeal in the 17th and 18th centuries, yet Greenwich's true heyday was during the 16th century, under the Tudors. Henry V's brother, the Duke of Gloucester, built the riverside Bella Court in 1427, and six years later enclosed

200 acres to make Greenwich Park. The Tudor king Henry VII remodeled it as the Palace of Placentia in 1500, then Henry VIII, born at Greenwich, adopted it as his favorite palace. His daughters, Mary and Elizabeth I, were born here, as was his son, Edward VI. Most importantly, from here he could watch his ships arriving with exotic cargoes and he could oversee his navy.

Little remains of this period. In the distance, what we see today is the central building. Anne of Denmark, James I's queen, initiated the changes, and introduced an entirely new style of architecture from the Continent.

Greenwich
🅰 Map p. 203

**Painted Hall &
Chapel**

✉ Old Royal Naval
College, King
William Walk,
SE10

☎ 020 8269 4747

🚇 DLR: Cutty Sark
DLR/rail:
Greenwich

www.oldroyalnaval
college.org

Sweeping away some of the
vernacular timber palace buildings, she employed Inigo Jones
to start building the Queen's
House in 1616. This Palladian villa
was England's first Renaissance
building and Jones's earliest
surviving English work. Another
queen, Charles I's Henrietta Maria,
completed and decorated it, and
Jones's son-in-law, John Webb,

returned and began by building
a riverside wing in 1664. He also
brought in Louis XIV's Versailles
gardener, André Le Nôtre, to
design a plan for the park, with
avenues spreading out from the
Queen's House up the hill. When
William and Mary came to the
throne, their extensive building
projects also included Greenwich.
They invited Sir Christopher Wren
to create a hospital for retired sailors, following the success of Royal
Hospital Chelsea, his hospital for
soldiers (see p. 180). Between
1696 and 1702, he created the
breathtaking sight we see today.
Demolishing the last of the Tudor
buildings, he added a mirror wing
to Charles's, with a great staircase
between them. The two U-shaped
buildings face each other, with the
Queen's House the main focus.

King William Walk

To visit the grand public rooms
of Wren's baroque hospital, once
home to 2,710 sailors, find the
West Gate entrance on King
William Walk. The gateposts are
topped with symbolic celestial and
terrestrial domes. The hospital,
now comprising buildings of the
University of Greenwich, is
mostly closed to visitors, but the
Painted Hall and **Chapel** can
be visited. The Painted Hall was
designed as the sailors' dining
room but rarely used. Wren's
design, Hawksmoor's architectural
decoration, and James Thornhill's
paintwork make this England's
grandest secular interior of the
period. Thornhill's ceiling, painted
between 1707 and 1726, shows
William and Mary handing down

Greenwich's Historic Riverside Pubs

For centuries, people have downed pints
and dined at Greenwich's riverside pubs.
Charles Dickens used to patronize the
Trafalgar Tavern *(Park Row, tel 020 8858
2909, www.trafalgartavern.co.uk),* which still
serves cask ales and whitebait, a dish of
tiny fried fish, as it did in his day. The 1837
building provides views of the Thames
from its large bay windows and ample
outdoor seating.

A couple of hundred yards downriver
is another history-steeped alehouse: the
Cutty Sark Tavern *(4–6 Ballast Quay,
tel 020 8858 3146, www.cuttysarktavern
.co.uk).* While Londoners have been making merry at the site since at least 1743,
when it was known as The Green Man, the
current building dates from 1810. The pub
anchored itself to its current identity in
the 1950s, when the clipper ship *Cutty Sark*
permanently docked in Greenwich.

---

then enlarged it, building bridges
to overcome the problem of the
main London–Dover road running
through the grounds. During the
Commonwealth, Cromwell's men
turned the Queen's House into a
biscuit factory.

Then Charles II, who spent his
exile in France and dreamed of
creating an English Versailles here,

Peace and Liberty to Europe, and a crushed Louis XIV holding a broken sword below them. When the chapel burned down in 1779, James Stuart designed its coolly classical replacement. Stuart's assistant, William Newton, controlled the refined decoration, some of London's finest. See especially the doorway between the chapel and the vestibule.

Back past the pier toward the tunnel opening, the *Cutty Sark* tea-clipper, built at Clydeside in Scotland in 1869, is the only survivor from a brief period when the fastest ships then available raced between the Far East and London with their high-value cargoes. The *Cutty Sark* sailed from China to England in 99 days and then, as a wool carrier, zipped from Australia to London in just 72. The clipper suffered extensive damage in a 2007 fire; it is currently being rebuilt and will reopen to the public in 2012.

Now is a good moment to see a bit of Greenwich town, which has an enjoyable market *(Wed.–Sun., www.shopgreenwich.co.uk; see* p. 165). Behind elegant Nelson Road and College Approach, the Victorian covered market survives near Hawksmoor's much-restored **St. Alfege Church** (1714). Walk up Stockwell Street, which turns into Croom's Hill at the **Fan Museum** (*tel 020 8305 1441, www.fan-museum.org*), where the social history and delicate craft of the fan is laid out in two Georgian town houses. The exhibit includes the 2,000-piece collection showcasing the beauty, quality, and range of designs.

Renovations at the National Maritime Museum include a covered courtyard.

National Maritime Museum

East of the Fan Museum, the National Maritime Museum—the world's largest nautical museum—traces the story of Britain and the sea. It is also one of the most beautiful museum complexes in Britain. The collection ranges from porcelain and glass to royal barges, and fills the Queen's House, Royal Hospital School, and the Old Royal Observatory in Greenwich Park on the hill.

The museum was founded in 1934. Its recent renovation includes a stunning glass-roofed courtyard designed by Rick Mather, plus state-of-the-art themed galleries with plenty of visitor participation.

The collection looks at Britain's navy, merchants, explorers, and their related trades. It considers explorations to the Arctic, mapping the British Empire, the great migration to North America, Cook's travels, and Nelson's battle triumphs. There are especially

Cutty Sark

Map p. 203

King William Walk, SE10

020 8858 2698

$$

DLR: Cutty Sark DLR/rail: Greenwich

www.oldroyalnaval college.org

NOTE: Closed until 2012

National Maritime Museum

Map p. 203

Romney Road, SE10

020 8858 4422

DLR: Cutty Sark DLR/rail: Greenwich

www.nmm.ac.uk

Royal Observatory

- 🗺 Map p. 203
- ✉ Blackheath Avenue, SE10
- ☎ 020 8858 4422
- 💲 $$$
- 🚉 DLR: Cutty Sark DLR/rail: Greenwich

www.nmm.ac.uk/ places/royal -observatory

Ranger's House

- 🗺 Map p. 203
- ✉ Chesterfield Walk, SE10
- ☎ 020 8853 0035
- 🕐 Closed Mon.– Tues. Nov.– March
- 💲 $$
- 🚉 DLR/rail: Greenwich Rail: Blackheath

fine collections of ship models, paintings, medals, uniforms, navigational instruments, and boats.

Highlights include finds from Henry VIII's flagship, the *Mary Rose*, which sank off Portsmouth in 1547; the gilded state barge designed by William Kent for Frederick, Prince of Wales, in 1732; Canaletto's painting "Greenwich Hospital from the North Bank of the Thames" (1747–1750); Captain Cook's reindeer-hide sleeping bag; and the huge collection devoted to Admiral Lord Nelson, including his silver, swords, uniform, and death coat, complete with fatal bullet hole.

INSIDER TIP:

Up the hill from the visitor center at the Prime Meridian, enjoy a lunch with a view at a little stand called The Honest Sausage.

—MARY JO SLAZAK
National Geographic Books subsidiary rights manager

The Queen's House: Do not miss the interior of the Queen's House. The hall is a perfect 40-foot cube and has Nicholas Stone's black-and-white floor laid in 1638, a Tulip Staircase, and a boldly cantilevered balcony. On the ceiling, Gentileschi's paintings, now in Marlborough House, were re-created by computer when the room was restored. The building now houses the Maritime Museum's fine-art collection.

The Royal Observatory

Up in the 200-acre (80 ha) park, the Royal Observatory consists of several buildings housing the museum's astronomical collection. **Flamsteed House** was built by Wren in 1675 for John Flamsteed, the first Astronomer Royal, and used by his successors until 1948. Timekeepers tick-tock in the rooms, and since 1833 the Time Ball on the eastern turret drops at 1 p.m., so passing sailors can check their clocks. In 1884 an international convention agreed that Greenwich would mark zero degrees longitude. The Greenwich Meridian passes through the courtyard, dividing the western and eastern hemispheres. This fountainhead of practical science opened a new planetarium and horology center in 2007.

Greenwich Park & Ranger's House

Greenwich Park has many fine trees dating back to Le Nôtre's landscaping for Charles II. Along the formal avenues, there are gnarled and twisted sweet chestnut, old cypress, paper birch, and prickly castor-oil trees, as well as Indian bean and tulip. From just below the Pavilion Tea House, the panoramic view of the East End, the City, and Westminster is spectacular. The refurnished, pretty, 18th-century redbrick Ranger's House is the setting for the eclectic but high-quality collection amassed by Julius Weinher. The German-born millionaire spent his money on everything from Italian majolica to medieval ivories and Memlinc paintings. ■

Easy escapes from London by train to the comparative calm of Windsor Castle, Oxford, the Cotswolds, Brighton, or York Minster

Excursions

Swans on the Thames at Windsor

Excursions

London can sometimes be simply too stimulating, too overwhelmingly urban and noisy, and relentlessly busy. It is comforting to know that this is a very easy city to leave. Yet the story of London until the 20th century was one of people arriving rather than leaving. England's great 19th-century railway system was built to bring people, trade, and supplies into London.

Today, while the congested roads discourage some potential travelers, the railway system has become a vital tool for escaping the city. London's grand Victorian stations invite you to dip into the clean air of England's lush countryside. Travel by train is easy and bargain ticket deals abound. *(National Rail inquiries, tel 0845 7484950, www.nationalrail.co.uk).*

For ideas on where to go, the British Tourist Authority information desk *(1 Regent Street, W1, www.visitbritain.com)* has details on monuments, historic houses, gardens, music festivals, and accommodations. The National Trust owns and cares for a large number of properties; the National Trust Handbook lists and explains the houses and gardens under its care. Membership brings unlimited free entry to their properties *(tel 0844 800 1895, www.nationaltrust*

.org.uk). English Heritage membership also offers free entry to their properties *(tel 0870 333 1181, www.english-heritage.org.uk).* For garden enthusiasts, the National Gardens Scheme's annual list of gardens open in England is essential *(www.ngs.org.uk),* as is the National Trust's guide to 200 gardens.

A 40-minute train ride westward from Waterloo station brings you to Windsor, a delightful outing. In addition to the castle, there are the twin towns of Windsor and Eton to explore, the Great Park, boat trips on the Thames, and Legoland. Trains from Waterloo go southwest to Salisbury, with its magnificent cathedral and close. The ancient monumental stones of Stonehenge stand a few miles to the north on Salisbury Plain, while Inigo Jones's Wilton House and the classic landscape gardens of Stourhead are to the west.

Eurostar trains run from St. Pancras to central Paris in less than 2.5 hours, a real daytrip or weekend opportunity. Lille (1.5 hours) and Brussels (2 hours) are even closer *(Eurostar inquiries, tel 0843 2186186, www.eurostar.com).*

From Paddington station, trains snake out westward to Oxford's dreamy college spires. The unashamedly grandiose Blenheim Palace is at nearby Woodstock. Beyond them lies the central Cotswold market town of Cirencester, surrounded by rolling, sheep-dotted hills and picturesque villages. Another line from Paddington leads to Shakespeare's birthplace, Stratford-upon-Avon, and the well-known towns of Broadway and Moreton-in-Marsh, best avoided in the crowded summer months. A third Paddington rail service brings you to the elegant Georgian crescents of Bath.

NOT TO BE MISSED:

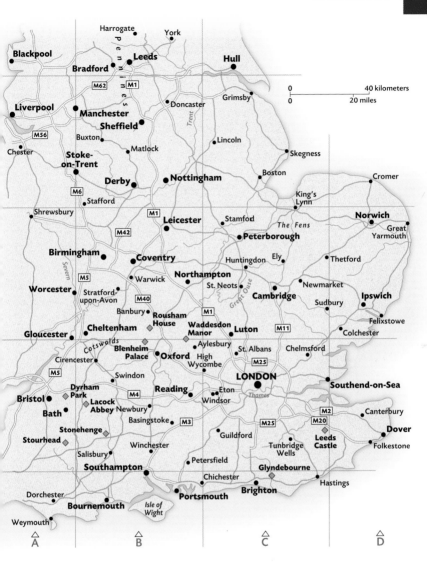

Trains leaving from Charing Cross, Victoria, and Waterloo stations go to the southeast. Here Canterbury's magnificent cathedral dominates the city, while romantic Leeds Castle, bought by Queen Eleanor in 1278, is near Maidstone. Trains from Victoria also speed down to Lewes for summer opera at Glyndebourne and to Brighton for seaside promenading, antique shops, and the Prince Regent's Pavilion.

Trains from Liverpool Street and King's Cross go north to Cambridge's colleges and cloisters, with Ely's and Peterborough's magical cathedrals nearby.

Farther afield, but perfectly manageable on a long daytrip or for a weekend, are York and Leeds. York has its fine Minster, Jorvik Viking Centre, and ancient city walls to explore, while handsome Leeds sits amid the rolling Yorkshire hills so vividly brought to life in the Brontë novels, with the North Yorkshire Moors National Park nearby. ■

Windsor

Set beside the Thames 20 miles (32 km) west of central London, Windsor is quick and easy to reach. The castle is magnificent, and is complemented by other things to see and do. A string of annual events includes the Royal Windsor Horse Show in May; the Windsor Carnival in June; the Royal Windsor Rose Show and polo matches in July; and the Windsor Festival in September. All are very jolly, friendly occasions.

The richly decorated surfaces of the King's Dining Room at Windsor Castle

Windsor

⬛ 221 C2

Visitor Information

✉ The Old Booking Hall, Windsor Royal Shopping, Thames St.

☎ 01753 743900 Accommodations: 01753 743907

www.windsor.gov.uk

Windsor Castle stands on a hill in the town center, its fairy-tale towers silhouetted against the sky. It was William the Conqueror who, in about 1080, threw up this defense as part of his ring of fortifications around London. The Norman castle was converted into a Gothic palace by Edward II. He founded the College of St. George in the Lower Ward and rebuilt the Upper Ward, while Edward IV built **St. George's Chapel** and Henry VIII added the grand gate in the Lower Ward. For King Charles II, who wanted to make Windsor his principal palace outside London, architect Hugh May created England's grandest suite of baroque **State Apartments,** decorated by woodcarver Grinling Gibbons. Later, George III brought in James Wyatt to enhance the castle's romantic character;

INSIDER TIP:

At Windsor Castle you can enjoy the pageantry of the Changing of the Guard without battling large crowds.

—LARRY PORGES
National Geographic Books editor

but it was George IV who employed Jeffrey Wyatville to raise Henry II's famous **Round Tower** to its present height of 215 feet (66 m) and improve the castle's medieval silhouette with extra towers. Wyatville also refurbished the State Rooms and completed the park's **Long Walk,** begun by Charles II.

Queen Victoria made Windsor her principal palace, so it was natural that when her consort, Prince Albert, died in the castle in 1861 she chose to create his memorial chapel here.

After a devastating fire on November 20, 1992 (see sidebar right), the Grand Reception Room, State Dining Room, Crimson Drawing Room, and other casualties were meticulously restored in a modern Gothic style. This style can be seen especially in the **Lantern Lobby.**

The State Apartments, embellished with art from the queen's unmatched collection, may be the central showpiece of the castle, but do not miss other special things. There is the exquisite **Queen Mary's Dolls' House,** designed by Sir Edwin Lutyens for the queen in 1924 to a scale

of 1:12; the **China Museum,** whose display cabinets contain Sèvres, Worcester, Meissen, and more; **St. George's Chapel,** built 1475–1528; and the **Albert Memorial Chapel,** created by Sir George Gilbert Scott.

At the foot of Windsor town, past the **Theatre Royal** *(Thames Street, tel 01753 853888, www .theatreroyalwindsor.co.uk)* and the house where Sir Christopher Wren lived, lies the Thames. Towpath walks are beautiful, and riverboats journey up- and down-river. Over the bridge lies **Eton,** whose college buildings were the haunt of such schoolboys as the Duke of Wellington.

The town is bounded in the south and east by **Windsor Great Park,** whose 4,800 acres (1,942 ha) contain many trees more than 500 years old. Just to the south, **Legoland** lives up to expectations. ∎

Windsor Castle

- ☎ 020 7766 7304
- 🕐 Open daily except during state occasions & official engagements. St. George's Chapel (tel 01753 865538) is closed to visitors on Sunday unless attending services.
- 💲 $$$$

www.royalcollection
.org.uk

Legoland

- ☎ 0871 2222001
- 🕐 Open late March–Oct.
- 💲 $$$$$

www.legoland.co.uk

The Windsor Fire

On November 20, 1992, fire spread through Windsor Castle after a spotlight ignited a curtain in the queen's private chapel. The flames consumed nine main rooms and about 100 smaller rooms in the 900-year-old royal fortress. Afterward, the fire sparked a national debate over who should pay for repairs: Queen Elizabeth II or the taxpayer-funded government, which owns the castle. Ultimately, the queen assumed most of the £37 million ($60 million) bill and, to help cover the costs, opened the State Rooms of Buckingham Palace for summer tours. The castle reopened in 1997. A new stained-glass window in the chapel depicts a fireman spraying water onto a burning castle.

Oxford

Lying between the Rivers Cherwell and Thames (called the Isis here), the honey-colored walls and spires of Oxford's ancient university buildings give the center of this busy city a timeless tranquility. By joining a guided walk, visitors can see colleges that are little changed in their layout and traditions since their medieval or Tudor foundation.

Looking over the Radcliffe Camera and All Souls College at Oxford University

Oxford

🗺 221 B2

🚆 Train takes 1 hour from Paddington station; National Express (08717 818181, www .nationalexpress .com) coach about 1 hour and 45 minutes from Victoria Coach station

Visitor Information

✉ Broad Street, near The Oxford Story, Oxford

☎ 01865 252200

www.oxfordcity .co.uk

Among the oldest colleges is **Merton** (*Merton St., tel 01865 276310*), founded in 1264. Its 14th-century Mob Quad contains the oldest library in England still in use. **Balliol** (*Broad St., tel 01865 277777*) has nurtured more politicians than any other college. Poet Percy Bysshe Shelley was "rusticated" (sent away for a term) for writing subversive pamphlets from **University College** on High Street, called The High (*tel 01865 276602*).

Magdalen (pronounced "Maudlin"; *The High, tel 01865 276000*) was built at the end of the 15th century and has a lovely deer park behind it. The largest college, **Christ Church** (*St. Aldate's, tel 01865 276150*), was founded by Cardinal Wolsey in 1525. Its chapel is also Britain's smallest cathedral, built in the 12th century as a priory church. In summer, a towpath stroll might go across **Christ Church Meadow** to Britain's oldest **Botanic Gardens,** (*tel 01865 286690, www.botanic-garden.ox.ac.uk, $*) whose most exotic plants are kept in riverside greenhouses.

To join undergraduates in a traditional Oxford pastime, test your skills by hiring a punt on the

Cherwell (pronounced "Char-well") from beside Magdalen Bridge or on the Isis from Folly Bridge near Christ Church, where boat trips depart. Summer events include Eights Week rowing competitions at the end of May.

Out at Garsington village, operas are staged at **Garsington Manor** (tel 01865 361636) in June, when the audience picnics in the gardens in fine clothes to create a *fête champêtre* atmosphere.

Oxford's impressive museums are open all year. The **Ashmolean** (Beaumont St., tel 01865 278000, closed Mon.), founded in 1683 and Britain's oldest public museum, houses Egyptian, classical, Oriental, and European art, plus silver and

INSIDER TIP:

The small, atmospheric Turf Tavern (4–5 Bath Place), popular with students and dons, is a great place to get a pint.

—PATRICIA DANIELS
National Geographic contributor

ceramics. The city's own story is told in the **Museum of Oxford** (St. Aldate's, tel 01865 252761); the university's is explained in the **Oxford Story** (Broad St., tel 01865 790055); and that of the universe is explored in the glorious building of the **University Museum of Natural History**, complete with dodo remains (Parks Road, tel 01865 272950). The **Pitt Rivers Museum** (Parks

Road, tel 01865 270927) is devoted to archaeology and anthropology. Other Oxford buildings to seek out include the **Bodleian Library,** founded in 1598, and the round **Sheldonian Theatre,** both on Broad Street; the domed **Radcliffe Camera,** part of the Bodleian Library, is next to the Sheldonian.

Around Oxford

There are three interesting country houses to visit in the vicinity of Oxford, each with a fine garden.

The Duke of Marlborough's 18th-century **Blenheim Palace** stands outside the charming village of Woodstock, 8 miles (13 km) northwest of Oxford on the A44. John Vanbrugh's huge Italianate palace is surrounded by a very English park. Tapestries, paintings, and fine furniture fill the gilded State Rooms and Long Library. The rolling acres of park include a narrow-gauge railway, a lake, and the Marlborough Maze.

Another grand house near Oxford is **Waddesdon Manor,** a French Renaissance château built by Baron Ferdinand de Rothschild between 1874 and 1889. Approximately 20 miles (32 km) northeast of Oxford, the house now belongs to the National Trust. French furniture gleams in the gilded salons, and the French-influenced gardens are clipped to perfection.

Less grand **Rousham,** 12 miles (19 km) north of Oxford on the A4260, is a 17th-century house standing in a garden little changed since it was landscaped by William Kent in the 18th century. ∎

Blenheim Palace

- 🅰 221 B2
- ✉ Woodstock, Oxfordshire
- ☎ 0800 849 6500
- 🕐 Daily
- 💲 $$$$$: includes park & most attractions. Supplement for fishing on the lake and rowboat rentals

www.blenheimpalace.com

Waddesdon Manor

- 🅰 221 B3
- ✉ Waddesdon, Buckinghamshire
- ☎ 01296 653226
- 🕐 Timed tickets obligatory
- 💲 $$$$

www.waddesdon.org.uk

Rousham House & Garden

- 🅰 221 B3
- ✉ Rousham, Oxfordshire
- ☎ 01869 347110
- 🕐 House open only by appt. Gardens open all year. No children.
- 💲 $$$

www.rousham.org

Salisbury & Stonehenge

South Wiltshire is best known for two truly magnificent sites: the soaring elegance of Salisbury Cathedral, set in its magnificent close, and Stonehenge's standing stones on the open grasslands of Salisbury Plain. This is ideal country for walking, horseback riding, cycling, and exploring unspoiled villages.

Horizontal lintels still crown some of the upright sarsen stones in Stonehenge's outer circle.

Salisbury

Ⓐ 221 B2

Visitor Information

✉ Fish Row, Salisbury

☎ 01722 334956

www.visitwiltshire .co.uk/salisbury/ home

Salisbury Cathedral

✉ The Close, Salisbury

☎ 01722 555120

🕐 Open daily. Evensong 5:30 p.m.

$ Donation. Various tours: $$

www.salisbury cathedral.co.uk

Salisbury

The Avon, Wylye, and Bourne Rivers twist their way through the chalk valleys to meet at New Sarum, or Salisbury. A good place to start exploring this city, however, is at **Old Sarum,** just north of the city. Here mounds, ditches, and walls tell the silent story of an Iron Age fort, a Roman settlement, a fortified Saxon town, and a Norman castle (*Castle Road, tel 01722 335398*) and **cathedral.**

It was Bishop Richard Poore who moved Old Sarum's cathedral to its present site. In 1220 he began the only medieval cathedral in England to be built in a single, unified style throughout. Completed in 1258, its 400-foot-tall (122 m) spire was added a

generation later. While the exterior is rich in traceried windows and ornate friezes, the interior's simple symmetry is emphasized by a lack of furnishings and by stained glass. There are some grand tombs, however, such as that of Bishop Giles de Bridport (1260). The Chapter House, in the cloisters, exhibits one of the four surviving copies of the Magna Carta.

Salisbury's **Cathedral Close** is the finest and largest of its kind in the country. Once the precinct of the ecclesiastical community serving the cathedral, it is now a peaceful square overlooked by elegant houses. Pierced by three strong gateways, its walls were built around 1330. The gates are still locked each night.

Several buildings in the close can be visited. **Mompesson House** (*The Close, Salisbury, tel 01722 335659, closed Thurs.–Fri. Nov.–Mar., $$, www.nationaltrust .org.uk*), run by the National Trust, was built for Charles Mompesson in 1701 and later decorated by Charles Longueville with fine plasterwork and a carved oak staircase. The Wardrobe dates from 1254, when it was built to store the bishop's clothing; today it houses the **Royal Gloucestershire, Berkshire & Wiltshire Regimental Museum** (*tel 01722 414536*). Sit beneath the magnificent roof of the **Medieval Hall** *(tel 01722 412472)* to see a 40-minute show recounting Salisbury's history. For information on Stonehenge and related sites, visit the **Salisbury & South Wiltshire Museum** *(The King's House, The Close, Salisbury, tel 01722 332151, Open Mon.–Sat. Oct.–May, Sun. June–Sept., $$, www.salisburymuseum.org.uk).*

Around Salisbury

Another elegant building, just west of the city, is **Wilton House,** home of the Herbert family since 1544. Its magnificent rooms are matched by a romantic park. For garden lovers, **Heale Garden** *(Middle Woodford, tel 01722 782504)* is a pretty 5-mile (8 km) drive north through the Wiltshire countryside, and **Houghton Lodge Gardens & Hydroponicum** *(near Stockbridge, tel 01264 810502)* are 16 miles (26 km)

east, beside the river Test in Hampshire.

Stonehenge

One of the most significant prehistoric sites stands on the rolling chalklands of Salisbury Plain. This mystical, enigmatic, and surely symbolic circle of giant standing stones may have marked the center of an ancient administrative, cultural, and social territory that was important as long ago as 3000 B.C. It stands near the sites of five prehistoric communities, marked by the remains of ceremonial and domestic structures, including burial mounds and the markings of Celtic farms and fields.

The original function of the stone circle has been discussed endlessly: Perhaps it was the center for a religious celebration of the winter and summer solstices, aligned to moon and sun; perhaps a gigantic astronomical stone calendar. At a later date, a 2-mile-long (3.2 km) avenue to the River Avon was added to mark the line of Midsummer's Day sunrise, and about 80 blue stones, some weighing 2 tons (1.8 tonnes), were transported 240 miles (386 km) from the Preseli Hills of South Wales. Later still, trilithons were added at the heart of the complex.

Stonehenge is a center for revived Druid ceremonies; several thousand people attend the summer solstice. To protect the stones from wear and vandalism, visitors are no longer allowed into the circle itself, but may walk around the circle close to the stones. ∎

Wilton House

- ✉ Wilton, Salisbury
- ☎ 01722 746729
- 🕐 Open Sun.–Thurs. April 22–Sept. 1
- 💲 $$$$

www.wiltonhouse.com

Stonehenge

- 🅰 221 B2
- ✉ Jct. of the A303 & A360
- ☎ 08073 331181
- 💲 $$$ (includes excellent audioguide)

www.english-heritage.org.uk/stonehenge

World Heritage Site

Stonehenge's famous circle is not the only local reminder of the ancient British peoples. The Stonehenge World Heritage site encompasses 6,500 acres (2,600 ha) of protected land containing the Cursus (a long rectangular earthwork), other henge monuments such as Woodhenge and Durrington Walls, neolithic and Bronze Age barrows (burial mounds), and an Iron Age hill fort.

Bath

Straddling the river Avon in a great bowl of softly curving hills, Bath was the Roman spa Aquae Sulis, popular from the first to the fifth centuries. The mineral-rich waters and natural hot spring have ensured the city's prosperity through the ages.

Bath
⚠ 221 A2

Visitor Information
✉ Abbey Church Yard, Abbey Chambers
☎ 870 444 6442 (outside U.K.) or 0906 7112000 (inside U.K.)

www.visitbath.co.uk

After speeding along high above the Avon Valley, the train from London slows down for a magnificent panorama of the city, with **Bath Abbey's** *(12 Kingston Buildings, tel 01225 422462)* pinnacled tower rising above Georgian terraces and crescents. The abbey is a good place to start a visit. It is the last complete monastic church to be built before the 16th-century Dissolution of the Monasteries.

Nearby, the **Roman Baths** complex, with temple, baths, and a museum of sculptures, coins, and

Bath's ancient baths are part of a Roman complex.

other remains, constitutes one of Europe's best Roman sites. Adjoining them, the Pump Room was the social center of 18th-century Bath, whose fashionable visitors included the Prince of Wales, later George IV. Architect Nicholas Grimshaw has incorporated some of the complex into Britain's only natural thermal spa.

It was during the 18th century that much of Bath was built, the mellow, local stone creating an elegant Georgian town that is lovingly preserved. Great Pulteney Street is particularly fine, reached across Robert Adam's Pulteney Bridge, built in 1770. Other remarkable buildings to seek out include **Guildhall** *(www.bathvenues .co.uk)*, on the High Street next to the old covered market, the beautiful **Theatre Royal** *(tel 01225 448844)*, on Milsom Street, and the **Octagon** building lying off it. The **Circus** and **Royal Crescent** are two superb buildings created by Bath's chief architects, John Wood the Elder and his son, John Wood the Younger. **No. 1 Royal Crescent** has been meticulously restored and furnished and is open to the public. It is worth comparing with the home of astronomer **William Herschel** *(19 New King St., tel. 1225 446865)*.

Bath abounds in museums, many celebrating its history. The **Building of Bath Museum** *(The*

EXPERIENCE: Taking the Waters in Bath

Make like a Roman and relax in the natural hot waters that have drawn people to Bath for centuries. While the original **Roman Baths** *(Pump Room, Stall St., tel 01225 477785, www.romanbaths.co.uk, $$$$)* are now a museum and historic site, the nearby **Thermae Bath Spa** *(tel 01225 477051, www.thermaebathspa.com)* still offers hot baths for today's visitors. A "Spas Ancient and Modern" package includes a tour of the Roman baths, soaking in mineral waters, and dining at the historic Pump Room, a neoclassical salon where the city's famous water flows from a fountain. Have a fortifying sip—the spa water is loaded with 43 minerals.

Vineyards, tel 01225 333895) tells of Georgian Bath, while the **Georgian Garden** at No. 4, The Circus, perfectly re-creates an 18th-century town garden. The **Book Museum** celebrates the craft of bookbinding and Bath's place in English literature; the story of one small Bath firm is told at the **Museum of Bath at Work** *(Julian Rd., tel 01225 318348)*. **Bath Postal Museum** *(8 Broad St., tel 01225 460333, www.bathpostalmuseum.org)* reminds visitors that the world's first stamp, was posted from Bath on May 2, 1840. The **Bath Boating Station** *(Forrester Rd., tel 01225 312900, www.bathboating. co.uk)* is a living museum of skiffs, punts, and canoes for rent.

Another museum worth visiting is the **Holburne Museum and Crafts Study Centre** *(Great Pulteney St. tel. 1225 466669, www.holburne.org)*, Sir William Holburne's collection of silver, porcelain, paintings, and more, housed in the 18th-century Sydney Hotel. In the basement of the grand 18th-century Assembly Rooms, the **Fashion Museum** *(Bennett St., tel 01225 477789, www.museumofcostume.co.uk)* has

an excellent collection covering Tudor times to the present.

Around Bath

On the southeastern outskirts of the city, the **American Museum in Britain** displays its quality collection in 18 re-created period rooms of the 17th to 19th centuries. **Bradford-on-Avon** is a delightful riverside town located about 8 miles southeast of Bath on the A363. Farther afield, but still easily reached, the National Trust runs three magnificent sights: **Dyrham Park,** 8 miles north on the A46, an early 18th-century house with deer park; **Lacock Abbey** *(Lacock, tel 01249 372501, abbey closed Tues. & Nov.–March, $$)*, 12 miles east of Bath, just off the A350, a country house founded as an abbey in the 13th century and now home to a museum commemorating Henry Fox Talbot, father of photography; and **Stourhead** *(Stourton, tel 01747 841152, house closed Wed.–Thur. & Nov.–March, www.nationaltrust. org.uk/main/w-stourhead, $$$$)*, 20 miles south of Bath off the B3092, a beautiful 18th-century English landscape garden. ■

American Museum in Britain

- ✉ Claverton Manor, Bath
- ☎ 01225 460503
- 🕐 Closed Mon. & Nov.–mid-March
- 💲 $$$

www.american museum.org

Bradford-on-Avon

Visitor Information
- ✉ 34 Silver St.
- ☎ 01225 865797

www.bradford onavon.co.uk

Dyrham Park

- 🅰 221 A2
- ✉ Near Chipping Sodbury, Wiltshire
- ☎ 01179 372501
- 🕐 House: closed Wed.–Thurs. & Nov.–March
- 💲 $$$

www.nationaltrust .org.uk/main/ w-dyrhampark

Stratford & the Cotswolds

The town where the poet, actor, and playwright William Shakespeare was born is now so bound up with its renowned citizen that avoiding crowds of fellow visitors is a problem. The same applies to the surrounding countryside and the Cotswolds that stretch southward from here. Try the off season; and always reserve tickets in advance for the Royal Shakespeare Theatre *(tel 0870 6091110)*.

Shakespeare's birthplace is furnished as it might have appeared in the 16th century.

Stratford-upon-Avon

⬛ 221 B3

Visitor Information

✉ Bridgefoot

☎ 0870 1607930

www.stratford-upon-avon.co.uk

Gloucestershire

⬛ 221 A2–B3

Visitor Information

✉ Corn Hall, Market Place, Cirencester

☎ 01285 654180

www.glos-cotswolds.com

✉ 77 Promenade, Cheltenham

☎ 01242 522878

www.visitcheltenham.info

For Shakespeare pilgrims, there are five key sites to see. In Stratford, **Shakespeare's Birthplace** on Henley Street *(tel 01789 204016, www.shakespeare.org.uk)*; **Nash's House and New Place** *(tel 01789 292325)* on Chapel Street, home of Shakespeare's granddaughter and site of his retirement house, where an Elizabethan knot garden has been planted; and the Tudor **Hall's Croft** *(tel 01789 292325)*, where his daughter and son-in-law, Dr. John Hall, lived, furnished in period style. Outside the town, you can visit his wife **Anne Hathaway's Cottage** *(tel 01789 292100)*, a thatched Tudor farmhouse at Shottery; and his mother Mary Arden's half-timbered house at **Wilmcote**.

Ten miles north of Stratford on the A46, **Warwick Castle** *(tel 0871 222 6688, www.warwick-castle .co.uk)* is one of England's finest, having grown from a wooden motte and bailey built by William the Conqueror in 1068 into a huge complex. A few miles north again, the ruins of **Kenilworth Castle** *(tel 01926 852078)* include a Norman keep, Great Hall, and gardens. **Ragley Hall** and its 400-acre (162 ha) park *(8 miles/13 km west of Stratford, tel 0800 093 0290, www.ragleyhall.com)* is matched by some smaller houses and gardens in the area, including **Snowshill Manor** *(tel 01386 852410)* and **Hidcote Manor Gardens** *(tel 01386 438333)*.

The Cotswolds

South of Stratford, sheep grazing the rolling hills of the Cotswolds brought prosperity that can be seen today in handsome stone-built market towns. **Cirencester** is the grandest, **Burford** has an impressive main street, and **Charlbury** is set in the timeless Evenlode Valley. **Tetbury** and **Chipping Norton** both testify to wool wealth. However, there may be too many visitors to enjoy the beauty of such towns as Bourton-on-the-Water, Moreton-in-Marsh, and Stow-on-the-Wold. ∎

Canterbury & Leeds Castle

Canterbury Cathedral, founded in A.D. 597, is the Mother Church of the Anglican Communion and the Seat of the Archbishop of Canterbury. As such, it is not only full of interest inside; it also dominates the city's history. To explore the streets and sights, you can walk alone or take a guided tour, gaze at the city from a punt, or ride through in a horse and carriage.

The present **Cathedral** building (tel 01227 762862, www.canterbury-cathedral.org), started in 1070, displays more than four centuries of architectural progress from the Norman choir and crypt to the high Gothic nave. The landmark Bell Harry Tower, 235 feet (72 m) high and built in 1495, is also Gothic. Archbishop Thomas à Becket was murdered in the northwest transept in 1170 by Henry II's knights because he had dared to criticize the king. The golden shrine to the saint became a major medieval pilgrimage site. (Geoffrey Chaucer's fictional pilgrims in *The Canterbury Tales* were typical.) The shrine itself was pillaged by Henry VIII, but candles still burn on the site in Trinity Chapel at the Cathedral's east end.

In the town, walk through the streets of half-timbered medieval buildings from the cathedral to **St. Augustine's Abbey** (Longport, tel 01227 378100), the **Roman Museum** (Longmarket, tel 01227 785575), and **The Canterbury Tales** (St. Margaret's Street, tel 01227 479227) where Chaucer's pilgrims' tales are reenacted.

Just east of Maidstone, **Leeds Castle** was one of Henry VIII's palaces. Built in the middle of a lake and surrounded by 500 acres (202 ha) of parkland, this is the epitome of the romantic castle. ■

Canterbury
🅰 221 D2
Visitor Information
✉ 12–13 Sun St., The Buttermarket (opposite cathedral entrance)
☎ 01227 862064
🕐 Closed Sun. Jan.–Easter
www.canterbury.co.uk

Leeds Castle
🅰 221 C2
✉ Broomfield, Maidstone
☎ 01622 765400
💲 $$$$
www.leeds-castle.com

Canterbury Cathedral's soaring Gothic nave

Brighton & Hove

The Prince Regent put Brighton on the map when he built his Royal Pavilion, an India-inspired palace. Ever since, Brighton has welcomed visitors and offered them entertainment.

Brighton

◭ 221 C1

Visitor Information

✉ Bartholomew Square

☎ 0906 7112255

www.visitbrighton .com

Glyndebourne

◭ 221 C1

Festival Opera

✉ Glyndebourne, Lewes, East Sussex

☎ 01273 813813

🕓 Performances late May–end Aug.

www.glyndebourne .com

Visit the **Royal Pavilion** *(tel 01273 290900)* to catch a glimpse of Regency high life. Nearby, you can get lost in the maze of lanes crammed with antiques shops, while a walk along the seafront passes Regency terraces and Palace Pier. Brighton also has an excellent **Museum & Art Gallery** *(Church St., tel 01273-290900)*, haunting Victorian memorials in **Lewes Road Cemeteries** *(tel 01273 604020)*, the **Booth Museum of Natural History** *(194 Dyke Road, tel 03000 290900)*, and the **Brighton Fishing Museum** *(201 Lower Kings Road Arches, tel 01273-723064)*, as well as a delightful theater and a calendar of arts festivals and fairs. North of the city center, there is Edwardian **Preston Manor** *(tel 01273 292770)*. In neighboring

Hove, the **Regency Town House** *(13 Brunswick Square, tel 01273 206306)* has been restored and is open to the public, while on the outskirts **Foredown Tower** *(Foredown Rd., Portslade, tel 01273-292092)*, a converted Edwardian water tower, gives views over the Sussex Downs.

Walks on the downs can be combined with visits to pretty Alfriston or Firle, villages within a few miles of each other. They lie about 15 miles east of Brighton, near **Charleston Farm House** *(tel 01323 811265)*, associated with the Bloomsbury Group. Opera enthusiasts can enjoy world-class opera in Michael Hopkins's theater at **Glyndebourne,** taking picnic supper on the lawns in their formal evening dress during the interval. ∎

EXPERIENCE: Brighton Activities

From antique motorcycles to paper unicorns, you never know just what you might find on Madeira Drive, Brighton's beachfront corridor and home to more than a dozen annual events *(see www .brightonrun.co.uk)*. In December the road practically ignites as residents parade with glowing, handmade paper lanterns in shapes ranging from whimsical clocks to unicorns and suns. Dubbed **"Burning the Clocks"** *(www.burningtheclocks.co.uk)* and held on the Winter Solstice, the celebration culminates when marchers toss the lanterns into a beach bonfire.

Madeira Drive also hosts a number of motorcycle events, including the **Pioneer Bike Run,** which invites owners of motorcycles built before 1915 to ride from London to Brighton. Some entrants are little more than bicycles with motors, and roadside repairs are common, but more than 300 vehicles sputter through the run every March.

In September the **National Speed Trials** *(www.brightonandhovemotorclub .co.uk/speedtrials_details.php)* zip in for 100-meter (109 yd) automotive sprints that date back to 1905.

Cambridge

Set in a loop of the Cam River in flat countryside, Cambridge is an idyllic, tranquil university city, quite different from bustling, hectic Oxford.

The oldest college is **Peterhouse,** *(tel 01223 338200),* founded in 1284. Each one that followed was a superb example of its architectural period. The most beautiful is **King's College** *(tel 01223 331417),* best seen from a boat on the river Cam or from the secluded walks of the "Backs," meadows across the river from the colleges. King's College Chapel is probably Britain's finest example of Perpendicular Gothic architecture.

Queens' *(tel 01223 335511)* has wonderful Tudor courts and the Mathematical Bridge built in 1749 without nails or bolts (but subsequent repair work has added them). **Trinity** *(tel 01223 338400)* has a Wren-designed library by the river. Undergraduates try to race around Great Court while the clock strikes twelve. Other colleges not to miss are **Clare, Magdalene, St. John's, Jesus,** and **Emmanuel.** Visitors may walk into their courtyards and chapels, and sometimes their gardens, or take a guided tour. (Access may be restricted at certain times.)

Punters take visitors down the river Cam in tranquil Cambridge.

Ely & Peterborough

Both these cities in the flat fenlands north of Cambridge have magnificent Norman cathedrals. Ely's is famous for its lantern tower and stained glass, Peterborough's for its west front and painted ceiling. Ely *(tel 01353 662062)* is an unspoiled market town on the Great Ouse River about 15 miles (24 km) north of Cambridge, Peterborough *(tel 01733 452336)* lies 25 miles (40 km) northwest of Ely. ■

Cambridge
🅰 221 C3
Visitor information
✉ Peas Hill, Cambridge
☎ 0871 226 8006
www.visitcambridge.org

York & Leeds

A three-hour train journey from London reaches the wild moors of Yorkshire in northern England. Here Romans, Saxons, Vikings, and Normans have all left their mark on York.

York

▲ 221 B5

Visitor Information

✉ Exhibition Square

☎ 01904 621756

www.york-tourism .co.uk

Visitors can walk the city walls, first built by the Romans, and explore the **Jorvik Viking Centre** *(Coppergate, tel 01904 615505)*, where they travel back through the centuries in "time-cars." But it is **York Minster** *(tel 01904 557216)* that dominates the narrow streets. Begun in the 13th century, it is England's largest Gothic church.

Other attractions include the **York Castle Museum** *(The Eye of York, tel 01904 687687)* with re-created period rooms, the huge **National Railway Museum** *(Leeman Rd., tel 08448 153139)*, **Merchant Adventurers' Hall**

(Fossgate, tel 01904 654818), built by York's medieval guilds, and the **City Art Gallery** *(Exhibition Square, tel 01904 687687)*, with paintings spanning 600 years.

Leeds

Across the moors lies **Leeds** *(visitor information, City Station, tel 0113 2425242, www.leeds.gov.uk)*, a handsome city whose markets and public buildings testify to centuries of wealth. In town, museums include the **City Art Gallery** *(The Headrow, tel 0113 2478248)*, notable for 20th-century works, and the **Royal Armouries Museum** *(Armouries Dr., tel 0113 2201999)*, where you can watch live displays of jousting and swordsmanship. The **Henry Moore Institute**—the sculptor studied in Leeds—puts on a variety of exhibitions. Three of Britain's national parks are within reach: the Yorkshire Dales, the North Yorkshire Moors, and the Peak District, all glorious places for walking. ■

York Minster stands tall over the city of York.

Travelwise

Bicycles for rent in Hyde Park

TRAVELWISE

PLANNING YOUR TRIP

When to Go

London is what you make of it. There are, however, seasons that are particularly good for certain interests, such as traditional events, gardens, or church music.

January, February, and **March** are good months for getting into popular plays and operas and enjoying museums in relative peace. Even the top restaurants are easier to book; and shoppers can take advantage of the sales. On the last Sunday of January, the beheading of Charles I is commemorated; February traditions include Chinese New Year celebrations in Soho.

Easter, which may fall in March or April, brings exceptional music when the Easter Passions are sung in the cathedrals, churches, and concert halls. At this time of year, there is plenty of horse racing, and the Oxford versus Cambridge boat race takes place between Putney Bridge and Hammersmith. In the parks, daffodils carpet the lawns while trees burst into leaf. Hyde Park is the setting for the Easter Parade and the Harness Horse Parade.

April and **May** mark an increase in cultural events. Arts festivals, houses that open only for the summer months, and fashionable sports such as polo at Ascot and the Windsor Horse Trials swing into action. A string of antiques fairs begins. There are flower shows at the Royal Horticultural Society's halls in Pimlico, culminating in the Chelsea Flower Show. The queen spends most of this time at Windsor, so the State Apartments may be closed. Watch for special events on the

first and last Mondays of May, both public holidays.

June brings hope for good weather. Arts festivals include Greenwich, Spitalfields, and the summer-long season of open-air concerts at Kenwood House and Marble Hill House. Traditional sporting events include The Derby at Epsom, Ascot Week, Henley Royal Regatta, the AEGON tournament at Queen's, and the All England Lawn Tennis championships at Wimbledon—all need advance reservations for good tickets. Traditional events peak, too, with Beating the Retreat, the Garter Ceremony at Windsor, and Trooping the Colour. Again, the queen is often at Windsor, when State Apartments close.

July and **August** are months when offices go quiet and many Londoners leave town. But museums and theaters fill up with visitors. To June's arts festivals add the City of London Festival and the nightly Henry Wood Promenade ("Prom") concerts at the Royal Albert Hall. With Londoners back from the summer break, **September** and **October** mix festivals on the Thames and in Covent Garden with major art shows, operas, and plays. In the parks, summer blooms give way to fall color.

November and **December** are strong on tradition: the State Opening of Parliament (October or November), Guy Fawkes' Day, the Lord Mayor's Show, and then the Christmas festivities. Shops and streets are decorated, theater tickets need to be reserved in advance, and an abundance of

music is performed in cathedrals, churches, and concert halls.

Climate

British weather is a daily surprise for every British person. Anything can happen on this island at the mercy of its surrounding seas, Gulf Stream, and prevailing winds: hot sun in April, sleet in August. This has two results in London: Weather is a constant topic of conversation; and, since anything can happen, few people carry umbrellas or raincoats.

For visitors, the motto is "be prepared." Ignore Londoners' laid-back approach to equipment and carry a fold-up umbrella, wear a waterproof coat, and consider waterproof shoes. Finally, any day planned outside needs a fallback indoor plan in case it rains, or worse.

Passports & Visas

Nationals of the United States, Canada, Australia, and New Zealand can enter the United Kingdom with just a passport (no visa is required).

HOW TO GET TO CENTRAL LONDON

From the Airports

Gatwick (tel 0844 335 1802, www.gatwickairport.com) The airport lies 30 miles (48 km) south of central London; traveling to London by rail is faster and more reliable than by road. There are two services: the more expensive Gatwick Express (tel 0845 8501530, www.gatwickexpress.com) to Victoria, a 30- to 35-minute ride, runs every 15 minutes by day and less frequently by night. Southern trains on the same route take longer as they are not nonstop.

Thameslink trains stop at London Bridge, Blackfriars, City Thameslink, Farringdon, and King's Cross Thameslink.

By road, the Airbus A5 (tel 020 08705 747777) bus takes 80 minutes and departs about once an hour, 5 a.m. to 8 p.m. A taxi costs more than £60 ($98).

Heathrow (tel 0844 335 1801, www.heathrowairport.com) London's main airport is 15 miles (24 km) west of central London, so rail and road are both options. Rail is more dependable during rush hours. By rail, the Heathrow Express (tel 0845 6001515, www.heathrowexpress.com) to Paddington, a 20-minute ride, runs every 15 minutes between 5:07 a.m. and 11:42 p.m. By Tube train, the Piccadilly line trains, a 40- to 60-minute ride, run regularly 5:02 a.m. to 12:00 a.m. through central London. National Express (tel 08717 818181, www.national express.com) runs from Heathrow Central Bus Terminal to Victoria Coach station every 30 minutes and takes 60 to 90 minutes. A taxi costs £30 to £50 ($49–$82), depending upon destination, congestion, and resulting trip time.

London City Airport (tel 020 7646 0000, www.londoncityairport.com) This small airport lies on the Isle of Dogs in Docklands, 9 miles (14 km) east of central London. It has a DLR station with links to Canary Wharf and Bank, both on the Tube. Services run every 8 to 15 minutes; journey time to Bank is 22 minutes. A prebookable bus shuttle (tel 0845 0959595, www.lcyshuttle.co.uk) runs to and from Canary Wharf and central London. A taxi takes 20 to 40 minutes and costs £20 to £25 ($32–$40).

Stansted (tel 0844 3351803, www.stanstedairport.com)

London's newest airport is 35 miles (56 km) northeast of central London, so rail is much faster than road. Stansted Express to Liverpool Street station takes 42 minutes, and runs every 15 minutes between 6 a.m. and 11:59 p.m. (1:30 a.m. Fri.–Sat.) By road, a taxi costs more than £60 ($98).

By Train or Bus
Eurostar trains (tel 020 7646 0088, www.eurostar.com) arrive at St. Pancras International (tel 020 7843 7688, www.stpancras.com) from Paris, Disneyland Paris, Brussels, and Lille.

National trains (tel 08457 484950, www.nationalrail.co.uk) arrive at Charing Cross, Euston, King's Cross, Liverpool Street, Paddington, Victoria, and Waterloo stations.

Long-distance bus services arrive at Victoria Coach station. National Express (tel 08717 818181, www.nationalexpress.com) is Britain's biggest company, Eurolines (tel 01582 404511) travels to the Continent.

GETTING AROUND
Public Transportation
Learning to enjoy London's public transportation system is the first step to enjoying exploring the capital. Taxis, although fun, are just one transportation experience, and when the traffic snarls the bills mount up very quickly, especially after 8 p.m., when much higher tariffs apply. Taking the Tube or a bus, as all Londoners do, saves time and can be great fun; and just ask if you are in doubt.

By Taxi
There are two kinds of taxi: the "black cab" and the minicab.

Black cabs (some painted other colors) are a distinct shape and are restricted in numbers, and their drivers have all passed the tough "The Knowledge" exams and know their city extremely well. They also have full insurance and are reliable to use to deliver parcels. To use one, either go to a taxi stand, phone a company such as Radio Taxis (tel 020 7272 0272, www.radiotaxis.co.uk) or Dial a Cab (tel 020 7253 5000, www.dialacab.co.uk), or hail one on the street that is displaying an illuminated yellow "For Hire" sign on top. The fare rises according to distance and time; charges rise evenings and weekends. The driver is obliged to use the straightest route to your destination unless you instruct him to do otherwise. To complain, call the Transport for London Taxi and Private Hire Directorate (tel 0845 6027000).

Minicabs often have untrained drivers and uninsured cars. Legally they may only be booked by phone and may not be picked up on the street—it is extremely unwise to do so. A minicab company should only be used by personal recommendation. An exception is Lady Cabs (tel 020 7272 3300, www.ladyminicabs.co.uk), which employs only women drivers and is preferred by some single women.

By Bus & Tube
Transport for London (tel 0843 2221234, www.tfl.gov.uk) runs the Tube (also known as the Underground) and most of the buses. Fares for both methods of transportation are structured according to nine concentric zones—zones 1 and 2 cover most of central London. Tickets can be bought individually for each trip, but the easiest, quickest, and most economical way to buy tickets is to choose an Oyster card.

An Oyster card can be bought at any Tube/DLR station for a refundable deposit of £3 ($4.90). You load money onto the card, either with cash and credit/debit cards at the ticket office, or using credit or debit cards at touch-screen machines. You then swipe the card on the round yellow disks at ticket barriers (and swipe again on exiting at the conclusion of your journey). Cards can also be used on all buses, but need only be swiped on entry. Oyster card fares are significantly less than ordinary single-ticket fares, and less than most Travelcards.

A Travelcard can be used on the Tube and bus system, plus the DLR and some rail services. There are various kinds of Travelcards, including one-day (valid before 9:30 a.m.), one-day (valid after 9:30 a.m.), one-week, weekend, and family cards. Each card can be bought for some or all of the zones. Once bought, you simply use it or show it on demand.

Both Oyster cards and Travel-cards can be bought online before you travel to the U.K. (http://visitor shop.tfl.gov.uk).

London's Bus System
There is nothing quite like rumbling through London on a bus, looking at the people, buildings, advertisements, and street art. To catch a bus, first find a bus stop, indicated by a pole with a red sign. This will list the bus numbers that stop there, together with their routes. Either pay with an Oyster card, Travelcard, or buy an individual ticket in advance.

The Tube (Underground)
This huge system of a dozen lines with about 300 stations snakes all over London and carries 2.5 million people a day. London's Tube (subway) is well lit, easy to use, and safe. First, plot your route on the Tube map. Then, buy a Travelcard, Oyster card, or individual ticket. Use this to pass through the automatic barriers, get on the right color-coded line, and ensure you are traveling in the right direction. To change lines, follow the signs to the connecting line on the platform. Use your ticket or card to exit through the barriers, then keep it flat for the next journey. When in doubt, ask; Londoners get lost, too.

Docklands Light Railway (DLR) (tel 020 7363 9700 or 0843 222 1234, www.tfl.gov. uk) This high-level railway runs from Bank and Tower Gateway stations, both connected to the Tube network, and on through Docklands.

Organized Sightseeing
Even the most independent traveler may find it helpful to take a tour sometimes. Bus tours give an overview of the city; walking tours open your eyes to a street's history and monuments; river tours provide a new perspective on London; and some tours simply get you into places usually closed to the public. Here is a selection; local tourist information centers will carry information on others and *Time Out* lists several in their "Around Town" section. Most telephone numbers provide detailed recorded information.

Bus Tours
Big Bus Company (tel 020 7233 9533, www.bigbustours.com); **Original London Sightseeing Tour** (tel 020 8877 1722, www .theoriginaltour.com).

River Tours
The useful website for all boat tours is www.tfl.gov.uk. See also p. 53.

Walking Tours
Citisights (tel 020 8806 3742, www.chr.org.uk); **Original London Walks** (tel 020 7624 3978, www.walks.com) has a huge variety of walks led by professionals and enthusiasts.

Tailor-Made Tours
To employ a guide with the highest qualifications, the Blue Badge, contact Tour Guides (tel 020 7495 5504, www.tourguides .co.uk).

Tours from the Air
Adventure Balloons (tel 01252 844222, www.adventureballoons .co.uk); **Cabair Helicopters** (tel 020 8953 4411, www.cabairhelicopters. com).

Specialist Tours
The many available include Super Tours of Westminster Abbey and St. Paul's Cathedral, tours of the Royal National Theatre, and tours of special houses such as Linley Sambourne House or Dennis Severs's House.

The Leisure Pass
A bargain way of visiting several fee-paying attractions (tel 0870 2429988, www.londonpass.com).

PRACTICAL ADVICE
Electricity
The supply is 230V, with a permitted range of 216.2–253V, and 50 cycles per second (kHz). Plugs are three-pin.
U.S. appliances need a voltage transformer and an adapter.

Money Matters
Sterling currency is used throughout Britain: 100 pence make 1 pound. Coins are in denominations of 1p, 2p, 5p, 10p, 20p, 50p, £1, and £2. Notes are in £5, £10, £20 and £50.

What's Going On?

Time Out (www.timeout.com), published on Tuesdays, provides exhaustive lists of London activities, together with reliable reviews and previews. Quality newspapers include *The Financial Times, Daily Telegraph, Independent, Guardian;* London's only evening paper is the *Evening Standard,* daily Monday to Friday. It has a large entertainment section. *Metro* is a free morning tabloid, widely available from dumpbins and many Tube stations. See also websites, this page.

Opening Hours

Major attractions are open seven days a week, though some open late on Sunday. Shops are open six days a week, but many open on Sundays from noon in key shopping areas. Late-night shopping takes place on Wednesday (Knightsbridge) and Thursday (Oxford Street, Regent Street, and Covent Garden).

Banks are open Monday to Friday from 9:30 a.m. to 5 p.m. Some branches also open 9:30 a.m. to 3.30 p.m. on Saturday. Late-opening Chequepoint branches include 550 Oxford Street and 71 Gloucester Road. Identification is essential when cashing traveler's checks.

Post Offices

Stamps can be bought at post offices and some newsstands and shops; Trafalgar Square Post Office, on William IV Street, stays open late. Mail boxes are red.

Public Holidays

January 1, Good Friday, Easter Monday, first Monday in May, last Monday in May, last Monday in August, December 25 and 26.

Restrooms

Otherwise known as toilets, lavatories, W.C.s (from water closet), conveniences, ladies, and gents. If the public rest rooms are unsavory, slip into the nearest large department store or hotel. In theaters, there are often few rest rooms and long lines for them.

Smoking

Smoking is now banned in all bars, pubs, restaurants, and other public places.

Telephones

The city code for London is 020. (When calling from the U.S., omit the initial "0.") To make a local call within London, either use coins or buy a BT phone card from a newsstand or other shop. Omit the 020 city code and just dial the eight-digit number. Outside London numbers usually have a three- or five-digit code and a six-figure number. Evenly spaced beeps mean the number is busy; a solid sound means the number is unobtainable.

To make an international call, an international, pre-paid phonecard is the best value, on sale at newsstands and other shops. Dial 00, then the country code, then the number. Before using the phone in your hotel room, check the mark-up charges with the receptionist, including for toll-free phone numbers; they may be substantial.

Directory assistance: 0800 953 0720 (free) gives a list of services. Also, www.ukphonebook.co.uk. Operator help: 100

Time Differences

GMT (Greenwich mean time) is standard time; BST (British summer time) is one hour ahead of GMT and runs from late March to late October. GMT is five hours ahead of U.S. eastern standard time.

Tourist Information

Visit Britain Offices Abroad

In the United States

Los Angeles 1766 Wilshire Blvd., Suite 1200, CA 90025, tel 310/481-2989

New York 551 Fifth Ave., Suite 701, NY 10176–0799, tel 1-800/462-2748

In Canada

Toronto 160 Bloor St. East, Ontario, M4W 189, tel 416/646-6674

Useful Websites

www.americanexpress.com

www.a-zmaps.co.uk

www.bbc.co.uk/london
  for news, travel, weather, entertainment, and sports

www.culture24.org.uk
  includes most London museum information

www.london.gov.uk
  the Greater London Authority

www.londonnet.co.uk
  information on restaurants, bars, nightlife, and more

www.londontown.com
  basic information on top sights, hotels, etc.

www.officiallondon theatre.co.uk
  the nonprofit organization gives on-the-day information on half-price theater tickets; you must buy them in person

www.pubs.com

www.riverthames.co.uk
  places and events along the river

www.streetmap.co.uk
  plan your day, then print out the street plan

www.tfl.gov.uk
  for all transport from buses and DLR to river services, plus journey planning help

www.ticketmaster.co.uk
  for tickets to shows and events

www.timeout.com
  for all London events

www.trailfinders.com
for all travel booking
www.uktravel.com
click on a Tube station to be
shown nearby attractions
www.visitbritain.com
the British Tourist Board
www.visitlondon.com
the London Tourist Board

Visitors with Disabilities

Facilities are generally good for visitors with disabilities. Artsline, 54 Charlton Street, NW1 (www .artsline.org.uk), has advice on access to arts and entertainment venues; their publication is *Disability Arts in London*. RADAR (the Royal Society for Disability and Rehabilitation) provides information on tour operators that cater specifically to disabled travelers (tel 020 7250 3222, www.radar .org.uk).

EMERGENCIES
Police, Fire & Ambulance

To summon any of these services, dial 999 from any telephone, free of charge. It is important that you tell the emergency services operator the address where the incident has taken place and the nearest landmark, crossroads, or house number; also, precisely where you are. Stay by the telephone until the service arrives.

Lost Property

Always inform the police, to validate insurance claims. Report a lost passport to your embassy (and always carry a separate photocopy of the information pages so another can be prepared quickly).

For lost property on the Tube, buses, black taxi cabs, and London Overground: Transport for London Lost Property Office (200 Baker Street, NW1 5R2, tel 020 79182000 or 0845 3309882, Mon.–Fri. 8:30–4, www.tfl.gov.uk).

Property lost on the DLR is held for 48 hours at Poplar Station (tel 020 7363 9550) and then forwarded to the office at 200 Baker St. (above).

Lost Credit Cards

Report any loss immediately to the credit card company, so credit can be stopped, and to the local police station; also telephone your bank.

Health Precautions

If you need a doctor or dentist, ask your hotel reception for advice. If the problem is minor, go to the nearest chemist (pharmacy) and speak to the pharmacist. To claim insurance, keep receipts for all treatments and medicines.
To call an ambulance, dial 999 (see Emergencies, this page).

National Health Service (N.H.S.) Hospitals

Hospitals with 24-hour emergency departments include:
University College Hospital, Gower Street (entrance in Grafton Way), WC1, tel 0845 1555000.
Chelsea and Westminster Hospital, 369 Fulham Road, SW10, Tel 8746 8000.

Other Facilities

Private hospitals (no emergency unit) include the **Cromwell Hospital,** Cromwell Road, SW5, tel 7460 2000.

Great Chapel Street Medical Centre (13 Great Chapel Street, W1, tel 020 7437 9360) is an N.H.S. surgery (doctor's office) open to all, but patients without the N.H.S. reciprocal agreement must pay.

For an optician and on-site workshop, try **Aitchison,** 127a Sloane St. SW1, tel 020 7730 4870. Those with more serious eye problems should seek help at **Moorfields Eye Hospital,** City

Road, EC1, tel 020 7253 3411.

For homeopathic practitioners and chemists, contact the **British Homeopathic Association,** Hahnemann House, 29 Park St. West, Luton, L413BE, tel 01582 408675, www.britishhomeopathic.org.

Chemists (Pharmacies)

Many drugs freely available in the U.S. cannot be bought over the counter in the U.K. Be sure to bring sufficient supplies of medicines from home. If more are needed, take the wrapping with full printed description of its contents to the chemist for advice on buying the nearest equivalent.

Chemists open from 9 a.m. until midnight include **Bliss Chemist,** 5 Marble Arch, W1, tel 020 7723 6116.

Sensible Precautions

Keep valuables locked in the hotel safe. Note, and preferably photocopy, any important information on passports, tickets, and credit cards, and keep this information in a separate place.

Keep only a small amount of money with you; put the rest in the hotel safe. Keep documents and money in a closed bag when you carry them. Do not leave your bag unattended, or on the floor of a restaurant, theater, or cinema. Do not travel alone at night, unless in a "black cab" or along well-lit streets and in buses with other people. Avoid parks after dark.

Embassies & Consulates
Canadian High Commission, Macdonald House, 1 Grosvenor Square, W1, tel 020 7258 6600, www.canadainternational.gc.ca.
Embassy of the United States of America, Grosvenor Square, W1, tel 020 7499 9000, http:// london.usembassy.gov.

Hotels & Restaurants

Location is the key to a successful London visit. There are hotels of every level of luxury, from simple to exotic, but their location is paramount: London is very big and hours can be wasted moving around. It is wise to work out where you will be spending your days and evenings, then choose a well-placed hotel that suits your lifestyle, dreams, and budget.

London's hotels have undergone a revolution, especially at the top end. The emphasis is on design-led hotels, such as Kit Kemp's Firmdale hotels, including the Soho with its fashionable bar. Myhotel, which opened in Chelsea in late 1998, was Terence Conran's first hotel, planned with a feng shui expert as an "oasis of calm." Subsequently, he lavishly transformed the Great Eastern Hotel (now the Andaz) in the City. Ian Schrager and Phillipe Starck have brought New York panache and success to London with new hotels, including the Sanderson and St. Martin's Lane.

Boutique hotels have long been established in South Kensington with such successes as the sumptuous Blakes. Now the choice has spread right across central London—to Hazlitt's in Soho, Charlotte Street in Fitzrovia, the Rookery in Clerkenwell, and Threadneedles in the heart of the City.

More traditional luxury hotels, such as the Ritz, Savoy, Berkeley, Claridge's, and Dorchester, are now joined by the Mandarin Oriental group's totally overhauled Hyde Park Hotel and the Waldorf Hilton. Other refurbished hotels include Le Méridien Piccadilly and Marriott's Grosvenor House. Indeed, lavish refurbishments abound at all levels, while newly built hotels spanning all price brackets open monthly.

It is, nevertheless, important to make reservations well ahead. London hotels are some of the world's most expensive, so when reserving, ask about special deals. These may include weekends or the quiet month of February—you may find

a better deal at a deluxe hotel than at a popular business hotel. New hotels often offer discounts while they deal with teething troubles. Some hotels have economic family rooms; others, such as the Citadines London Trafalgar Square, have a kitchen in each room. When reserving you may be asked for a deposit or for your credit card number. Check the room rate carefully: It should include the hefty 20 percent VAT, but occasionally prices are given without this.

If anything goes wrong, talk to the duty manager. If the problem is not solved, speak to the manager, then put it in writing.

Visit London has a hotel information and reservation section on its website (www.visitlondon.com) and publishes the reliable booklet "Where to Stay & What to Do." It also handles serious complaints.

Some of the nicest hotels are in old buildings. If you have particular needs in comfort, services, or anything else, check that your hotel can provide them.

Visitors with disabilities can obtain information on suitable places to stay from **Tourism for All** (c/o Vitalise, Shap Road Industrial Estate, Shap Road, Kendal, Cumbria LA9 6NZ, tel 0845 1249971 or +44 1539 814 683 from outside the U.K., www. tourismforall.org.uk).

Apartments

Those visiting for longer periods may wish to rent a serviced apartment on a weekly basis. Rates can be very competitive even in the city center. Agencies specializing in vacation rentals include **CHS London Ltd,** (tel 020 8772 1939,

www.chslondon.com). **The King's Wardrobe** (6 Wardrobe Place, Center Lance, EC4, tel 020 7792 2222, www.bridgestreet .co.uk) has modest, well-priced apartments right near St. Paul's Cathedral. **No. 5 Maddox Street,** (5 Maddox Street, W1, tel 020 7647 0200, www.living-rooms .co.uk) has contemporary suites equipped with workstations, balconies, and minimalist decor. **Citadines London Trafalgar Square** (18–21 Northumberland Avenue, WC2, tel 0800 376 3898 or international reservations +33 1 4105 7905, www.citadines.com) has 189 simple studios and one- and two-bedroom apartments in an unbeatable location. Citadines also has properties in Barbican, Holborn, and South Kensington.

Restaurants

London's food revolution began in the 1980s and continues today. In London, if you know where to go, you can find impressive cooking of almost every cuisine in the world, from Thai to modern Californian, from Indian to north Italian. The result is that the London restaurant world spins fast in an upward spiral. Chefs are the stars, emerging from the shadow of their mentors to open strings of their own restaurants, to write columns for newspapers, publish cookbooks, and star in television series. A sous-chef of a major restaurant in January opens his own restaurant in March, a second, off-beat brasserie in June, and publishes his first book by the autumn. Sommeliers and front-of-house managers can also determine the success of a restaurant. High-fashion restaurants, mentioned in gossip columns and reviewed repeatedly, need to be reserved well in advance; even then, tables will be kept for regular favored clients. Certain tables may be unacceptable, such as ones beside the kitchen, near the restrooms, or by the drafty door; do not hesitate to refuse these. In summer, it requires luck or an early arrival to win a prized outdoor table on the sidewalk or in restaurant back gardens.

Prices are often high, so it is important to check such details as the existence of a cover charge per person. The service charge may or may not be included—if not, ten percent should be added for a satisfactory meal, slightly more for exceptional service. If in doubt, ask. To eat some of London's finest food at a reasonable price, there is usually a good value set menu at lunchtime. As for the wine lists, if the restaurant is any good, its wine buyer will have chosen a good house wine. If you prefer tap water (quite safe to drink in London), be certain to ask for it specifically.

Few restaurants have a dress code, but in better restaurants, it is usual to dress up in keeping with glamorous surroundings and skillfully prepared food. Traditional restaurants such as the Savoy expect a jacket and tie. Smoking is completely prohibited inside restaurants, bars, pubs, and public places. It is considered rude to use a mobile phone at the table.

The increasing number of fashionable bars in central London demand nice dress, too. Some are in the deluxe hotels; others at the front of restaurants. Pubs, on the other hand, tolerate all forms of dress and often serve good food. A handful are included in the following selection.

Remarkable hotel restaurants and bars are noted within the following hotel entries. Beware: Some well-known chefs move locations regularly; if you want to enjoy a specific chef's creations, check that he or she is still working on site. To be sure of a table at almost any of the restaurants listed below, a reservation is essential. If you have particular needs in cuisine or comfort, check that your chosen restaurant can provide them.

Apart from restaurants within hotels, closures for public holidays, Christmas, New Year's, and Easter may vary from year to year, so it is best to check.

Hotels and restaurants have been organized by price, then in alphabetical order.

Abbreviations:
L = lunch
D = dinner

■ THE THAMES

There is a limited number of rooms with good Thames views, so reservations are essential. (For a wider choice of Thames views, see the South Bank, pp. 248–249.) Riverside pubs are some of the best in London, and many serve excellent food; those listed here are near the main sights to visit.

HOTELS

🏨 THE SAVOY
🍴 $$$$$
STRAND
WC2
TEL 020 7836 4343
FAX 020 7240 2398
www.fairmont.com/savoy
Ideal stylish location for mixing City with West End. Reopened in October 2010, after a major refurbishment. The 62 rooms have river views. American Bar, Pavilion Room teas, and River Room restaurant all top notch.
🛈 268 🚇 Charing Cross

PRICES

HOTELS
An indication of the cost of a double room in the high season is given by $ signs.
$$$$$	Over $280
$$$$	$200–$280
$$$	$120–$200
$$	$80–$120
$	Under $80

RESTAURANTS
An indication of the cost of a three-course meal without drinks is given by $ signs.
$$$$$	Over $80
$$$$	$50–$80
$$$	$35–$50
$$	$20–$35
$	Under $20

RESTAURANTS

🍴 TATE BRITAIN REX WHISTLER
$$$
TATE BRITAIN
MILLBANK
SW1
TEL 020 7887 8825
www.tate.org.uk
There are no river views in this basement, but Rex Whistler's mural covers the walls, and there is breakfast, lunch, or tea to be had between picture-gazing sessions upstairs.
🚇 Pimlico 🕁 Closed D.

🍴 TATE MODERN RESTAURANT
$$$
BANKSIDE, LEVEL 7
SE1
TEL 020 7887 8888
www.tate.org.uk
Worth dressing up to enjoy the breathtaking views of the City, the buzzy bar, and the good food; book to avoid standing in line.

🚇 Southwark/London Bridge
🕐 Closed Sun.–Thurs. D

🍴 **TATE MODERN CAFÉ 2**
$$
BANKSIDE, LEVEL 2
SE1
TEL 020 7401 5014
www.tate.org.uk
Sleek but informal ground-floor Thameside café is ideal for simple, robust food pre- or post-museum exploration.
🚇 Southwark/London Bridge
🕐 Closed Sat.–Thurs. D

WATERSIDE PUBS
(in order from west to east)

🍴 **LONDON APPRENTICE**
$
CHURCH STREET
ISLEWORTH
TW7
TEL 020 8560 1915
www.thelondonapprentice
.co.uk
A few yards from the car entrance to Syon House. Good food and notable beers.
🚇 Hounslow East (then bus H37)/Richmond

🍴 **THE BULL'S HEAD**
$
STRAND-ON-THE-GREEN
KEW
W4
TEL 020 8994 1204
www.pubs.com
A variety of beers on a pretty towpath, ideal before or after Kew Gardens. Food served noon to 10 p.m. daily.
🚇 Kew Gardens/Gunnersbury Park

🍴 **THE DOVE**
$
19 UPPER MALL
W6
TEL 020 8748 5405
www.pubs.com
Short walk from Chiswick House along a pretty towpath. Simple, 300-year-old pub, good atmosphere, plenty of

rowing to watch while eating traditional bread and cheese or a Thai dish.
🚇 Ravenscourt Park/Hammersmith

🍴 **TOWN OF RAMSGATE**
$
62 WAPPING HIGH STREET
E1
TEL 020 7481 8000
www.pubs.com
Traditional, possibly smugglers', pub a short walk from the Tower of London.
🚇 Wapping

🍴 **MAYFLOWER**
$
ROTHERHITHE
SE16
TEL 020 7237 4088
www.pubs.com
Cozy pub close to the pier where the *Mayflower* sailed for America in 1620.
🚇 Rotherhithe

🍴 **THE CUTTY SARK**
$
4–6 BALLAST QUAY
LASSELL STREET
GREENWICH
SE10
TEL 020 8858 3146
www.cuttysarktavern.co.uk
Delightful old village pub with open fire serving warming soups, whitebait, ribs, and steaks. Outside benches.
🚇 Greenwich (DLR)
🚤 to Greenwich (5-minute walk along towpath)

◼ THE CITY
Restaurants in the City are booming, and a short taxi ride reaches the impressive restaurants of Clerkenwell and Islington—useful for post-theater meals, too.

HOTELS

🏨 **ANDAZ**
$$$$$
40 LIVERPOOL STREET

EC2
TEL 020 7961 1234
FAX 020 7961 1235
http://london.liverpoolstreet
.andaz.hyatt.com
Conran took a grand Victorian railway station and stylishly transformed it into a modern City hotel, though now renamed and run by Hyatt.
🛏 267 🚇 Liverpool Street

🏨 **ROOKERY**
$$$$
12 PETER'S LANE
COWCROSS STREET
EC1
TEL 020 7336 0931
FAX 020 7336 0932
www.rookeryhotel.com
Under the same management as the successful Hazlitt's (q.v.), simple but tasteful rooms in Georgian rowhouses, and one stunning suite.
🛏 33 🚇 Farringdon

🏨 **THREADNEEDLES**
$$$$
5 THREADNEEDLE STREET
EC2
TEL 020 7657 8080
FAX 020 7657 8100
www.theetoncollection.com
The City's original boutique hotel is inside a fine former Midland Bank building, equipped with plasma TVs and other gadgets.
🛏 69 🚇 Bank

RESTAURANTS

🍴 **CLUB GASCON**
$$$$
57 WEST SMITHFIELD
EC1
TEL 020 7796 0600
www.clubgascon.com
Diners select three—four if appetites are big—scrupulously prepared Gascony dishes made with the best ingredients; foie gras is almost obligatory.
🚇 Barbican/Farringdon
🕐 Closed Sat. L, Sun. L & D

🏨 Hotel 🍴 Restaurant 🛏 No. of Guest Rooms 🚇 Tube 🕐 Closed

RHODES TWENTY FOUR
$$$$
24TH FLOOR, TOWER 42
OLD BROAD STREET
EC2
TEL 020 7877 7703
www.rhodes24.co.uk
Dress up for lunch or early dinner and enjoy Gary Rhodes's faultless food with bird's-eye London views.
🚇 Bank/Liverpool Street
🕐 Closed Sat.–Sun.

LES TROIS GARCONS
$$$$
1 CLUB ROW, SHOREDITCH
E1
TEL 020 7613 1924
www.lestroisgarcons.com
Chandeliers and stuffed animals form part of the extravagant décor of this converted pub, now a popular restaurant serving food that combines classical French and contemporary British influences.
🚇 Liverpool Street
🕐 Closed Sun.

CAFÉ DU MARCHÉ
$$$
CHARTERHOUSE MEWS
22 CHARTERHOUSE SQUARE
EC1
TEL 020 7608 1609
www.cafedumarche.co.uk
French brasserie dishes include *daube en boeuf* and *tarte aux fruits* in this very relaxed, informal escape from city pressures.
🚇 Barbican/Farringdon
🕐 Closed Sat.–Sun. L, Sun. D

FREDERICK'S
$$$
CAMDEN PASSAGE
N1
TEL 020 7359 2888
www.fredericks.co.uk
One of Islington's oldest restaurants, serving modern European food in a double-height conservatory. Confit of lamb, roast salmon, and beef wellington are all good, and there are plenty of vegetarian dishes.
🚇 Angel 🕐 Closed Sun.

MORO
$$$
34–36 EXMOUTH MARKET
EC1
TEL 020 7833 8336
www.moro.co.uk
Husband and wife Sam and Sam Clark cook innovative dishes, many influenced by Spain. Try *cecina* (dry-cured beef) with artichokes and Spanish almond cake.
🚇 Farringdon 🕐 Closed Sun.

SOMETHING SPECIAL

ST. JOHN
In his fashionably spare restaurant beside Smithfield meat market, Fergus Henderson has revived British dishes that most British people had forgotten about. The emphasis is on meat: plenty of offal, venison, pork, and more usual meats; plus homemade breads. Wickedly delicious old-fashioned puddings and English cheeses.
$$$
26 ST. JOHN STREET
EC1
TEL 020 7251 0848
www.stjohnrestaurant.co.uk
🕐 Closed Sat. L, Sun. D

CICADA
$$
132–136 ST. JOHN STREET
EC1
TEL 020 7608 1550
www.rickerrestaurants.com
Large, modern interior with central bar and friendly atmosphere for enjoying all kinds of Asian food, including seared salmon and crab and ginger dumplings.
🚇 Farringdon 🕐 Closed Sat. L, Sun.

THE EAGLE
$$
159 FARRINGDON ROAD
EC1
TEL 020 7837 1353
www.pubs.com
Jolly atmosphere in this converted pub with scrubbed floors. The short menu written on a blackboard might include wholesome Italian sausages with butter beans or grilled swordfish.
🚇 Farringdon
🕐 Closed Sun. D

MODERN PANTRY
$$
47–48 ST. JOHN'S SQUARE
EC1
TEL 020 7250 0833
www.themodernpantry.co.uk
Two attractive Georgian townhouses play host to a takeout service (the pantry); a bustling, informal café on the ground floor; and an equally informal restaurant spread across dining rooms on the floor above. It's fashionable but unpretentious. Weekend brunch is especially popular, so be sure to book.
🚇 Farringdon 🕐 Café open daily, restaurant closed Sun.–Mon.

PATERNOSTER CHOP HOUSE
$$
WARWICK COURT
PATERNOSTER SQUARE
EC4
TEL 020 7029 9400
www.paternosterchophouse.com
Great location overlooking the remodeled square and cleaned St. Paul's Cathedral. Best at lunchtime; reliable British dishes.
🚇 St. Paul's 🕐 Closed Sat., Sun. D

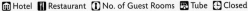

🏨 Hotel 🍴 Restaurant 🛏 No. of Guest Rooms 🚇 Tube 🕐 Closed

🍴 SMITHS OF SMITHFIELD

$$

67–77 CHARTERHOUSE STREET
EC1
TEL 020 7251 7950
www.smithsofsmithfield.co.uk
Head up past the noisy dining room to the top (fourth) floor for peace, splendid views across Smithfield to St. Paul's, and good food: tender steaks and desserts such as fruit-filled summer pudding and "British cheese from Neal's Yard with oatcakes."
🚇 Farringdon 🕐 Top floor closed Sun. D

🍴 WAPPING FOOD

$$

WAPPING HYDRAULIC POWER STATION
WAPPING WALL
E1
TEL 020 7680 2080
www.thewappingproject.com
Funky industrial building where customers enjoy a sharp menu plus art installations, classic movies, and a good bar.
🚇 Wapping/Shadwell 🕐 Closed Sun. D

▦ WESTMINSTER

At the heart of London, the capital's grandest hotels have exceptional restaurants and jolly bars, which make excellent rendezvous spots.

HOTELS

🏨 ATHENAEUM

🍴 **$$$$$**

116 PICCADILLY
W1
TEL 020 7499 3464
FAX 020 7493 1860
www.athenaeumhotel.com
The elegant comfort and high level of service draw guests back to Athenaeum's rooms and apartments, as do Windsor Lounge teas and the spa.

Higher rooms have park views.
ⓘ 156 🚇 Hyde Park

🏨 BROWN'S

🍴 **$$$$$**

ALBEMARLE STREET
W1
TEL 020 7493 6020
FAX 020 7493 9381
www.brownshotel.com
Traditional English elegance in the heart of old Mayfair. Totally refurbished. Roaring fires, and creaking floorboards; an echo of Mayfair mansions. Especially good traditional tea.
ⓘ 117 🚇 Green Park

SOMETHING SPECIAL

🏨 CLARIDGE'S

The queen's state guests move here after Buckingham Palace. Huge corner suites. Glorious public rooms include the grand dining room, design by Thierry Despont and Diane von Furstenberg, food by Gordon Ramsay.

$$$$$

BROOK STREET
W1
TEL 020 7629 8860
FAX 020 7499 2210
www.claridges.com.uk
ⓘ 203 🚇 Bond Street

🏨 THE CONNAUGHT

🍴 **$$$$$**

CARLOS PLACE
W1
TEL 020 7499 7070
FAX 020 7495 3262
www.the-connaught.co.uk
Considered the most discreet of London hotels, where the famous can remain anonymous. Recently refurbished, and boasts Michelin-starred food from Hélène Darroze and two fine bars, the Coburg and Connaught.
ⓘ 122 🚇 Bond Street

🏨 THE DORCHESTER

🍴 **$$$$$**

PARK LANE
W1
TEL 020 7629 8888
FAX 020 7409 0114
www.thedorchester.com
Lavishly redone, including the rooftop Oliver Messel rooms and a luscious spa. Guests and visitors can enjoy fine Promenade teas, the zippy bar, and restaurants: the traditional Grill, three-Michelin-star Alain Ducasse, and opulent China Tang (Cantonese).
ⓘ 250 🚇 Hyde Park Corner

🏨 FOUR SEASONS

🍴 **$$$$$**

HAMILTON PLACE
PARK LANE
W1
TEL 020 7499 0888
FAX 020 7493 1895
www.fourseasons.com/london
Refurbished in 2010, an intelligently designed hotel with excellently appointed rooms and suites, especially Conservatory rooms; some of London's top chefs have worked in the Four Seasons restaurant (modern European). A second hotel is at Canary Wharf, Docklands.
ⓘ 192 🚇 Hyde Park Corner

🏨 LANDMARK HOTEL

$$$$$

222 MARYLEBONE ROAD
NW1
TEL 020 7631 8000
FAX 020 7631 8080
www.landmarklondon.co.uk
The spectacular Winter Garden, a palm court that operates all day, sets the tone for this converted grand late-Victorian building. Large bedrooms with good bathrooms. Surprisingly well-located.
ⓘ 300 🚇 Marylebone

🏨 Hotel 🍴 Restaurant ⓘ No. of Guest Rooms 🚇 Tube 🕐 Closed

🏨 LE MERIDIEN
🍽 PICCADILLY
$$$$$
21 PICCADILLY
W1
TEL 020 7734 8000
FAX 020 7437 3574
**www.lemeridienpiccadilly
.co.uk**
Located at the crossroads of
St. James's, Mayfair, and
theaterland. Guests enjoy fine
rooms, a splendid health club
and spa, stylish afternoon
tea in the Oak Room, and
excellent bars.
ℹ️ 266   🚇 Piccadilly Circus

🏨 THE METROPOLITAN
🍽 $$$$$
19 OLD PARK LANE
W1
TEL 020 7447 1000
www.metropolitan.como.bz
The Metropolitan has a reputation for cutting-edge cool
design and matching guests,
who book into its rooms and
apartments. Getting a reservation at its Nobu restaurant
(Japanese) is hard, though the
once-exclusive Met Bar is now
less trendy than it was.
ℹ️ 150   🚇 Hyde Park Corner

🏨 THE RITZ
🍽 $$$$$
150 PICCADILLY
W1
TEL 020 7493 8181
FAX 020 7493 2687
www.theritzlondon.com
Exquisite hotel overlooking
Green Park, whose painted
and gilded dining room is
London's most beautiful. Tea
is disappointing but the bar is
a promenade for the stylish.
Note the formal dress code:
no jeans or sneakers, and men
must wear jacket and tie.
ℹ️ 136   🚇 Green Park

🏨 THE STAFFORD
🍽 $$$$$
16–18 ST. JAMES'S PLACE

SW1
TEL 020 7493 0111
FAX 020 7493 7121
www.kempinski.com
One of London's most luxurious small hotels, tucked down
an alley off St. James's Street.
Delightful dining room, fine
wines stored in 350-year-old
cellars.
ℹ️ 105   🚇 Green Park

🏨 TRAFALGAR
🍽 $$$$
2 SPRING GARDENS
W1
TEL 020 7870 2900
FAX 020 7870 2911
www.thetrafalgar.com
Designed to attract younger
guests, this lifestyle hotel
has sharp service, good
design, and the popular
Rockwell Bar and roof bar.
ℹ️ 129   🚇 Charing Cross

🏨 DURRANTS
$$$
26–32 GEORGE STREET
W1
TEL 020 7935 8131
www.durrantshotel.co.uk
The hotel opened when
its Georgian terrace was quite
new, in 1790, and descen-
dants of that family maintain
its homely tone today.
ℹ️ 92   🚇 Bond Street

RESTAURANTS

🍽 LE GAVROCHE
$$$$$
43 UPPER BROOK STREET
W1
TEL 020 7408 0881
www.le-gavroche.co.uk
Calm decor, perfect service,
and an extensive wine list
form the backdrop for Michel
Roux's theater, which has been
running for over 25 years and
is now directed by his son,
Michel Roux Junior. Perfect
French dishes include *darne de
boeuf à l'ancienne.* 🚇 Marble
Arch   🕐 Closed Sat. L & Sun.

PRICES

HOTELS

An indication of the cost of
a double room in the high
season is given by **$** signs.

$$$$$	Over $280
$$$$	$200–$280
$$$	$120–$200
$$	$80–$120
$	Under $80

RESTAURANTS

An indication of the cost of
a three-course meal without
drinks is given by **$** signs.

$$$$$	Over $80
$$$$	$50–$80
$$$	$35–$50
$$	$20–$35
$	Under $20

🍽 GREENHOUSE
$$$$$
27A HAY'S MEWS
W1
TEL 020 7499 3331
**www.greenhouserestaurant
.co.uk**
Michelin-starred chef Antonin
Bonnet creates imaginative
European fusions for his
elegant but friendly dining
room.
🚇 Green Park   🕐 Closed Sat.
L, Sun.

🍽 BENARES
$$$$
12A BERKELEY SQUARE HOUSE
BERKELEY SQUARE
W1
TEL 020 7627 8886
www.benaresrestaurant.com
Atur Kocchar, who made
Tamarind (q.v.) so special,
focuses on the dishes of
his native area of India, the
ancient city of Benares and its
surrounding area.
🚇 Green Park/Bond Street

⊓ BENTLEY'S OYSTER BAR & GRILL

$$–$$$$

11–15 SWALLOW STREET

W1

TEL 020 7734 4756

www.whitestarline.org.uk

Bentley's opened in 1916, and still occupies the same beautiful neo-Gothic building almost a century later. Tucked away in a tiny side street, yet just moments from busy Piccadilly and Regent Street, this is an iconic London restaurant, revitalized in 2005 by a superb update that has respected the beautiful arts and crafts–inspired interior. Eat fine fish and seafood either in the lively (and less expensive) Oyster & Champagne Bar downstairs or in the more sedate dining rooms upstairs.

🚇 Piccadilly Circus

⊓ LE CAPRICE

$$$$

25 ARLINGTON STREET

SW1

TEL 020 7629 2239

www.le-caprice.co.uk

This and The Ivy (see p. 250, tables even more of a premium) are run with supreme efficiency by one team. Atmosphere is clublike, with chic customers greeting each other over champagne and *risotto nero* or baked fish, all fashionably modern. European.

🚇 Green Park

SOMETHING SPECIAL

⊓ LOCANDA LOCATELLI

One of the recent stars of London's dining scene. The modish and understated contemporary dining rooms are a celebrity favorite, but the style and sleek service are underpinned by superb Italian cooking. The seasonal meat, fish, and pasta dishes are often winningly straightforward—*minestrone di verdura* (vegetable soup), *tortellini in*

brodo (meat parcels in broth), or *sgombro alla griglia in crosta di erbe* (grilled mackerel in a light herb crust).

$$$$

8 SEYMOUR STREET

W1

TEL 020 7935 9088

www.locandalocatelli.com

🚇 Marble Arch

⊓ MATSURI

$$$$

15 BURY STREET

SW1

TEL 020 7839 1101

www.matsuri-restaurant.com

The title is Japanese for "festival." The food is theatrical but precise. Try the sushi, simple okonomi-yaki, or the full teppan-yaki experience. Second, more contemporary, branch on High Holborn.

🚇 Green Park

⊓ LA PORTE DES INDES

$$$$

32 BRYANSTON STREET

W1

TEL 020 7224 0055

www.blueelephant.com

Following a success in Brussels (hence the French), this extravagantly decorated, large and beautiful restaurant serves very high quality, if pricey, Indian food.

🚇 Marble Arch 🕐 Closed Sat. L

⊓ SKETCH: THE LECTURE ROOM

$$$$

9 CONDUIT STREET

W1

TEL 020 7659 4500

www.sketch.uk.com

A dizzy combination of Mourad Mazous, founder of nearby Momo (q.v.), Parisian chef Pierre Gagnaire, and a grand Mayfair mansion decked in uncompromisingly contemporary design by Gabhan O'Keefe. Great café

and dining rooms.

🚇 Oxford Circus/Piccadilly Circus 🕐 Closed Sat.–Mon. L, Sun. D, Mon.

⊓ THE SQUARE

$$$$

6–10 BRUTON STREET

MAYFAIR

W1

TEL 020 7495 7100

www.squarerestaurant.com

Philip Howard's modern European dishes, with a French emphasis, served in a high-ceilinged, large-windowed space. The terrine of foie gras and the guinea fowl and artichokes with cured ham are especially good.

🚇 Green Park 🕐 Closed Sat. L, Sun. L

⊓ TAMARIND

$$$$

20 QUEEN STREET

W1

TEL 020 7629 3561

www.tamarindrestaurant .com

Serious Indian cooking. Original recipes, often gleaned from traditional Indian homes, are cooked to conserve their distinctive spices and aromas, such as chicken marinated in green chili and mustard.

🚇 Green Park 🕐 Closed Sat. L

⊓ L'AUTRE PIED

$$$

5–7 BLANDFORD STREET

W1

TEL 020 7486 9696

www.lautrepied.co.uk

Less expensive than its sister restaurant, Pied à Terre, but no less serious in its approach to cooking—the sophisticated, French-influenced meat and fish dishes have earned a Michelin star.

🚇 Baker Street/Bond Street

🍴 THE AVENUE

$$$

7–9 ST. JAMES'S STREET

SW1

TEL 020 7321 2111

www.danddlondon.com

Restrained, elegant design, plus good value wines complement British and other European dishes such as chilled cucumber soup with Colchester crab.

🚇 Green Park

🕐 Closed Sat. L, Sun.

🍴 CAFÉ BAGATELLE

$$$

WALLACE COLLECTION,

HERTFORD HOUSE,

MANCHESTER SQUARE,

W1

TEL 020 7563 9505

www.eliancerestaurants.co.uk

Laze over late breakfast, a coffee, lunch, or afternoon tea in the covered courtyard of one of London's great mansions, now home to the Wallace Collection, which includes the best private collection of French art outside Paris.

🚇 Bond Street/Marble Arch

🕐 Closed D

🍴 THE CINNAMON CLUB

$$$

THE OLD WESTMINSTER LIBRARY

30–32 GREAT SMITH STREET

SW1

TEL 020 7222 2555

www.cinnamonclub.com

Spacious late-Victorian municipal grandeur sets the tone for a stylish marriage of Western and Indian cuisine—and pricey wines; try the Rajasthani roast saddle of venison, and be adventurous with dessert. Serves breakfast on weekdays.

🚇 Westminster/St. James's Park

🕐 Closed Sat. L, Sun.

🍴 MAZE

$$$

MARRIOTT

10–13 GROSVENOR SQUARE

W1

TEL 020 7107 0000

www.gordonramsay.com

Worth penetrating the lackluster hotel to eat Jason Atherton's stunning Spanish-inspired food in David Rockwell's room.

🚇 Bond Street.

🍴 THE PROVIDORES & TAPA ROOM

$$$

109 MARYLEBONE HIGH STREET

W1

TEL 020 7935 6175

www.theprovidores.co.uk

Peter Gordon's fresh combinations of Asian and Middle Eastern ingredients keep the ground-floor tapas bar and upstairs restaurant brim full.

🚇 Baker Street/Bond Street

🍴 UNION CAFÉ

$$$

96 MARYLEBONE LANE

W1

TEL 020 7486 4860

www.brinkleys.com

Light, airy café serving modern European dishes that emphasize fresh ingredients gleaned from all over England; for instance, chargrilled royal bream. Breakfast also.

🚇 Bond Street 🕐 Closed Sun. D

🍴 IL VICOLO

$$$

3 CROWN PASSAGE

KING STREET

SW1

TEL 020 7839 3960

www.toptable.co.uk

Seek out this hideaway to join local St. James's art dealers and Christie's experts for good value, home-style Italian food served with speed and a smile.

🚇 St. James's/Green Park

🕐 Closed Sat., Sun. L

🍴 MASALA ZONE

$$

9 MARSHALL STREET

W1

TEL 020 7287 9966

www.masalazone.com

Good imaginative pan-Indian food with style and at affordable prices. An ideal pause for shoppers. Six other central London locations.

🚇 Oxford Circus

■ SOUTH BANK

The strip along the south bank of the Thames is now one of the city's most exciting and innovative areas.

HOTELS

🏨 LONDON MARRIOTT
🍴 COUNTY HALL

$$$$$

COUNTY HALL, WESTMINSTER BRIDGE ROAD

SE1

TEL 020 7928 5200

FAX 020 7928 5300

www.marriott.co.uk/hotels

Hotel in part of the London administrators' 1930s building. Some rooms have river views and the leisure facilities, including pool, are first class.

🛏 200 🚇 Westminster/Waterloo

🏨 LONDON BRIDGE

$$$$

8–18 LONDON BRIDGE STREET

SE1

TEL 020 7855 2200

FAX 020 7855 2233

www.london-bridge-hotel.co.uk

This well-equipped modern hotel is just south of London Bridge, a short walk from the popular Borough market and the City. No river views.

🛏 138 🚇 London Bridge

🏨 MAD HATTER

$$$

3–7 STAMFORD STREET

SE1

TEL 020 7401 9222

FAX 020 7401 7111

🏨 Hotel 🍴 Restaurant 🛏 No. of Guest Rooms 🚇 Tube 🕐 Closed

www.fullershotels.com
A welcome new arrival located behind South Bank theaters, near Blackfriars Bridge, a short walk to the City or taxi to the West End. No river views.
(i) 30 **[Tube]** Blackfriars

[Hotel] PREMIER INN
$$
COUNTY HALL, BELVEDERE ROAD
SE1
TEL 0871 5278648
FAX 0871 5278649
www.premierinn.com
Excellent location for this no-frills, good value hotel tucked behind the deluxe London Marriott. No river views.
(i) 313 **[Tube]** Westminster/Waterloo

RESTAURANTS

[Restaurant] BLUEPRINT CAFÉ
$$$$
THE DESIGN MUSEUM
28 SHAD THAMES STREET
SE1
TEL 020 7378 7031
www.conran.com
This light, modern restaurant offers fine views of Tower Bridge and the nicest service; riverview tables a premium. Head chef Jeremy Lee combines European culinary influences with those of his native Scotland.
[Tube] Tower Hill **[Closed]** Closed Sun. D

[Restaurant] ANCHOR & HOPE
$$$
36 THE CUT
SE1
TEL 020 7928 9898
A great gastro-pub in a useful location, serving bold British food. Take note: no booking, and you may have a long wait at busy times. The best dishes are the simple ones such as duck heart, beef rump, Tamworth pork.
[Tube] Southwark/Waterloo
[Closed] Closed Mon. L, Sun. D

[Restaurant] CANTINA VINOPOLIS
$$$
1 BANK END
SE1
TEL 020 7940 8333
www.cantinavinopolis.com
A wine museum, wine bar and brasserie sprawling under the railway arches. A convenient spot to stop between sightseeing and theater-going on the South Bank. Don't miss Wine Wharf, part of the complex (Stoney St. tel 020 7940 8335, www.winewharf.co.uk) for an exceptional selection of wines.
[Tube] London Bridge **[Closed]** Closed L Mon.–Wed., Sun. D

[Restaurant] LIVEBAIT
$$$
43 THE CUT
SE1
TEL 020 7928 7211
www.livebaitrestaurants.co.uk
A favorite fish restaurant among Londoners, who sit at closely packed tables to eat worldwide fish dishes—monkfish fajitas, teriyaki-glazed halibut, palourde clams, and cod with couscous.
[Tube] Waterloo/Southwark

[Restaurant] RANSOME'S DOCK
$$$
35–37 PARKGATE ROAD
BATTERSEA
SW11
TEL 020 7223 1611
www.ransomesdock.co.uk
It merits a taxi ride to this former ice factory, where Martin and Vanessa Lam's excellent modern European dishes include Loch Fyne scallops, Trelough duck breast, and hot prune and Armagnac soufflé. Notable wines at fair prices.
[Tube] Sloane Square (then no. 19 bus or a 20-minute walk or a taxi)

[Restaurant] BERMONDSEY KITCHEN
$$
194 BERMONDSEY STREET
SE1

TEL 020 7407 5719
www.bermondseykitchen
.co.uk
The easy relaxed atmosphere, open kitchen, and bar add to the enjoyment of good modern European food—don't miss the hot chocolate pudding. Opens for brunch 9:30 a.m. Sat.–Sun.
[Tube] Borough/London Bridge

[Restaurant] ROYAL OAK
$
44 TABARD STREET
SE1
TEL 020 7357 7173
Worth seeking out is this beautifully maintained pub for its local friendliness and its beer from Harveys of Lewes. Good steak and kidney pudding. No music.
[Tube] Borough

TRAFALGAR SQUARE & SOHO

HOTELS

[Hotel] ST. MARTIN'S LANE
$$$$$
45 ST. MARTIN'S LANE
WC2
TEL 800/ 697-1791 (U.S.) OR 0800 4969 1780 (INTERNATIONAL)
FAX 020 7300 5501
www.stmartinslane.com
Hovering between West End theaters and Covent Garden restaurants, Philippe Starck's dramatically minimalist rooms and extensive bars attract design-conscious clients.
(i) 204 **[Tube]** Covent Garden/Leicester Square

SOMETHING SPECIAL

[Hotel] HAZLITT'S
Once the home of writer William Hazlitt (1778–1830), this gracious building is now a townhouse hotel in the heart of Soho. There are antiques in the beautifully furnished rooms. Ideal for theater and

museum visits. As this is a landmark hotel, there are no elevators. Minimal room service.

$$$$
6 FRITH STREET
W1
TEL 020 7434 1771
FAX 020 7439 1524
www.hazlittshotel.com
ⓘ 30 🚇 Tottenham Court Road

🏨 SOHO HOTEL

$$$$
4 RICHMOND MEWS
DEAN STREET
W1
TEL 020 7559 3000
www.firmdale.com
Designer Kit Kemp's sixth London hotel (see website for the others) mixes country style with urban simplicity in a bare brick building. Lovely bathrooms. Buzzing bar and restaurant.
ⓘ 91 🚇 Tottenham Court Road

🏨 DEAN STREET
🍴 TOWNHOUSE

$$$
71 DEAN STREET
W1
TEL 020 7434 1775
www.deanstreettownhouse.com
This chic Soho hotel opened in 2010 in a converted four-story Georgian house with a rich history. Public spaces are opulent, while the rooms have original features and a decorative palette of mostly soft browns and off-whites. The popular dining room (open to non-patrons) has a traditional, clublike look and atmosphere, and serves classic British food at breakfast, lunch, tea, and dinner.
ⓘ 39 🚇 Tottenham Court Road

RESTAURANTS

🍴 ELENA'S AT L'ÉTOILE

$$$$
30 CHARLOTTE STREET
W1
TEL 020 7636 7189
www.elenasletoile.co.uk
Having made her name at the Soho landmark L'Escargot (48 Greek Street, tel 020 7437 2679), Elena Salvoni ran this century-old Soho restaurant until her forced retirement in 2010. Little has changed since her departure. French food includes brill with horseradish and parsley crust.
🚇 Goodge Street/Tottenham Court Road 🕐 Closed Sat. L, Sun.

🍴 HAKKASAN

$$$$
8 HANWAY PLACE
W1
TEL 020 7927 7000
www.hakkasan.com
Dress up to fit in with the other stylish patrons at this large, sleek, and dimly lit restaurant, which serves excellent and sophisticated contemporary Asian food. Prices are high, but you can eat for less at lunch.
🚇 Tottenham Court Road

SOMETHING SPECIAL

🍴 THE IVY

Getting a table is the difficult part. Once achieved, the sharp staff ensures a memorable meal in this old Soho restaurant. Lunchtime clientele eat roast fish and irresistible puddings while enjoying Howard Hodgkins and Alan Jones art hung on the walls.
$$$$
1–5 WEST STREET
COVENT GARDEN
WC2
TEL 020 7836 4751
www.the-ivy.co.uk

PRICES

HOTELS
An indication of the cost of a double room in the high season is given by **$** signs.

$$$$$	Over $280
$$$$	$200–$280
$$$	$120–$200
$$	$80–$120
$	Under $80

RESTAURANTS
An indication of the cost of a three-course meal without drinks is given by **$** signs.

$$$$$	Over $80
$$$$	$50–$80
$$$	$35–$50
$$	$20–$35
$	Under $20

🚇 Leicester Square/Covent Garden

🍴 QUO VADIS

$$$$
26–29 DEAN STREET
W1
TEL 020 7437 9585
www.quovadisoho.co.uk
This Soho restaurant offers excellent service and a smart interior. The menu offers classic British and European meat, fish, and seafood dishes, plus good-value set lunch and pre-theater menus.
🚇 Leicester Square/ Tottenham Court Road 🕐 Closed Sun.

🍴 BERTORELLI'S

$$$
19 CHARLOTTE STREET
W1
TEL 020 7636 4174
www.santeonline.com
A classy, modern Italian restaurant. Maddalena Bonino's cooking for the upstairs room includes grilled squid and

smoked chicken risotto.
🚇 Goodge Street/ Totten-
ham Court Road 🕒 Closed
Sat. L, Sun.

🍴 MON PLAISIR
$$$
21 MONMOUTH STREET
WC2
TEL 020 7836 7243
www.monplaisir.co.uk
A traditional, long-established
French bistro. Choose from a
good range of reliable main
dishes, but end with the crème
brûlée.
🚇 Covent Garden/Leicester
Square 🕒 Closed Sun.

🍴 THE NATIONAL
GALLERY DINING
ROOMS
$$$
NATIONAL GALLERY
TRAFALGAR SQUARE
WC2
TEL 020 7747 2525
www.nationalgallery.org.uk
If you need a break from
the tip-top art, take lunch
overlooking Trafalgar Square;
book early for the best views.
There's also a café on the
ground floor.
🚇 Charing Cross/Leicester
Square

🍴 ALPHABET
$$
61–63 BEAK STREET
W1
TEL 020 7439 2190
With an enviable reputation
across London, this bar con-
centrates on drink, not food.
The well-made cocktails and
impressive, affordable wines
make it very popular with
Londoners.
🚇 Oxford Circus/Piccadilly
🕒 Closed Sun.

🍴 CANTON
$$
11 NEWPORT PLACE
WC2
TEL 020 7437 6220
Discerning Chinese patrons
come to this simple diner to
pay fair prices for delicious
roast duck and its fine sauces;
crab and oysters are good
here, too.
🚇 Leicester Square

🍴 CHUEN CHENG KU
$$
17 WARDOUR STREET
W1
TEL 020 7437 1398
One of the last restaurants
to serve dim sum from the
trolley (11 a.m.–6 p.m.). Arrive
early to try fresh steamed
dumplings, steamed snails, and
about 30 other morsels.
🚇 Leicester Square/
Piccadilly Circus

🍴 PIERRE VICTOIRE
$$
5 DEAN STREET
W1
TEL 020 7287 4582
www.pierrevictoire.com
Find hearty-sized portions
of no-fuss French food and
a bottle of wine enjoyed in
a calm, unhurried, candlelit
room; and do not miss out on
the *tarte au citron*.
🚇 Tottenham Court Road

🍴 CAFÉ IN THE CRYPT
$
CRYPT OF ST. MARTIN-IN-THE-
FIELDS
TRAFALGAR SQUARE
WC2
TEL 020 7839 4342
www.stmartin-in-the-fields
.org
Ideal for a cheap, cheery,
and peaceful pause. Delicious
wholesome food at bargain
prices includes casseroles and,
among the desserts, apple pie
and custard.
🚇 Charing Cross/Embank-
ment

🍴 MISATO
$
11 WARDOUR STREET
W1
TEL 020 7734 0808
www.allinlondon.co.uk
Worth standing in line for
the delicious katsu, teriyaki,
and dim sum in this popular,
cramped café.
🚇 Leicester Square

▌ COVENT GARDEN
TO LUDGATE HILL

Hotels range from grand to
bargain in this superb location.
There are many restaurants, but
fewer of quality than might be
expected: The area has been hit
by the exit of Fleet Street's newspapers and the simultaneous rise
of City restaurants to the east.

HOTELS

🏨 COVENT GARDEN
$$$$$
10 MONMOUTH STREET
WC2
TEL 020 7806 1000
FAX 020 7806 1100
www.firmdale.com
The wood-paneled drawing
room and atmospheric Tiffany
library, together with the
individualized, brightly colored
rooms, make this seem far
from urban London's hub.
ℹ️ 58 🚇 Covent Garden

🏨 CROWNE PLAZA
🍴 LONDON—THE CITY
$$$$$
19 NEW BRIDGE STREET
EC4
TEL 0871 9429198
FAX 020 7438 8088
www.ichotelsgroup.com
Superbly located between
Ludgate Hill and Fleet Street,
and with a vibrant bar and the
excellent Refettorio restaurant,
this is an ideal hotel for mixing
business with pleasure.
ℹ️ 203 🚇 Blackfriars

SOMETHING SPECIAL

ONE ALDWYCH

One of London's most dynamic contemporary renovations. Built in 1907 for the *Morning Post* newspaper, now transformed by Gordon Campbell-Gray and Mary Fox Linton into a state-of-the-art hotel. Serious art on the walls, sumptuous and extensive health spa. Indigo restaurant and formal adjoining Axis restaurant.

$$$$$

1 ALDWYCH

WC2

TEL 020 7300 1000

FAX 020 7300 1001

www.campbellgrayhotels.com

🛈 105 🚇 Charing Cross

🏨 HAYMARKET HOTEL

$$$$

1 SUFFOLK PLACE

SW1

TEL 020 7470 4000

www.firmdale.com

One of the Firmdale group's stable of invariably excellent and intimate hotels, with an ideal location—the Haymarket is at the heart of the theater district. Rooms are calm, quiet, and very comfortable, and facilities include a gym and swimming pool.

🛈 50 🚇 Piccadilly/Leicester Square

🏨 THE FIELDING HOTEL

$$$

4 BROAD COURT, BOW STREET

WC2

TEL 020 7836 8305

FAX 020 7497 0064

www.thefieldinghotel.co.uk

Quiet, simple accommodation in a pedestrian lane across from Covent Garden Opera.

🛈 25 🚇 Covent Garden

RESTAURANTS

🍴 CHRISTOPHER'S

$$$$

18 WELLINGTON STREET

WC2

TEL 020 7240 4222

www.christophersgrill.com

A grand former casino houses Christopher Gilmour's restaurant, just off Aldwych. Quality American food in the basement bar/café and the beautiful upstairs dining room.

🚇 Covent Garden 🕐 Closed Sun. D

🍴 J SHEEKEY

$$$$

32–34 ST. MARTIN'S COURT

WC2

TEL 0871 2238016

www.j-sheekey.co.uk

Modern lighting and a fresh look contrast well with the original 1890s wood paneling, creating an individual style. The menu, with a strong emphasis on traditional British seafood dishes, also includes modern dishes. Try the oak-smoked eel, or Cornish cock-crab.

🚇 Leicester Square

🍴 MURANO

$$$$

20 QUEEN STREET

W1

TEL 020 7495 1127

www.schoolofhartnett.co.uk

Gordon Ramsay protégé and TV chef Angela Hartnett opened this refined Italian Mayfair restaurant as chef-patron to great acclaim in 2008, and it continues to excel. A three-course set lunch might include a salad of wood pigeon with a citrus fruit sherry vinaigrette. Dress code is "smart," but a jacket and tie are not required.

🚇 Green Park 🕐 Closed Sun.

🍴 RULES

$$$$

35 MAIDEN LANE

WC2

TEL 020 7836 5314

www.rules.co.uk

Established in 1798, this art-filled, quality traditional English restaurant is the place to eat such dishes as potted duck, Highland deer, and steak, kidney, and oyster pudding.

🚇 Covent Garden

SOMETHING SPECIAL

🍴 BLEEDING HEART

A little off the beaten track, but well worth seeking out. The bar, bistro, and restaurant in a warren of rooms off Holborn offer the perfect combination of good atmosphere, a wide choice of wines, and authentic French food.

$$$

BLEEDING HEART YARD, OFF GREVILLE STREET

EC1

TEL 020 7242 2056

www.bleedingheart.co.uk

🚇 Farringdon 🕐 Closed Sat.–Sun.

🍴 JOE ALLEN

$$$

13 EXETER STREET

WC2

TEL 020 7836 0651

www.joeallen.co.uk

Comfortingly American menu served in a continuously buzzy basement. Reliable Caesar salad, clam chowder, ribs, and pecan pie. American cocktails.

🚇 Covent Garden

🍴 THE PORTRAIT

$$$

NATIONAL PORTRAIT GALLERY

WC2

TEL 020 7312 2490

www.npg.org.uk/visit/food

Perched on top of the renovated galleries, this is an ideal place to pause between portraits. Stunning London views and efficient food, but can be noisy.

🚇 Leicester Square

🕐 Closed Sat.–Wed. D

🍴 SIMPSONS-IN-THE-STRAND

$$$

100 STRAND

WC2

TEL 020 7836 9112

www.simpsonsinthestrand
.co.uk

Almost a caricature of a traditional English restaurant, Simpsons was founded in 1828 as a coffeehouse. A full English breakfast is the best meal to eat here in the Grand Divan dining hall.

🚇 Charing Cross/
Covent Garden

🕐 Closed 9 p.m. Sun.

🍴 THE SEVEN STARS

$$

53 CAREY STREET

WC2

TEL 020 7242 8521

www.pubs.com

This pub dates from 1604 and offers good food as well as fine real ales.

🚇 Chancery Lane

🍴 WORLD FOOD CAFÉ

$$

1ST FLOOR, 14 NEAL'S YARD

WC2

TEL 020 7379 0298

www.worldfoodcafeneals
yard.co.uk

Quality vegetarian food with the owner's photographs hung on the walls. Try the impressive salads, Egyptian falafels, lemon tart, and mango-yogurt drink.

🚇 Covent Garden 🕐 Closed 5.00 p.m. Mon.–Wed., Sun. D

▪ BLOOMSBURY

This area has a full range of good hotels, all within walking distance of the Bloomsbury museums, Covent Garden, and West End theaters.

HOTELS

🏨 CHARLOTTE STREET
🍴 HOTEL

$$$$$

15–17 CHARLOTTE STREET

WC1

TEL 020 7806 2000

FAX 020 7806 2002

www.firmdale.com

Smart yet friendly and relaxed hotel inside a period building, with a small gym and reliable Oscar restaurant.

ℹ 52 🚇 Tottenham Court Road

🏨 SANDERSON

$$$$$

50 BERNERS STREET

W1

TEL 020 7300 1400

FAX 020 7300 1404

www.sandersonlondon.com

As with its sister hotel, St. Martin's Lane, the Schrager-Starck partnership creates minimalist rooms but crowded public spaces; try the Long Bar and the spa.

ℹ 150 🚇 Oxford Circus

🏨 ACADEMY

$$$$

21 GOWER STREET

WC1

TEL 020 7631 4115

FAX 020 7636 3442

www.theetoncollection.com

Set in five Georgian rowhouses, with opulent furnishings and discreet art, this professionally run fairy-tale view of English interiors works well.

ℹ 49 🚇 Goodge Street

🏨 THE MONTAGUE ON
THE GARDENS

$$$$

15 MONTAGUE STREET

WC1

TEL 020 7637 1001

FAX 020 7637 2516

www.montaguehotel.com

Centrally located, this styl-ish hotel is imaginatively deco-rated, with attention to detail. Bedrooms offer bold decor and quality furnishings.

ℹ 100 🚇 Kings Cross/
Holborn

🏨 MORGAN HOTEL

$$$

24 BLOOMSBURY

WC1

TEL 020 7636 3735

FAX 020 7636 3045

www.morganhotel.co.uk

Superbly located, this modest and good-value family-run hotel by the British Museum has both rooms and small apartments.

ℹ 21 🚇 Tottenham Court Road

🏨 HARLINGFORD HOTEL

$$

61–63 CARTWRIGHT GARDENS

WC1

TEL 020 7387 1551

FAX 020 7387 4616

www.harlingfordhotel.com

Despite the budget rates, all guests enjoy ensuite bathrooms, contemporary decoration, friendly manage-ment and adjacent garden and tennis court.

ℹ 44 🚇 Russell Square/
Euston

🏨 GENERATOR

$

37 TAVISTOCK PLACE

WC1

TEL 020 7388 7666

FAX 020 7388 7644

www.generatorhostels.com

Steel, chrome, and exposed pipes plus its huge size, jolly bar, and Internet room keep the setting sleek, the prices low, and the guests hip and happy. Mostly shared dorm-style rooms.

ℹ 848 beds 🚇 Russell Square

🏨 Hotel   🍴 Restaurant   ℹ No. of Guest Rooms   🚇 Tube   🕐 Closed

RESTAURANTS

🍴 ASK
$$
48 GRAFTON WAY
W1
TEL 020 7388 8108
www.askcentral.co.uk
Arguably the best of London's pizza chain restaurant groups, this branch has the usual wide variety of pizzas and other good dishes, plus sharp service.
🚇 Warren Stret

🍴 BACK TO BASICS
$$
21A FOLEY STREET
W1
TEL 020 7436 2181
www.backtobasics.uk.com
Local fish restaurant housed in a former corner shop. Try Dover sole with tarragon and mahimahi with lentil vinaigrette, and leave space for bread and butter pudding with whiskey sauce.
🚇 Goodge Street/Oxford Circus

🍴 POLPO
$$
41 BEAK STREET
W1
TEL 020 7734 4479
www.polpo.co.uk
Polpo is an intimate and attractive Venetian-style *bacaro*, or wine bar, that offers *cicheti*, the Italian equivalent of tapas, and a fine choice of wines from mainly small northern Italian producers. Appropriately, it occupies part of an 18th-century Soho building that was once home to the Venetian painter Canaletto. Reservations taken for lunch only.
🚇 Oxford Circus/Piccadilly Circus 🕐 Closed Sun. D.

🍴 WAGAMAMA
$
4 STREATHAM STREET
WC1
TEL 020 7323 9223
www.wagamama.com
Japanese noodle bar a skip from the British Museum. No reservations, possibly some waiting for the chicken ramen, *gyoza* (stuffed dumplings), and edamame. Success has given birth to 19 branches throughout town.
🚇 Tottenham Court Road

■ REGENCY LONDON & NORTH

For ease of use, restaurants covering this long strip are listed south to north.

HOTELS

🏨 DORSET SQUARE
$$$
39 DORSET SQUARE
NW1
TEL 020 7723 7874
FAX 020 7724 3328
www.dorsetsquare.co.uk
Tim and Kit Kemp's first London hotel—see their website for the rest—with their trademark professionalism, individual attention, and British relaxed atmosphere.
🛏 37 🚇 Marylebone

🏨 HAMPSTEAD VILLAGE GUESTHOUSE
$$
2 KEMPLAY ROAD
HAMPSTEAD
NW3
TEL 020 7435 8679
FAX 020 7794 0254
www.hampsteadguesthouse.com
Very pretty setting for an ideal bed-and-breakfast home, with good breakfasts and the Heath for morning walks. There is also a cottage.
🛏 9 🚇 Hampstead

RESTAURANTS

PICCADILLY

SOMETHING SPECIAL

🍴 THE WOLSELEY
See and be seen for lunch in the magnificent 1921 former car showroom, enjoying a glass of champagne and then steak frites and fish. Book well ahead. Also open for stylish breakfast, tea, and dinner.
$$$$
160 PICCADILLY
W1
TEL 020 7499 6996
www.thewolseley.com
🚇 Green Park

🍴 THE CRITERION
$$$
224 PICCADILLY
W1
TEL 020 7930 0488
www.criterionrestaurant.com
Standing right beside the Eros statue at Piccadilly Circus, with marble walls and mosaic ceiling, it offers modern European food and live music Friday and Saturday from 7 p.m.

🚇 Piccadilly Circus 🕐 Closed Sun. L

🍴 DOVER STREET
$$$
8–10 DOVER STREET
W1
TEL 020 7629 9813
www.doverst.co.uk
Diners in the bars and restaurant enjoy some of London's best live jazz, blues, Latin, and soul music. Smart-casual dress code; no sport shoes.
🚇 Piccadilly
🕐 Closed Sat. L, Sun.

REGENT STREET

🍴 VILLANDRY
$$$
170 GREAT PORTLAND STREET
W1
TEL 020 7631 3131
www.villandry.com
Having feasted on an impeccable snack or full lunch rounded off with some of Villandry's superbly sourced cheeses, there is the irresistible adjoining food store for buying more of their tip-top ingredients.
🚇 Great Portland Street
🕐 Closed Sun. D

🍴 RIBA CAFÉ AND BAR
$
ROYAL INSTITUTION OF BRITISH ARCHITECTS
66 PORTLAND PLACE
W1
TEL 020 7631 0467
www.riba.org
Find the sleek 1930s building among Adam's grand mansions, check out the events program, and then head upstairs for a stylish breakfast or light lunch—on the roof terrace in summer.
🚇 Great Portland Street
🕐 Closed D, Sun. L & D

PRIMROSE HILL

🍴 LEMONIA

$$$
89 REGENT'S PARK ROAD
NW1
TEL 020 7586 7454
Near Primrose Hill, this local favorite serves Greek Cypriot dishes such as *louvia* (black-eyed beans and spinach), squid, and pudding of Greek yogurt, honey, and nuts.
🚇 Chalk Farm 🕐 Closed Sat. L, Sun. D

HAMPSTEAD

🍴 HIGHGATE BULL
$$$
13 NORTH HILL
N6
TEL 0845 4565033
Among the many pubs here, Bull wins for its historic building, outdoor terrace, quality beers, good service, and excellent food—from steaks to afternoon tea.
🚇 Highgate

🍴 JIN KICHI
$$
73 HEATH STREET
NW3
TEL 020 7794 6158
www.jinkichi.com
Well-established Japanese izakaya-style restaurant, with loyal local clientel. Delicate dishes include chicken and shiso leaf.
🚇 Hampstead 🕐 Closed Mon., Tues.–Fri. L

🍴 LOUIS PATISSERIE
$
32 HEATH STREET
NW3
TEL 020 7435 9908
www.london-eating.co.uk
Ideal stop during a visit to Hampstead or after a healthy walk on the Heath. Good apple danish pastries compete with interesting Hungarian ones such as cinnamon pretzels.
🚇 Hampstead 🕐 Closed 6 p.m.

◼ KENSINGTON & SOUTH KENSINGTON

There are several townhouse hotels in this residential area on the west side of central London, plus good restaurants much patronized for dinner by local residents.

HOTELS

🏨 BAGLIONI
$$$$$
60 HYDE PARK GATE
SW7
TEL 020 7368 5700
www.baglionihotels.com
Inside a Victorian mansion opposite Kensington Palace, the atmosphere is easy, the decor chic modern, the rooms equipped with everything including espresso machines. Serious spa.
🛏 68 🚇 High Street Kensington

🏨 ASTER HOUSE
$$$
3 SUMNER PLACE
SW7
TEL 020 7581 5888
www.asterhouse.com
Welcoming and relaxed, and part of a fine, white stucco South Kensington terrace. Excellent service, with fine attention to detail, and a delightful, plant-filled conservatory for breakfast.
🛏 13 🚇 South Kensington

🏨 GALLERY HOTEL
$$$
8–10 QUEENSBERRY PLACE
SW7
TEL 020 7915 0000
FAX 020 7915 4400
www.eeh.co.uk
Flagship hotel of the Elegant English Hotels chain (which includes the Gainsborough and Willett in London), good value in well-furnished period buildings.
🛏 36 🚇 South Kensington

🏨 THE GORE

$$$

190 QUEEN'S GATE
SW7
TEL 020 7584 6601
www.gorehotel.com
Opened over a century ago,
the Gore carefully preserves
its Victorian details with pan-
eled rooms, potted ferns, rugs,
and glorious stained-glass
windows. The same building
houses the fine quality Bar
One Ninety and Bistro One
Ninety (tel 020 759 6705).
🛏 50   🚇 South Kensington

🏨 MAYFLOWER

$$$

26–28 TREBOVIR ROAD
SW5
TEL 020 7370 0991
FAX 020 7370 0994
www.mayflowerhotel.co.uk
Modern, well-appointed
rooms of character with a
touch of the exotic, such
as colonial ceiling fans; plus
adjoining apartments. There
are also two sister hotels
nearby.
🛏 48   🚇 Earl's Court

🏨 SUMNER

$$$

54 UPPER BERKELEY STREET
MARBLE ARCH
W1
TEL 020 7723 2244
FAX 0870 7058767
www.thesumner.com
The excellent 5 Sumner Place
hotel in South Kensington has
morphed itself into a grander
refurbished townhouse in
Marylebone, installing its
notably caring staff.
🛏 20   🚇 Marble Arch

🏨 VICARAGE HOTEL

$$$

10 VICARAGE GATE
W8
TEL 020 7229 4030
FAX 020 7792 5989
www.londonvicaragehotel.com
The grand lobby of this Victorian stucco townhouse leads
to more restrained rooms, and
the ambience is relaxed.
🛏 17   🚇 High Street
Kensington/Notting Hill

🏨 RUSHMORE

$$

11 TREBOVIR ROAD
SW5
TEL 020 7370 3839
FAX 020 7370 0274
www.rushmore-hotel.co.uk
Frescoed wall, draped beds, an
elegant breakfast room, and
good service make this
a bargain deal.
🛏 22   🚇 Earl's Court

RESTAURANTS

🍴 ABINGDON

$$$

54 ABINGDON ROAD
W8
TEL 020 7937 3339
www.theabingdonrestaurant
.com
Great atmosphere at this
modern bistro in a converted
corner pub. Try tuna, grilled
steak with pommes frites, or
duck leg confit.
🚇 High Street Kensington

🍴 CLARKE'S

$$$

124 KENSINGTON
CHURCH STREET
W8
TEL 020 7221 9225
www.sallyclarke.com
In the late 1970s, Sally
Clarke's Cal-Ital food
introduced new ideas to
many young chefs. Fresh
juices, home-baked breads,
chargrilled duck, and perfect
cheeses are all part of a
good meal here. Brunch on
Saturday mornings.
🚇 Notting Hill Gate
🕐 Closed Sun. D

🍴 HEREFORD ROAD

$$$

3 HEREFORD ROAD
W2
TEL 020 7727 1144
www.herefordroad.org
Despite a slightly austere dining room, Hereford Road has
been a success since it opened
in 2007. Part of an increasingly
trendy neighborhood, it
serves unfussy and perfectly
prepared classic British
food—braised beef, roast calf's
kidney, potted crab—at prices
that are more than fair for
the area.
🚇 Bayswater

🍴 KENSINGTON PLACE

$$$

201–209 KENSINGTON CHURCH
STREET
W8
TEL 020 7727 3184
www.kensingtonplace
-restaurant.co.uk
Plate-glass public eating in
a loud, big room. Modern
food includes grilled scallops
with pea puree and mint
vinaigrette—and don't miss
the breads.
🚇 Notting Hill Gate

🍴 LAUNCESTON PLACE

$$$

1A LAUNCESTON PLACE
W8
TEL 020 7937 6912
www.launcestonplace
-restaurant.co.uk
A sophisticated setting suits
this restaurant's modern
British dishes, such as Denham
Castle lamb, Tamworth
sucking pig, or West Coast
scallops.
🚇 Gloucester Road/
High Street Kensington
🕐 Closed Mon. L

🍴 WHITS

$$$

21 ABINGDON ROAD
W8
TEL 020 7938 1122
www.whits.co.uk
Gentle-paced popular bar and
restaurant where the wine list

🏨 Hotel   🍴 Restaurant   🛏 No. of Guest Rooms   🚇 Tube   🕐 Closed

and food are equally reliable. Known for its generous portions and fresh ingredients from primarily British sources. 🚇 High Street Kensington 🕐 Closed Sat.–Tues. L, Sun–Mon. D

🍴 LA BRASSERIE
$$
272 BROMPTON ROAD
TEL 020 7581 3089
www.labrasserielondon.com
La Brasserie is that rare thing—a brasserie that really looks and feels French. Great food throughout the day, including breakfast and afternoon tea, at good prices. Convenient for the Conran Shop and other South Ken stores.
🚇 South Kensington

■ CHELSEA, BELGRAVIA & KNIGHTSBRIDGE

Smart Londoners and foreign diplomats set the tone for elegant, discreet hotels and up-market eating, even in shops.

HOTELS

🏨 THE BERKELEY
🍴 $$$$$
WILTON PLACE
SW1
TEL 020 7235 6000
www.the-berkeley.co.uk
Now part of the Maybourne Hotel Group (who also own Claridge's and the Connaught), the emphasis is on super-luxury all the way. The Berkeley is a modern hotel run on traditional lines: open fire in the lobby, lavish flower arrangements, spacious rooms, valet service. Excellent top-floor health club and swimming pool, equaled by the bar and restaurants that include Marcus Wareing's Pétrus.
ℹ 214 🚇 Hyde Park Corner

🏨 THE CAPITAL
🍴 $$$$$
22 BASIL STREET
KNIGHTSBRIDGE
SW3
TEL 020 7589 5171
FAX 020 7225 0011
www.capitalhotel.co.uk
Egyptian cotton sheets cover the beds in this immaculate, design-aware hotel that has both rooms and apartments. Eric Chavot cooks notably in the Capital restaurant.
ℹ 49 🚇 Knightsbridge

🏨 GORING
🍴 $$$$$
BEESTON PLACE
GROSVENOR GARDENS
SW1
TEL 020 7396 9000
FAX 020 7834 4393
www.goringhotel.com
Run by the Goring family since 1910, this hotel promises excellent hospitality and service, and each room is individually designed and decorated. The excellent restaurant serves both traditional and contemporary British cuisine. The clublike bar is also first-rate.
ℹ 71 🚇 Victoria

SOMETHING SPECIAL

🏨 THE HALKIN
The innovator: London's first design-aware hotel. Inspired by classic Italian style; notably the good air-conditioning and lighting control, staff dressed in Armani, and a Michelin-starred contemporary Thai restaurant called Nahm.
$$$$$
HALKIN STREET
SW1
TEL 020 7333 1000
FAX 020 7333 1100
www.halkin.como.bz
ℹ 41 🚇 Hyde Park Corner

🏨 JUMEIRAH CARLTON TOWER
🍴 $$$$$
CADOGAN PLACE
SW1
TEL 020 7235 1234
FAX 020 7235 9129
www.jumeirah.com
Impressive modern hotel, whose sky-high swimming pool and health club indicate top-quality services at all levels; Chinoiserie Lounge for tea, Rib Room and Oyster Bar for traditional food. Convenient for Harrods and other shopping.
ℹ 220 🚇 Knightsbridge

🏨 THE LANESBOROUGH
🍴 $$$$$
HYDE PARK CORNER
SW1
TEL 020 7259 5599
FAX 020 7259 5606
www.lanesborough.com
Located on Hyde Park Corner, this modern traditional hotel created inside a grand 19th century neoclassical building offers lavish furnishings and extremely comfortable bedrooms. The Conservatory restaurant, with its palms and fountains, serves international cuisine.
ℹ 95 🚇 Hyde Park Corner

🏨 MANDARIN ORIENTAL HYDE PARK
🍴 $$$$$
66 KNIGHTSBRIDGE
SW1
TEL 020 7235 2000
FAX 020 7235 2001
www.mandarinoriental.com/london
A splendid Edwardian landmark, extravagantly refurbished. Large rooms (request a park view), lavish bathrooms, and many fine Hyde Park views. Two outstanding restaurants include the French Bar Boulud, overseen by Daniel Boulud, and the first London venture from Britain's

own three-star chef, Heston Blumenthal, called Dinner by Heston Blumenthal.

📍 198 🚇 Knightsbridge

🏨 THE KNIGHTSBRIDGE
$$$$
10 BEAUFORT GARDENS
SW3
TEL 020 7584 6300
FAX 020 7584 6355
www.firmdale.com
Good location for Knightsbridge shopping, and smart rooms to match. No bar, restaurant, or gym, but great room service menu.

📍 44 🚇 Knightsbridge

🏨 B&B BELGRAVIA
$$$
64–66 EBURY STREET
SW1
TEL 020 7259 8570
FAX 020 7259 8591
www.bb-belgravia.com
Away from chintz, this is freshness and contemporary quality introducing a new understanding of a "B&B," from quality bed linen and power showers to fresh breakfast ingredients.

📍 17 🚇 Victoria

🏨 MORGAN HOUSE
$$
120 EBURY STREET
SW1
TEL 7730 2384
www.morganhouse.co.uk
A charming bed-and-breakfast home in pretty, well-located Pimlico; good breakfasts; some rooms share bathrooms. Includes rooms for up to four people.

📍 11 🚇 Victoria

RESTAURANTS

🍴 GORDON RAMSAY
$$$$
68 ROYAL HOSPITAL ROAD
SW3
TEL 020 7352 4441

www.gordonramsay.com
Celebrated chef Gordon Ramsay creates his modern French dishes in this small, intimate restaurant. Dishes might include lobster ravioli or langoustine and salmon poached in light bisque. Good value three-course set lunch.

🚇 Sloane Square (10-minute walk) 🕐 Closed Sat. & Sun.

🍴 EBURY
$$$
11 PIMLICO ROAD
SW1
TEL 020 7730 6784
www.theebury.co.uk
Worth the detour to enjoy one of London's top gastropubs with bar, brasserie, and upstairs restaurant; great decor, charming staff, and accomplished European dishes. Leave room for the desserts, each matched with a dessert wine.

🚇 Sloane Square/ Victoria

🍴 RASOI VINEET BHATIA
$$$
10 LINCOLN STREET
SW3
TEL 020 7225 1881
www.rasoi-uk.com
Vineet Bhatia's inventive and often superb dishes founded on the diverse Indian cuisines and then taken to new heights.

🚇 Knightsbridge 🕐 Closed Sat. L

🍴 SALLOOS
$$$
62–64 KINNERTON STREET
SW1
TEL 020 7235 4444
www.squaremeal.co.uk
Mr. Salahuddin's classy Pakistani restaurant, founded in 1979, serves his family recipes. The focus is meat, including marinated lamb chops, chicken shish kebab, and quails, all eaten with

warm naan breads.

🚇 Knightsbridge 🕐 Closed Sun.

🍴 TOM'S KITCHEN
$$$
27 CALE STREET
SW3
TEL 020 7349 0202
www.tomskitchen.co.uk
Tom Aitkin's modern bistro is busy and bustling, with an open kitchen, wood-fired oven, and spit-roast and grill. It offers classic modern British cooking, with hints of Italian, French, and American cuisine. Breakfasts are particularly good (especially the pancakes) and there's an appealing bar on the upper floor.

🚇 Sloane Square/South Kensington

🍴 THE THOMAS CUBITT
$–$$
44 ELIZABETH STREET
SW1
TEL 020 7730 6060
www.thethomascubitt.co.uk

This airy and tastefully decorated contemporary pub with food sits well on Elizabeth Street, which is full of similarly chic and perfectly pitched outlets. Eat casually downstairs from the bar menu or in the small, more formal dining rooms upstairs.
🚇 Sloane Square/Victoria

■ WEST LONDON

Some special hotels and some good restaurants to combine with sightseeing.

HOTELS

🏨 THE HEMPEL
$$$$$
31–35 CRAVEN HILL GARDENS
W2
TEL 020 7298 9000
FAX 020 7402 4666
www.the-hempel.co.uk
Anouska Hempel's second hotel has both rooms and apartments. She pushes minimalism farther than any other hotelier would dare—natural fabrics, slate, sand-blasted glass, a Zen garden, H-Bar, and I-Thai restaurant (Italian/Thai).
🛏 42 🚇 Lancaster Gate/Queensway

🏨 ABBEY COURT
$$$$
20 PEMBRIDGE GARDENS
W2
TEL 020 7221 7518
FAX 020 7792 0858
www.abbeycourthotel.co.uk
Designers Guild fabrics are used in the individually decorated rooms of this friendly townhouse hotel. All rooms have plenty of books and a relaxing Jacuzzi bath.
🛏 22 🚇 Notting Hill Gate

🏨 THE PORTOBELLO HOTEL
$$$$
22 STANLEY GARDENS
W1
TEL 020 7727 2777
FAX 020 7792 9641
www.portobellohotel.com
Townhouse hotel tucked away in leafy and exclusive residential Notting Hill. Its stuccoed Victorian facade belies a delightfully idiosyncratic and high-quality interior much loved by guests.
🛏 21 🚇 Holland Park/Notting Hill Gate

🏨 THE ROCKWELL
$$$$
181–183 CROMWELL ROAD
SW5
TEL 020 7244 2000
www.therockwell.com
One of London's best recent openings occupies a listed, historic building. Rooms are all different, though all share elegant and understated contemporary styling. Triple-glazing blocks the noise from busy Cromwell Road. The location is good for Gloucester Road and the stores of Kensington High Street.
🛏 40 🚇 Earl's Court

🏨 COLONNADE
$$$
2 WARRINGTON CRESCENT
LITTLE VENICE
W9
TEL 020 7286 1052
FAX 020 7286 1057
www.theetoncollection.com
Leafy, romantic Little Venice is the rural setting for the sumptuous Victorian hotel with classically decorated rooms; worth the edge-of-town location.
🛏 43 🚇 Warwick Avenue

RESTAURANTS

🍴 THE RIVER CAFE
$$$$$
THAMES WHARF
RAINVILLE ROAD
W6
TEL 020 7386 4200
www.rivercafe.co.uk
Famous across the world for inspirational cookbooks bearing its name, the fountainhead of Ruth Rogers's and the late Rose Gray's success is worth the effort of booking well in advance and dedicating time to reach the off-beat location.
🚇 Hammersmith, then taxi or 20-min. walk

🍴 LA TROMPETTE
$$$$
5–7 DEVONSHIRE ROAD
W4
TEL 020 8747 1836
www.latrompette.co.uk
Worth the journey out (combine with Kew, Chiswick, or Syon, perhaps) to enjoy the impressive French dishes of James Bennington, together with his well-chosen wines and charming staff; a memorable and good-value treat.
🚇 Turnham Green 🕐 Closed Sun. D

SOMETHING SPECIAL

🍴 THE BELVEDERE
A quality restaurant in one of London's beautiful parks. The Belvedere was formerly the summer ballroom of the Jacobean mansion Holland House. Now it is one of London's most romantic settings, serving reliable, not exceptional, French cuisine. Best for lunch, when there is a good-value set menu.
$$$
ABBOTSBURY ROAD
HOLLAND PARK
W8
TEL 020 7602 1238
www.belvedererestaurant.co.uk
🚇 Holland Park
🕐 Closed Sun. D

🍽 CHEZ KRISTOF
$$$
111 HAMMERSMITH GROVE
W6
TEL 020 8741 1177
www.chezkristof.co.uk
Jan Woronieki (of Baltic
and Wodka) turns to French
regional cooking here, with
great results.
🚇 Goldhawk Road

🍽 THE FIFTH FLOOR
$$$
HARVEY NICHOLS
KNIGHTSBRIDGE
SW1
TEL 020 7235 5250
www.harveynichols.com
The ultimate shopping dream:
four floors of Harvey Nichols
fashion sandwiched between
chic restaurants. This one is the
smartest, serving dishes such
as quail with pumpkin ravioli
and creamy risotto. Also open
for breakfast and tea. There
is a trendy bar next door, a
simpler café, and a sublime
food store nearby.
🚇 Knightsbridge 🕐 Closed
Sun. D

🍽 JULIE'S
$$$
135 PORTLAND ROAD
W11
020 7229 8331
www. juliesrestaurant.co.uk
Julie's has been a chic and
romantic fixture for West
Londoners in the know since
1969, its main lure an eclectic
maze of homey dining rooms
and alcoves with a distinctly
bohemian air. Tucked away
in an enclave of prime real
estate, it is perfect for a
quiet drink at the bar or a
full meal of mostly British-
influenced dishes. Request
a table upstairs in the wine
bar, where the food is the
same and the setting is more
appealing.
🚇 Holland Park

🍽 RIVA
$$$
169 CHURCH ROAD
SW13
TEL 020 8748 0434
www.squaremeal.co.uk
Enjoy Francesco Zanchetta's
almost perfect rustic Italian
food. Classic regional dishes
include fritelle, *osso buco alla
milanese* with saffron risotto
more than merit the long
journey from the center of
town.
🚇 Hammersmith (then
bus 33, 72, 209, or 283)
🕐 Closed Sat. L and period
in Aug.

◾ EAST LONDON
The revitalization of East London, from the Tower to Canary
Wharf, has included the birth
of its own bar and restaurant
scene.

HOTEL

🏨 FOUR SEASONS
CANARY WHARF
$$$$$
46 WESTFERRY CIRCUS
E14
TEL 020 7510 1999
FAX 020 7510 1998
www.fourseasons.com
Canary Wharf's first deluxe
hotel, a stunning building and
setting run by the reliable
Four Seasons chain that pam-
pers guests with all modern
conveniences including pool,
spa, and tennis courts.
ⓘ 142 🚇 Canary Wharf

RESTAURANTS

🍽 BISTROTHEQUE
$$$
23–27 WADESON STREET
E2
TEL 020 8983 7900
www.bistrotheque.com
Find a great bar upstairs, a
casual but notable French

restaurant all in a former
warehouse.
🚇 Bethnal Green 🕐 Closed
L Mon.–Fri.

🍽 CAFÉ SPICE NAMASTE
$$$
16 PRESCOT STREET
E1
TEL 020 7488 9242
www.cafespice.co.uk
Modern, highly inventive
Indian cooking by Cyrus
Todiwala. Try the tandoori
duck, Goan seafood pilau,
and whichever new dish he
has created.
🚇 Tower Hill 🕐 Closed Sat.
L, Sun.

🍽 PLATEAU
$$$
CANADA PLACE
CANADA SQUARE
E14
TEL 020 7715 7100
www.daddlondon.com
Suitably dramatic glass
building on this stunning
waterside site. Bar, grill, and
restaurant all good.
🚇 DLR/Canary Wharf
🕐 Closed Sat. L, Sun. & bank
holidays

🍽 BRICK LANE BEIGEL
BAKE
$
159 BRICK LANE
E1
TEL 020 7729 0616
The fact that more than
7,000 bagels leave Sammy's
tiny, unremarkable café on a
Saturday night confirms its
status as the best in town.
Quality smoked salmon,
cream cheese, and breads.
🚇 Liverpool Street
🕐 Open 24 hours

🏨 Hotel 🍽 Restaurant ⓘ No. of Guest Rooms 🚇 Tube 🕐 Closed

Shopping

There are various ways of shopping in London. You may come with a specific shopping list, you may want to see the latest fashions, or you may simply wish to window shop with the possibility of a purchase. Whichever it is, London has several shopping centers and offers several ways of shopping.

Although shops are traditionally open between 9 a.m. and 5 p.m., opening hours are no longer fixed times. Many Oxford Street, Regent Street, and High Street Kensington shops remain open until 7 or 8 p.m. on Thursday; most Knightsbridge and Chelsea shops do the same on Friday; and most stores in key shopping areas, including those on Tottenham Court Road, are open on Sunday. Seasonal sales take place in January, extending into February, and July, extending into August.

Most shops accept the major credit cards. There is often a fee for using travelers' checks.

The VAT, currently 20 percent, is payable on almost everything (exceptions include books, food, and children's clothes). All non-U.K. passport holders and those officially resident outside the U.K. are exempt from the VAT if they are taking the goods out of the U.K. within three months. The tax must be paid, then reclaimed. There is one system for those living in EC countries, another for those living outside the EC. Shopkeepers are usually good at helping customers complete the necessary forms.

London shoppers are well protected by the law. For instance, a shopkeeper displaying a credit card sign is obliged to accept that card; goods in sales should be perfect unless they are labeled otherwise; and if an object fails to perform its job, there should be a full refund.

Department Stores

The one-stop shopping that department stores offer has advantages. Some well-known stores:

Fenwick, 63 New Bond Street, tel 020 7629 9161. Fashion, cosmetics, and fabrics.

Fortnum & Mason, 181 Piccadilly, tel 020 7734 8040. High prices, but the own-brand goods make perfect presents.

Harrods, Knightsbridge, tel 020 7730 1234. The epitome of these grand, multi-floored shops. It is often derided by Londoners who then admit they go there for one department.

Harvey Nichols, 109–25 Knightsbridge, tel 020 7235 5000. Classy clothes for women.

John Lewis, Oxford Street, tel 020 7629 7711. Good for reasonably priced, sensible homeware.

Liberty, Regent Street, tel 020 7734 1234. Goods range from sumptuous fabrics to the best china and glass.

Marks & Spencer, 458 Oxford Street, tel 020 7935 7954. An obligatory visit to M&S for underwear the world wears.

Peter Jones, Sloane Square, tel 020 7730 3434. John Lewis's slightly more stylish sister.

Selfridges, 400 Oxford Street, tel 0800 123400. Vast store with notable food and cosmetics. Currently considered by shopaholics to rival Harrods.

Souvenirs

Museum and gallery shops have quality goods ranging from desk diaries featuring their treasures to full sets of tableware and related toys. Examples of these can be found at:

The BBC Shop, Broadcasting House, Wood Lane, tel 020 8225 8230. A wide range of BBC-based gifts, including books and videos.

British Museum, Great Russell Street, tel 020 7328 8299. Three shops plus a children's shop.

Natural History Museum, Cromwell Road, tel 020 7942 5000. Thousands of dinosaur souvenirs.

Queen's Gallery, Buckingham Palace Road, tel 020 7321 2233. Quality goods, often bearing the royal stamp of authenticity.

Science Museum, Exhibition Road, tel 020 7942 4000. Projects for budding scientists.

Tate Britain, Millbank, tel 020 7887 8000.

Tate Modern, Bankside, tel 020 7887 8000. Both Tates have excellent stocks of books and designer gifts.

Victoria & Albert Museum, Cromwell Road, tel 020 7492 2000. Collection-inspired goods.

Specialty Shops

This is where the fun lies, although some homework with the map may be needed to avoid crisscrossing London. Certain kinds of shops tend to group together, such as in Bond Street or Sloane Street for fashion, Brompton Cross, Soho, and Clerkenwell for contemporary design and jewelers, and St. James's and Mayfair for upscale art. Here are some ideas:

Accessories

James Smith & Sons, 53 New Oxford Street, tel 020 7836 4731. Every kind of umbrella and walking stick.

Swaine Adeney Brigg & Sons and **Herbert Johnson,** 54 St. James's Street, tel 020 7409 7277. For classic accessories including umbrellas and hats.

Tiffany & Co., 25 Bond Street, tel 020 7409 2790. For total extravagance.

Art at Auction

The two top auction houses are:

Christie's, 8 King Street, St. James's, tel 020 7839 9060.

Sotheby's, 34–35 New Bond Street, Mayfair, tel 020 7293 5000.

It is also well worth visiting:

Bonhams, 101 New Bond Street, tel 020 7447 7447.

Phillips, 26 Albemarle Street, tel 020 7318 4010.

Specialty Bookstores

Books for Cooks, 4 Blenheim Crescent, tel 020 7221 1992. Possibly the world's best for cookery and cuisine.

Henry Sotheran, 2–5 Sackville Street, tel 020 7439 6151.

Maggs Brothers, 50 Berkeley Square, tel 020 7493 7160. Locate that out-of-print, first edition, or rare antiquarian book.

Travel Bookshop, 13–15 Blenheim Crescent, tel 020 7229 5260. Excellent travel specialist immortalized in the movie *Notting Hill.*

Decor and Designs

Designers Guild, 277 King's Road, tel 020 7351 5775.

Divertimenti, 33–34 Marylebone High Street, tel 020 7935 0689.

Heal's, 196 Tottenham Court Road, tel 020 7636 1666.

Designer Fashion

Many top designers, such as Vivienne Westwood and Burberry, have their flagship stores in or near New Bond Street, in Mayfair. Branches are usually in Knightsbridge (Sloane Street, Brompton Road), Kensington, and/or Covent Garden. Large department stores such as Harvey Nichols and Selfridges also house top designer lines (see p. 261).

Other well-known names to seek out include:

Agnès B, 35 Floral Street, tel 020 7379 1992.

Betty Jackson, 311 Brompton Road, tel 020 7589 7884.

Issey Miyake, 52 Conduit Street, tel 020 7581 4620.

Jean Paul Gaultier, 171–175 Draycott Avenue, tel 020 7584 4648.

Paul Smith, 122 Kensington Park Road, tel 020 7727 3553.

Stella McCartney, 30 Bruton Street, tel 020 7518 3100.

Zandra Rhodes, 81 Bermondsey Street, tel 020 7403 5333.

Gifts

Alessi Oggetti, 22 Brook Street, tel 020 7518 9091. For chic designer objects.

Asprey, 167 New Bond Street, tel 020 7493 6767. Ultimate deluxe gifts, but for most people just ultimate window shopping.

Bibendum, 113 Regent's Park Road, tel 020 7722 5577. Fine selection of wines.

Carluccio's, Carrick Street, tel 020 7836 0990. Designer delicatessen with cheeses, herbs, and cosmetics.

Falkiner Fine Papers, 76 Southampton Row, tel 020 7831 1151. Beautiful paper.

Paxton & Whitfield, 93 Jermyn Street, tel 020 7930 0259. Cheeses.

Shoes

Specialty shoe shops include:

Emma Hope, 53 Sloane Square, tel 020 7259 9566.

Manolo Blahnik, 49 Old Church Street, Chelsea, tel 020 7352 3863.

Natural Shoe Store, 13 Neal Street, tel 020 7836 5254.

Sports Equipment

Lillywhites, 24–36 Lower Regent Street, tel 0870 3339600. Whatever the sport, this shop has the equipment and outfit.

Toys & Games

Hamleys, 188 Regent Street,

tel 0871 7041977. A seven-floor wonderland for kids and adults, but it's more congenial to go to the fourth floor of Harrods, where they take orders.

Unusual Sizes

Base, 55 Monmouth Street, tel 020 7240 8914.

Evans, 538–540 Oxford Street, tel 0844 9840262. Stocks fashionable clothes in sizes 14 to 32, plus the French & Teague 1647 range, plus clothes for petite women.

Street Markets

Market goods range from fine antiques, as at Camden Passage to fruits and vegetables, as in Berwick Street, Soho (see p. 165).

Camden Market, Camden High Street. This and its adjoining markets provide a huge sprawl of stalls, street culture, and bargain shopping of all kinds.

Portobello Road Market, Portobello Road. Over a mile long, selling quality antiques and fruits and vegetables (see p. 164).

Entertainment

One of the most exciting, if frustrating, things about London is that there is so much theater, music, cinema, and other entertainment that it is impossible to see everything you would like to see. The range is wide, too, from serious opera, cinema, and sacred music to jazz restaurants, spectator sports, and extravagant musicals. And that does not include the plays, often the biggest draw for visitors. It would be impossible to list every entertainment venue in London. But here are some tips and essential information to help you find the right entertainment for your taste.

Information

Time Out, published every Tuesday, has impressively comprehensive entertainment listings. Their often acerbic reviews should not be taken too seriously. The *London Evening Standard,* published daily Monday through Friday, is London's monopoly evening newspaper, featuring day-after reviews, plus plenty of listings.

The Guardian newspaper publishes a detailed listings magazine free with its Saturday edition. See also websites p. 239

Cinema

London's cinema is not as good as some other European cities such as Paris. That said, there is a good mix of Hollywood, independent, European (subtitled, not dubbed), and oldies.

Large-Screen Theaters

The best places to see commercial first runs include:

Empire, Leicester Square, tel 0871 4714714.

Odeon West End, Leicester Square, tel 0871 2244007.

Other theaters include:

National Film Theatre, South Bank, tel 020 7928 3232. Independent theater with two cinemas showing a mixed program.

BFI London IMAX Cinema, 1 Charlie Chaplin Walk, South Bank, tel 0870 7872525.

Everyman, Hampstead, tel 0871 9069060. Shows fine films, old and new in repertory.

Clubbing

London has the most dynamic and varied nightlife in the world. The most exciting nights are weekdays, not weekends. Many clubs operate one night a week and have specific dress codes. To find your way, consult *Time Out.* As a start, check out Bar Rumba, Fabric, Egg, and Ministry of Sound.

Comedy

Comedy Café, 66 Rivington Street, tel 020 7739 5706.

The Comedy Store, 1a Oxendon Street, www.thecomedystore .co.uk. Budding comics face an unforgiving audience.

Dance

Bhavan Centre, 4a Castletown Road, tel 020 7381 3086. Quality, traditional Indian dance.

Royal Opera House, Covent Garden, tel 020 7304 4000. Home to the Royal Ballet, sharing time with the Royal Opera.

Sadler's Wells Theatre, Rosebery Avenue, tel 0844 4124300

The Coliseum, St. Martin's Lane, tel 0871 9110200. Major world dance companies in summer and at Christmas; otherwise, opera.

The Place, 17 Dukes Road, tel 020 7121 1100.

The **South Bank, Royal Opera House** and **Barbican Centre** (see Theater section) are also major dance venues.

Dance Umbrella, tel 020 8741 4040, offers an annual festival of dance and performances at nine major venues around the city.

Music

Classical

It is said that there are a thousand concerts given across London each week. The capital has four world-class orchestras, many small ensembles, and countless venues. Major venues include:

Barbican Centre, Silk Street, EC2, tel 020 7638 4141 (information), 020 7638 8891 (box office)

Royal Albert Hall, Kensington Gore, tel 0845 4015045. London's circular concert hall and venue for the Proms.

Royal Festival Hall, Queen Elizabeth Hall, and **Purcell Room** on the South Bank, tel 0844 8750073.

Wigmore Hall, 36 Wigmore Street, tel 020 7935 2141.

Contemporary

Big stars play major venues such as:

O_2 **Academy Brixton,** 211 Stockwell Road, tel 0844 4772000 (box office); 0905 0203999 (enquiries); fee for calls. The lesser, or newer, ones play here.

Earl's Court Exhibition Centre, tel 020 7385 2515.

Hackney Empire, 291 Mare Street, tel 020 8985 2424.

The O_2 Arena, North Greenwich, tel 0844 8560202 (Ticketmaster). Formerly the Millennium Dome, now an extremely popular music and events venue.

Wembley Arena and Stadium, tel 0844 9808001 (stadium), 0844 8150815 (arena).

Festivals

Major festivals include the Hampton Court Palace Festival, the City of London Festival, the Henry Wood Promenade Concerts (BBC "Proms"), the Spitalfields Festival, and the Almeida Festival. Jazz festivals include Ealing Jazz Festival (tel 020 8825 6640), Europe's largest, and the London Jazz Festival (tel 020 7324 1880).

Jazz

Find some of the best jazz in town at:

Bull's Head, 373 Lonsdale Road, Barnes, tel 020 8876 5241. Good jazz in a friendly riverside pub.

Dover Street, 8–9 Dover Street, tel 020 7629 9813. Popular basement bar.

Jazz Café, 5 Parkway, tel 020 7688 8899. Favorite among the young.

Pizza Express Jazz Club, 10 Dean Street, tel 0845 6027017. Quality pizzas and mainstream jazz.

Ronnie Scott's, 47 Frith Street, tel 020 7439 0747. Run by jazz musicians for jazz lovers.

Music & Dance with Food

London is less good at upscale restaurants with dancing—the **Savoy's River Room** (see p. 242) is an exception—than is at more modest places such as **Salsa!,** 96 Charing Cross Road, tel 020 7379 3277, **Costa Dorada,** 47–55 Hanway Street, tel 020 7636 7139, and **Sarastro,** 126 Drury Lane, tel 020 7836 0101, where budding opera singers entertain (usually Sun. & Mon.).

Opera

The Coliseum (see Dance). English National Opera performs in English for seasons alternating with dance.

Royal Opera House (see Dance). Home to the Royal Opera and the Royal Ballet.

Sadler's Wells (see Dance) and **Holland Park Theatre** (tel 0845 2309769) also host opera.

Theater

Theater Information & Tickets

Tickets for almost any show can be bought legally. It is extremely unwise to buy from a ticket tout. Ticketmaster (tel 0844 8440444) is a reliable agency, with a reservation fee. Harrods (direct line 020 7225 6666) has amazingly good allocations for a hefty fee. Beware: Theaters taking phone reservations may also charge a fee.

Artsline (tel 020 7388 2227, answering machine; www.artsline .org.uk) gives free advice on London arts for visitors with disabilities.

Ideally, either go to the theater (where there are seating plans) or go to the half-price ticket booth, called TKTS (Leicester Square, WC2, www.officiallondontheatre .co.uk or www.tkts.co.uk). Here you can save up to 50 percent on seat prices. It is open Monday through Saturday from 10 a.m. to 7 p.m., Sunday 11 a.m. to 4 p.m., selling tickets for that day's performance only. One person may buy up to four tickets (credit cards accepted; £3 service charge per ticket). Beware imitators around the square.

Commercial Theaters

The commercial theaters of the West End stage plays and musicals with broad appeal. Here are a few:

Almeida, Almeida Street, tel 020 7359 4404. Lures top actors to perform highbrow plays.

Barbican Centre, Silk Street, EC2, tel 020 7638 8891 Regional and foreign theater companies.

Donmar Warehouse, 41 Earlham Street, tel 0844 8717624.

Hampstead Theatre, Swiss Cottage Centre, tel 020 7722 9301.

Old Vic, Waterloo Road, tel 0844 8717628. Shakespeare and other classic drama.

Royal Court, Sloane Square, Chelsea, tel 020 7565 5000. Known for new writing.

The Gate, 11 Pembridge Road, tel 020 7229 0706.

The Kings Head, 115 Upper Street, tel 020 7226 8561 (inquiries), 0844 2090326 (box office).

Theatre Royal Stratford East, tel 020 8534 0310.

Young Vic, The Cut, tel 020 7922 2922.

"The Fringe"

The Fringe consists of little theaters scattered across London, the venues often small and basic, many of them in pubs, often promoting young people and new ideas. Try these:

Etcetera Theatre, Oxford Arms Pub, 265 Camden High Street, tel 020 7482 4857.

The Finborough, Hen & Chickens, 109 St. Paul's Road, tel 020 7244 7439.

Other Theaters

Regent's Park (see p. 147)
Shakespeare's Globe (see p. 103)

State-Supported Theater

The state supports the Royal National Theatre, which has three stages, each with several plays in production concurrently. Plays range from Greek to contemporary first runs.

Royal National Theatre, South Bank, tel 020 7452 3400, tickets 020 7452 3000. Three theaters under one roof.

Royal Shakespeare Company, Aldwych, tel 0870 9500940. The company currently has no permanent London home, but it often performs at the Roundhouse, Chalk Farm (tel 0844 4828008).

INDEX

ILLUSTRATIONS CREDITS

All photos by Alison Wright unless otherwise noted.

National Geographic
TRAVELER
London

Published by the National Geographic Society

John M. Fahey, Jr., *Chairman of the Board and Chief Executive Officer*

Timothy T. Kelly, *President*

Declan Moore, *Executive Vice President; President, Publishing*

Melina Gerosa Bellows, *Executive Vice President, Chief Creative Officer, Books, Kids, and Family*

Prepared by the Book Division

Barbara Brownell Grogan, *Vice President and Editor in Chief*

Jonathan Halling, *Design Director, Books and Children's Publishing*

Marianne R. Koszorus, *Director of Design*

Barbara A. Noe, *Senior Editor*

Carl Mehler, *Director of Maps*

R. Gary Colbert, *Production Director*

Jennifer A. Thornton, *Managing Editor*

Meredith C. Wilcox, *Administrative Director, Illustrations*

Staff for This Book

Patricia Daniels, *Project Editor*

Kay Kobor Hankins, *Art Director*

Kate Baylor, *Illustrations Editor*

Michael McNey and Mapping Specialists, *Map Production*

Rob Waymouth, *Illustrations Specialist*

Rachael Jackson, John Maloney, Larry Porges, Jane Sunderland, *Contributors*

Manufacturing and Quality Management

Christopher A. Liedel, *Chief Financial Officer*

Phillip L. Schlosser, *Senior Vice President*

Chris Brown, *Technical Director*

Nicole Elliott, *Manager*

Rachel Faulise, *Manager*

Robert L. Barr, *Manager*

National Geographic Traveler: London
(Third Edition)
ISBN: 978-1-4262-0821-8

First edition: Edited and designed by AA Publishing (a trading name of Automobile Association Developments Limited, whose registered office is Norfolk House, Priestley Road, Basingstoke, Hampshire, England RG24 9NY. Registered number: 1878835).

Area map illustrations drawn by Chris Orr Associates, Southampton, England

Cutaway illustrations drawn by Maltings Partnership, Derby, England

Printed in China

11/TS/1

The National Geographic Society is one of the world's largest nonprofit scientific and educational organizations. Founded in 1888 to "increase and diffuse geographic knowledge," the Society works to inspire people to care about the planet. National Geographic reflects the world through its magazines, television programs, films, music and radio, books, DVDs, maps, exhibitions, live events, school publishing programs, interactive media and merchandise. *National Geographic* magazine, the Society's official journal, published in English and 33 local-language editions, is read by more than 40 million people each month. The National Geographic Channel reaches 370 million households in 34 languages in 168 countries. National Geographic Digital Media receives more than 15 million visitors a month. National Geographic has funded more than 9,600 scientific research, conservation and exploration projects and supports an education program promoting geography literacy. For more information, visit www.nationalgeographic.com.

For more information, please call 1-800-NGS LINE (647-5463) or write to the following address:

National Geographic Society
1145 17th Street N.W.
Washington, D.C. 20036-4688 U.S.A.

For information about special discounts for bulk purchases, please contact National Geographic Books Special Sales: ngspecsales@ngs.org

For rights or permissions inquiries, please contact National Geographic Books Subsidiary Rights: ngbookrights@ngs.org

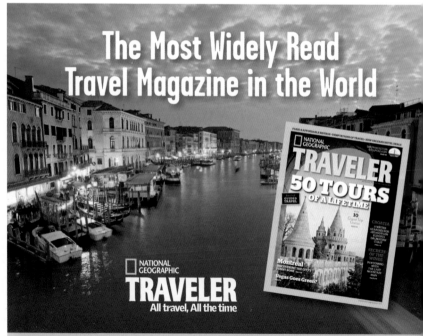